A CHURCH OF
HER OWN

ALSO BY SARAH SENTILLES

Taught by America: A Story of Struggle and Hope in Compton

A CHURCH OF HER OWN

What Happens When a Woman Takes the Pulpit

SARAH SENTILLES

MARINER BOOKS / HOUGHTON MIFFLIN HARCOURT
Boston   New York

For the ministers who shared their stories,
for Amy and Maylen who minister to me,
and for all women who keep other women strong.

First Mariner Books edition 2009
Copyright © 2008 by Sarah Sentilles

For information about permission to reproduce selections from this book,
write to Permissions, Houghton Mifflin Harcourt Publishing Company,
6277 Sea Harbor Drive, Orlando, Florida 32887-6777.

www.hmhbooks.com

Excerpt from *Beloved* copyright © 1987 by Toni Morrison, used by permission
of Alfred A. Knopf, a division of Random House, Inc.

Excerpts from "The Thunder, Perfect Mind," pp. 298, 301, 302 from *The Nag
Hammadi Library in English,* 3rd, completely revised edition, by James M.
Robinson, general editor. Copyright © 1978, 1988 by E. J. Brill, Leiden, The
Netherlands. Reprinted by permission of HarperCollins Publishers.

Library of Congress Cataloging-in-Publication Data
Sentilles, Sarah.
A church of her own: what happens when a woman takes the pulpit/
Sarah Sentilles.
p. cm.
Includes bibliographical references and index.
1. Women clergy. I. Title.
BV676.S46 2008
262'.14082—dc22 2007037894
ISBN 978-0-15-101392-0
ISBN 978-0-15-603332-9 (pbk.)

Text set in Adobe Garamond
Designed by Liz Demeter

PRINTED IN THE UNITED STATES OF MERICA

DOC 10 9 8 7 6 5 4 3 2 1

As in all the churches of the saints, women should be silent in the churches. For they are not permitted to speak, but should be subordinate, as the law also says. If there is anything they desire to know, let them ask their husbands at home. For it is shameful for a woman to speak in church. Or did the word of God originate with you? Or are you the only ones it has reached?

—I CORINTHIANS 14:34–36

Peter said to Mary, "Sister, we know that the Savior loved you more than all other women. Tell us the words of the Savior that you remember, the things which you know that we don't because we haven't heard them."

Mary responded, "I will teach you about what is hidden from you." And she began to speak these words to them.

—THE GOSPEL OF MARY 6:1–4

Contents

I am writing this preface almost a year after the murder of a student at a school a few miles from where I live and two months after the passage of Proposition Eight, the amendment that wrote discrimination into California's constitution and took away the right of everyone in the state to marry. On Tuesday, February 12, 2008, Lawrence King, an eighth-grader, was fatally shot by a classmate in the computer lab at E. O. Greene Junior High School in Oxnard, California. The murder was classified as a hate crime. The victim was targeted in part, reports indicate, because he was gay and sometimes wore makeup and jewelry to school. My friend Kaia Tollefson wrote that Lawrence King was murdered not because he was gay but because his killer was raised in a society that endorses the ridicule, discrimination, and violence that GLBTQ people endure every day.

As someone who has spent the past ten years studying Christian theology and its effects, I lay some of the blame for this boy's murder and the passage of Proposition Eight at the feet of church communities. Many congregations are working against homophobia, but many more continue to bless, sanction, and promote it. Other church communities insist that there are faithful people on both sides of the argument about homosexuality—equally valid ways to think about what the Bible says or doesn't say, what Jesus would or wouldn't do, what God demands—and that the challenge is to learn to live with one another even when we disagree. But I don't believe "getting along" is the challenge. The challenge is to create a world in which children don't get shot when they wear high heels to school. The congregation of one of the ministers I interviewed flies a Pride flag outside its church. The parishioners fly that flag because they recognize that the loudest voice against GLBTQ people is a religious one. I quote their minister in the book, but I think it is worth quoting her again. "I am so sick of people saying there's room for faithful people on both sides," she said. "It's bigotry. The bigotry of good church folks permits the violence of ordinary folks."

Right now, some congregations in the Episcopal Church—the tradition in which I was almost ordained—are threatening schism over this very issue, and it's probably no coincidence that some churches are voting to leave the Episcopal Church at a time when we have our first female presiding bishop, Katharine Jefferts Schori. (I interviewed her for this book.) Sexism and heterosexism are linked. The arguments used to keep women out of ordained ministry are connected to the arguments used to bless discrimination against GLBTQ folks. Those of us who call ourselves religious—ministers, congregations, divinity schools, seminaries, faith communities, and people who would never set foot inside a church—have a role to play in ending discrimination and hate.

Since the publication of this book, I have had conversations with many people who want to make churches better places for women—thereby making them better places for everyone. They asked, How can we help? What should we do? Where can we find encouragement? How can we support the ministers we know? How can we better prepare ourselves for the sexism we will encounter when we are ordained? The first thing we can do is talk to one another about sexism—admit that it exists, recognize that it is taking a toll on our communities and our relationships with God, hold ourselves accountable for the effects of our policies and theologies. Women seeking ordination can form groups to share their experiences and strategize. Congregations can create groups to address sexism in their liturgies and their churches. Faculties at seminaries and divinity schools can look critically at how they prepare their students for the sexism they will encounter as ministers. I studied all kinds of liberation theologies at Harvard Divinity School, but I rarely had a conversation about the oppressive practices of church communities where I would someday work. There is a gap between what students are learning in school and what is happening in churches. Looking critically at the experiences of women ministers offers an opportunity to build a bridge across this gap, making both sides stronger and more just.

A note about terminology: I use the phrase "woman minister" several times in this book, a phrase one of my friends dislikes because it smacks of the epithet "woman driver." The phrase is certainly problematic—as one of the ministers I interviewed pointed out, no one says "man minister"—but I chose to use it for several reasons. First, I use "woman minister" instead of "female minister" because I think "woman minister" is more inclusive. "Woman" refers to gender identity, not simply biological sex. Some of the ministers I interviewed are transgender, and some identify as women, not necessarily as females. Second, people usually say "woman driver" when a woman gets in their way—cuts them off, drives too slowly or too fast, or just happens to be sharing the road in a way that bothers them. When they say "woman driver," they are also saying women can't drive, men drive better than women, and having women on the road is frightening. By writing "woman minister" instead of "female minister," I am pointing out something similar—that having a woman as a minister remains a strange and frightening experience for many people. But there is also a big difference between "woman minister" and "woman driver." When someone drives badly and happens to be a woman, her poor driving is often attributed to her gender rather than to a simple lack of skill. Women ministers, however, are not singled out only when they make mistakes. One of the main arguments in this book is that they are perceived as women ministers—not just ministers—even if nothing goes wrong. *A Church of Her Own* reveals the real effects of this perception and what these effects disclose about how both women and ministers are (mis)understood.

Because I believe in the importance of talking about sexism and being committed to working against it, I have created a discussion guide that I hope will be helpful. You can find the guide on my web-site: www.sarahsentilles.com. I encourage you to gather with others to talk about the issues raised in *A Church of Her Own*, to wrestle with theology, to reflect on what you believe and why, to ask critical questions about how your community supports, or fails to support, women and ministers, to look closely at how welcoming your "welcoming" congregation actually is, to think about the connections between justice and faith.

Some readers have criticized this book as being a biased, unbalanced report about women's experiences in ministry. These critics are correct. I never set out to write a "balanced" book about sexism in churches. Let me be clear about it from the beginning: sexism is bad, and I am on a mission to stop it. A few of the readers who accused me of being biased were women ministers, and they wrote that the book did not reflect their experience working in churches. They do not experience sexism as ordained women, they said, and they wished I had spent more time writing about ministers like them. I am glad to hear that some women are having fantastic experiences in churches, but I am surprised that their response to reading about other women's not so fantastic experiences is "Why didn't you write more about me?" If the stories collected in these pages do not reflect what you know, how wonderful for you! You give me hope! But it seems to me your sexism-free existence requires something of you. You have an obligation to support your sisters who are suffering in churches, maybe even in a church right next door to your own.

When *A Church of Her Own* was published, I received phone calls, e-mails, and letters from many ministers, and most said the same thing: *What a relief. I thought I was the only one.* Reading about other women's struggles confirmed that what was happening to them was part of a larger pattern, that they weren't crazy. *A Church of Her Own* helped these ministers understand their own experiences with sexism and empowered them to do something about it—to tell their stories, to form advocacy groups, to talk to other ministers, to begin a conversation with their congregations about sexism, to change their churches. I wrote this book so ministers would know they are not alone—and so the rest of us might be brave enough to admit that sexism happens in our church communities, to recognize that we must fight against it, and to believe we can build a more just world.

THE MOST SEXIST HOUR

Ten years ago, I changed my entire life so I could be ordained as an Episcopal priest. I moved from Los Angeles, California, to Cambridge, Massachusetts, to attend Harvard Divinity School; got a job at an Episcopal church in a suburb of Boston, where I ran the church school and youth group programs and was sometimes allowed to preach; and entered the ordination process in the Massachusetts diocese. To make a long story short: Things did not go well. I thought it was my fault.

When I lived in Los Angeles, I attended All Saints Episcopal Church in Pasadena. The people there were doing the kind of work I wanted to do in the world—fighting injustice and racism, combating poverty, working for civil and religious rights for everyone— all while creating a sanctuary, a place where I felt seen, cared for, held. Although I lived in Venice, a couple of blocks from the beach, I drove all the way to Pasadena, quite a trek during Southern California's rush hour, three times a week. Less than a year after my first Sunday at All Saints, I became a member of the church and an Episcopalian. Because I had been baptized and confirmed as a Catholic, it was not necessary for the Episcopalians to do those rituals over again, nor was I required to convert. I was, instead, "received," and that is exactly what it felt like.

Before I went to All Saints, I never fit into any institutional religion. The God in my heart and of my prayers had always been different from the one preached about from the pulpit or professed in creeds. The voices of that faith community in California surprised me, spoke to me, echoed my deepest beliefs and most radical doubts, called me to be an instrument of peace. I decided to become a priest.

But All Saints was my first encounter with the Episcopal Church, and I misinterpreted that particular church as indicative of what I might find in the Episcopal Church as a whole. When I moved to Cambridge to go to divinity school, I could not find a church that felt like home. I grew to hate going to church, not because I hated church but because I loved it. I believed in what church could be, in what might be possible when people come together week after week to think about the world and how God might be calling us to make it a better place. It was this radical hope that made my stomach hurt every time I found myself sitting in a pew listening to a terrible sermon; reciting bad theology; and awkwardly juggling the weekly program, the *Book of Common Prayer*, the hymnal, and *Enriching Our Worship*.

Even when I realized that All Saints was the exception and not the rule, I still wanted to be a priest. I convinced myself that once ordained I would be able to help create another church like All Saints. I wouldn't be annoyed by sermons if I were the one preaching them, right?

My plan had (at least) one crucial flaw: To be ordained, I had to survive the ordination process. This proved impossible, and when it all fell apart—the process, my faith, my understanding of God—I figured I had been deluded to think being a priest is what I was meant to be, crazy to have dared to believe I might belong. I thought it was about me—that my theology was not traditional enough, my Christology not orthodox enough, my politics not conservative enough. I felt very alone. I started getting migraines. The way I was treated during the ordination process confirmed my worst beliefs about myself: It's true, Sarah, you do not belong. You are not good enough. You have done something wrong. Ashamed, I withdrew from the process and stopped going to church altogether. Mine was a conversion in reverse.

Then I began to pay attention to the experiences of other women from my divinity school, and I realized that the brightest, most creative women I knew were also having trouble. Either they struggled through the ordination process in mainline Protestant denominations like I did, or, once ordained and working in churches, they were silenced, humiliated, and abused. These women—women who were brilliant and capable and loved Jesus, who were faithful, who brought down the house when they preached, who had dedicated their lives to serving God—were being driven out of churches or were leaving the ministry altogether. Many were depressed. Some were angry. Most were ashamed.

What was happening?

A Church of Her Own began as my attempt to answer that question. I started asking women about their experiences in churches, and then I listened. In each interview, whether in person or by telephone, I usually had to give only one prompt: Why don't you tell me about your history in the church? Then they would talk, sometimes for hours. I listened to my friends. I listened to their friends. I listened to women I read about in the newspaper, or who had written articles in books, or who were friends of friends of friends of friends. I listened to strangers. I interviewed women across races and denominations and classes, women who had been ordained for just a year and women who had been ordained for decades. I listened to women who had amazing experiences in churches, women who found churches difficult places to be, and women who made their own kind of church. All of their experiences revealed the failure of churches to celebrate and support women in ministry and betrayed a deep misogyny alive and well in most Christian denominations.

I concentrated my listening efforts on women ministering in mainline Protestant denominations, but I also interviewed Catholic women. The contrast between Catholic and Protestant women's stories could not have been more dramatic. While many of the Protestant women I interviewed internalized their experience of sexism, taking it personally and believing, like I did, that what happened to them was somehow their fault, the Catholic women I interviewed understood sexism as institutional, not individual. The blatant misogyny of the Roman Catholic prohibition of the ordination of women gives women something around which to organize, galvanizes them, forces them to conceive of and fight against sexism as systemic. Embracing their church's radical social justice tradition, they understand the fight for women's rights as part of a larger fight—against poverty, injustice, imperialism, racism, heterosexism, and the destruction of the environment. Watching their Protestant sisters suffer, they recognize that ordaining women is not the end of the struggle but just the beginning. What is required is nothing less than a revolution of the priesthood itself. Surprisingly, Catholic women's stories helped me see how devastating Protestant sexism is.

We Protestants like to pretend sexism does not exist in *our* churches, and yet ordained ministry continues to be one of the most male-dominated of all professions. Even though the ministry was one of the first professions to encounter proposals to admit women, it was one of the last actually to do so, and the acceptance of women clergy is far from universal or uncontested today. Churches as cultural institutions have played historically repressive roles in the lives of women. Therefore, neutrality on or denial about so-called women's issues is not enough. Churches—as communities, as denominations, as institutions, as Christians—must be actively antisexist. Even more, they must be feminist, which simply means, to quote my divinity school professor's bumper sticker, that we must believe in the radical notion that women are human beings.

Many of the Protestant women I interviewed were "good girls." Before they abandoned their jobs, their churches, their vocations, or their good-girl selves, they tried to be the ministers they imagined their congregations expected them to be. They wanted to do well, to be liked, to keep their jobs. They conformed to imagined expectations, even when they were not sure exactly what those expectations were, even when no one in the congregation ever approached them directly to tell them to change the way they dressed or give different sermons or tone down their politics. They intuited what others wanted them to do, and they tried to follow those wishes, even if it meant checking parts of themselves at the door. I, too, have always been a good girl, a rule follower, a performer. I have spent much of my life doing what is expected of me so I will be loved—or at least so I won't get in trouble. Listening to women's stories helped me understand this good-girl part of myself and revealed her as a dangerous myth. Many of the women I talked with said that when they experienced outright hostility or subtle opposition to their politics or gender or body type or race or sexual preference, they actually thought, "If they really knew me, they would like me," and then spent the next few weeks or months or years trying to prove how likeable they were. Establishing your likability is not a good recipe for resisting oppression. It is, however, a good recipe for shame.

To write this book, I had to face my own shame. Listening to the stories of other women—women who, like me, thought what had happened to them was their fault, who felt alone and afraid—I got in touch with my rage, first on their behalf, and then on my own. What happened to me was not an isolated incident but rather part of an effort to keep women out of positions of authority and to keep religion from changing. I am not a conspiracy theorist. I don't imagine that there are secret gatherings late at night in hidden rooms where people strategize about how to ruin women's lives or keep the church as a males-only club. In a way, it would be much simpler if that were the case. Fighting sexism in the church would be as easy as banging down a door and demanding that everyone conspiring around the table come out with his or her hands up. Sexism is more insidious than that. It dresses in the garments we all wear. It speaks our language. It works in concert with other forms of discrimination. It blesses some of the most fundamental ways we have of understanding ourselves and each other.

Not one of the people who acted against the women I interviewed would identify him- or herself as a sexist or a racist or a homophobe. Each would insist she or he had the best intentions, and, perhaps, he or she did. Despite some of the best intentions of mentors or congregants or colleagues, though, women ministers endure abuse, blame, and exclusion. Even as they assume leadership positions, women continue to pay the high price of unexamined, religiously sanctioned sexism. They pay the price when they are driven out of the ordination process. They pay the price when they are paid less than their male counterparts, when they are offered part-time or interim work, when they are passed over for senior-level positions at thriving churches, or when they are forced to work multiple jobs because many churches willing to hire women can't afford to pay them. They pay the price when they challenge the ways we think about God or about church or about ourselves and are punished by their congregations. They pay the price when their bodies become too female to ignore—when they are pregnant, or lesbian, or single—or when they are not female enough: too loud, too proud, too strong, too brave.

And they are not the only ones who pay a price. Mainline Protestantism is losing out to everything—conservative evangelicalism, megachurches, storefront churches, Catholic activism, secularism, and Sunday yoga classes (which is where you will find me). The mainline drain can be traced directly to the failure of churches to tap the deep resources of women called to ministry who could revitalize the church. The problems faced by women ministers cannot be dismissed as "women's" problems. They belong to all of us, whether you have a female minister in your church or not, whether you attend church or not, whether you think your congregation is sexist or not, even whether you are Christian or not. None of us—even those of us outside the church—is exempt from the reverberations of religious institutions' failings. Churches' treatment of women and women's reactions to this treatment are symptoms of a larger problem, indicative of the broader ways the church needs to change. What we do and say and believe in church is connected to what we do and say and believe in our everyday lives. Our theology is linked to the state of the world—to war and poverty and environmental destruction and reckless consumerism—and it is time that we held ourselves accountable.

Several years ago, I heard Harvard Law School professor Lani Guinier deliver a speech in which she compared the struggles of marginalized groups in institutions to canaries in coal mines. The experiences of marginalized groups alert us to the racism, classism, misogyny, and bigotry in our world, revealing that there is something toxic in our atmosphere. But, Guinier pointed out, unlike the miners who heeded the canaries' warnings, we blame our version of the canaries, not the noxious gases.

A 1993 United Methodist survey on the retention of female clergy found that there is an oppressive silencing of the promising, bright voices that have left local church ministry. If we listen to the silence—and to the whispering and to the voices raised in anger—the experiences of women ministers might help us all breathe better, maybe even help us create a revitalized church and a more just and life-giving world.

The stories I heard probably differ little from stories women in any number of professions might tell. In some ways, churches are not more sexist or racist or homophobic than other institutions. But in most workplaces the law mandates that employers cannot discriminate based on sex, race, class, religion, sexual orientation, ethnicity, or ability. No such law exists for churches. The Roman Catholic Church and the Southern Baptist Church can legally refuse to ordain women. The United Methodist Church can legally refuse to ordain openly gay people. It is not that corporations and universities and law firms and police departments don't discriminate, but they cannot say out loud that they do. Churches can. Their members can write GOD HATES FAGS in large letters on poster board; can exclude women from positions of authority; can insist that only straight White men can get ordained. Who can stop us, they ask. We are following the will of God.

This is what makes sexism in the church different than sexism in other institutions. In a religious context, our relationship with God and our relationship with women are inextricably linked. If we change our relationship with women, we inevitably change our relationship with God. We have been told that religious sexism is supported by passages in the Bible, by thousands of years of tradition, by the writings of church patriarchs, and by God. Historical critics, progressive biblical scholars, and feminist theologians try to explain away sexism in our sacred texts, putting offending passages in context, redefining words, pointing out mistranslations, and claiming God and Jesus as essentially liberative. But what if you can't erase sexism? What if you ordain women even though the Bible forbids it? If the Bible says women should be silent in the church, if ancient doctrine says women cannot be priests because Jesus did not ordain any women, if God created woman as somehow less than man, and we ordain women *anyway,* then how we understand the Bible, tradition, and God will be fundamentally and irrevocably altered. Ordaining women forces us to ask questions about what we believe and why we believe it, ushering us into an adult relationship with faith. If you ordain women in spite of what the Bible or the Vatican or God says, then you must recognize that you are consciously, intentionally, picking and choosing what you believe—which parts of the Bible and tradition you follow, what you call sacred, what you value, what kind of God you worship. Ordaining women unravels belief and offers it back to us, revealing that we are always in the process of constructing, destroying, and re-creating our belief systems.

While it is belief that has kept women out of the church, it is also belief that keeps women in the church. Many of the women I interviewed believe the church is where God is calling them to be, and it is this belief that allows some of them to stay despite the abuse they endure at the hands of congregations, colleagues, other ministers, or the institution. Some stay out of stubbornness, others out of hope, others out of the knowledge that the church is as fallible as any other human institution. Others could not stay, but even when they left the institutional church, they were still ministers. Working in nonprofits or hospitals or prisons or schools they were as ministerial as when they stood in the pulpit or at the altar.

On my first day of work at an Episcopal church in a suburb of Boston, the rector pulled me into her office. (In the Episcopal Church, a rector is the priest in charge of a self-supporting church and is elected by the vestry of that church.) "Do you notice anything about my desk?" she asked.

I looked at her desk for a long time. I took in the neat piles of books and papers, the Bible and the *Book of Common Prayer,* the long list of things she had to do. "No," I said.

"Do you see this rock?" she asked, pointing to a large gray rock sitting on top of a pile of papers.

"Yes," I said.

"It looks like a paperweight, doesn't it? But I have it here within reach in case I need to use it to protect myself," she said. "You should do the same." Then she told me how frightening it is to be a woman in the church, not just at night when a stranger might wander into the empty building off the street, but all the time, every day.

The women and men who fill the pages of this book are brave. Sharing their stories with me involved great risk. Because of this risk and the fear of repercussions, some of the people I interviewed asked me to disguise their identities (changed names are indicated with an asterisk at first mention). All of them asked that I change the names of their churches, colleagues, and congregations. Each tried to protect not only herself but also the people in her care.

In a question-and-answer session following a speech he delivered in 1963 at Western Michigan University, Rev. Dr. Martin Luther

King Jr. referred to eleven o'clock on Sunday morning as the most segregated hour in the United States. He said, "We must face the fact that in America, the church is still the most segregated major institution in America. At eleven o'clock on Sunday morning when we stand and sing and Christ has no east or west, we stand at the most segregated hour in this nation. This is tragic. Nobody of honesty can overlook this." He went on to say that the church must repent and "remove the yoke of segregation from its own body." Almost a half century later, eleven o'clock remains one of the most segregated hours in America, and, I think, one of the most sexist. At eleven o'clock, people in pews all over the country kneel and pray to a male God, stand and sing to a male God, and, although women typically make up the majority of congregations, are usually led by male ministers.

What happens to the women who dare to transform the most segregated, sexist hour in America?

Part One

VOCATION

CALL

I turned one the year the first women were ordained in the Episcopal Church. On July 29, 1974—the same year girls were allowed to play in Little League—eleven women known as "The Philadelphia Eleven" were "irregularly" ordained by retired bishops in the Episcopal Church. I imagine these eleven women as a posse, a band of superheroines, robed, wearing knee-high boots, and sporting bullet-deflecting bracelets like Wonder Woman. Bracelets would have been useful for deflecting what came at them after that day. Many in the church fought against their ordinations. Hard. Although there was no specific canon in Episcopal Church law prohibiting ordaining women to the priesthood, the rules did require a recommendation from the standing committee to do so. The Philadelphia Eleven had no such recommendation. Less than a month after their irregular ordinations, the House of Bishops called an emergency meeting, denounced the ordinations, and declared them invalid. Charges were also filed against the bishops who ordained the eleven women. Nevertheless, in 1976, official ordinations followed the irregular ones. Women were priests. Supporters were elated, opponents furious. Leaders in the Episcopal Church responded to the opponents by voting in 1977 that if an individual bishop did not want to ordain women in his diocese, he did not have to. This policy was still on the books as recently as 1997, and was even debated at the 2003 General Convention, although arguments about women were overshadowed by arguments about the consecration of the first openly gay bishop, Gene Robinson. Three dioceses in the American Episcopal Church— Quincy, Illinois; Fort Worth, Texas; and San Joaquin, California— continue to prohibit the ordination of women, and more than half of the thirty-eight provinces in the Anglican Communion, including the Church of England, refuse to ordain women as bishops.

Other denominations started ordaining women more than a hundred years before the Episcopal Church did: Congregationalists in 1853 (Antoinette Brown); Universalists in 1863 (Olympia Brown); and the Methodist Protestant Church in 1880 (Anna Howard Shaw). Some beat the Episcopalians by just a decade or two: the Methodist Church in 1950, the African Methodist Episcopal Church in 1960, the Presbyterian Church in 1964, and the Lutheran Church in 1970. Claiming their exclusion of women is sanctioned by God and the Bible, some Christian groups—the Roman Catholic Church, Eastern Orthodox Church, and Lutheran Church–Missouri Synod, to name a few—still refuse to ordain women.

Because most mainline Protestant denominations only extended the right of ordination to women in the last few decades, this timeline wrongly suggests that the ordination of women is a modern problem, a result of the women's movement, a contemporary issue with which churches are just beginning to wrestle. Such a view allows opponents of women's ordination to claim that their prohibition against ordaining women is "orthodox," "traditional," and "Christian." Historical evidence, however, reveals that the leadership of women in church communities is not new at all. In fact, since the founding of the first Christian communities, women have acted as leaders. What is new—at least relatively—is *refusing* to allow women positions of authority in churches. Given the evidence, you might even argue that ordaining women is more orthodox than not ordaining them. Paul's pronouncement in his letter to the Corinthians that "women should be silent" reveals that women were making all kinds of noise in church. Why else would he need to tell them to shut up?

Concentrating on the year that denominations granted women the right to ordination obscures the fact that well before denominations permitted women to be ministers, women were *acting* as ministers. It puts too much weight on ordination, which historically has not been the central criterion for identifying someone as a minister. Even though the hierarchy of the Catholic Church partly justifies its refusal to ordain women by insisting that Jesus only ordained men, the truth of the matter is that Jesus did not ordain anyone—male or female. Denominational policy regarding the ordination of women has never corresponded to the actual practice of women in ministry. This remains true today: The Roman Catholic Church does not ordain women, but many Catholic churches in the United States are effectively headed by women due to the shortage of ordained male priests. Policies about women's ordination carry symbolic meaning well beyond their pragmatic consequences. Denominations that refuse to ordain women resist something more than actual female bodies preaching in pulpits and standing at altars; they resist modernity and the "liberal agenda." Denominations that allow the ordination of women do not necessarily support actual female bodies in positions of authority; they embrace modernity and progressivism (at least in theory).

In their book *In Their Own Right,* Carl J. and Dorothy Schneider mark 1656 as the beginning of the history of female clergy in America. That was when British Quaker "Public Friends" Mary Fischer and Ann Austin landed in the Massachusetts Bay Colony, "only to be arrested, imprisoned, examined for marks of witchcraft, and shipped back to England." While authorities in some churches assigned women only the work they thought appropriate for their sex—teaching Sunday school—others allowed women to engage in activities that looked an awful lot like ordained clergy work, such as running prayer meetings in which they gave testimony and preached, spreading the gospel as evangelists, giving public speeches, and traveling all over the world as missionaries. With or without official sanction, women did the work and challenged communities' understandings of both women and ministers. Anne Hutchinson arrived in the Massachusetts Bay Colony in 1634, and, much to the horror of the Puritan civil and church powers there, held weekly meetings for the religious betterment of women during which she preached and criticized the sermons of other local clergy. African American women—both free women and slaves—preached and ran weekly prayer meetings. Women like Sophie Murray, Elizabeth Cole, Rachel Evans, and Harriet Felson Taylor were well-known African Methodist Episcopal (AME) preachers. Jarena Lee, convinced that God wanted her to preach, approached Richard Allen, the founder and bishop of the AME Church, and asked for his permission. He did not grant her permission, so Lee married a minister and tried to live her life as a minister's wife. Years later, while she was sitting in church, the male minister leading the service lost track of what he was doing. Lee jumped up and took over, and her performance convinced Allen that she was indeed called by God to preach. She became an itinerant preacher and traveled thousands of miles to deliver sermons. Although the hierarchy of the church refused to license her as a preacher, calling her instead an "official traveling exhorter," Lee described herself as the "first female preacher of the First African Methodist Episcopal Church." Quaker women also engaged in ministry even though their religious institution did not acknowledge them. Lucretia Mott—a teacher, mother of six, and activist—began her ministry in 1818, speaking in Quaker meetings and organizing a female antislavery society. In 1840, she attended the World's Anti-Slavery Convention in London—where women were only allowed to watch, not to participate—and there she met Elizabeth Cady Stanton and agreed to form an organization to promote women's rights.

In the same way that the prohibition of ordained women does not translate into an absence of women ministers, permitting the ordination of women does not translate into an abundance of them. Although many Christian denominations currently profess that ordination is open to women, such a rule does not an egalitarian system make. Survey after survey administered in denomination after denomination for the last fifteen years reveals that, in the words of a United Methodist study in 1993 on the retention of female clergy, "the gifts of God for the people of God are being rejected." Women ministers have different experiences than their male counterparts, and these different—read more *difficult*—experiences are shaped by sexism and often compounded by racism. Female ministers are paid less than male ministers with equal or less experience; male ministers are more likely to be hired as senior ministers than female ministers; more female ministers are offered part-time or interim work than their male colleagues; men are more liable than women to be senior pastors of larger, wealthier congregations; the higher the position in the church, the less likely a woman will be accepted in it; women clergy are leaving local church ministry at a higher rate than men, and if these women are women of color, they are less likely to return to church ministry than their White female colleagues; women wait longer than men for their first call to a congregation; many women leave parish ministry as a result of terrible experiences with senior ministers; and women endure sexual harassment, individual discrimination, and systemic discrimination on a regular basis. And yet, when asked, most congregants don't think sexism is a problem in the church.

In a way these surveys, like the version of history that begins with the year women were officially ordained, are misleading. They create the sense that the difficulties faced by women ministers are new, that we have only just discovered that women have a hard time in the church. Surveys generate a Columbus effect, allowing us to shout, *look what we discovered!* Only the fact that we do not know our history allows us to think this way. One of my professors in divinity school, feminist theologian and biblical scholar Elisabeth Schüssler Fiorenza, continually reminded us of the importance of knowing women's history. If we do not know about the struggles that came before us, we will repeat the past without learning from it.

Consider the life of Antoinette Brown. In 1847, she applied to seminary at Oberlin. Although the seminary faculty did not want to let her enter the program, they were also not comfortable denying anyone the chance to learn more about religion. They allowed her to attend classes but refused to enroll her officially as a student, declined to call on her in class, and would not give her a student license to preach. Although she completed all the requirements for a degree, they failed to grant her a diploma. While she was a student, Brown wrote a biblical exegesis of the passage in Paul's letter to the Corinthians where he writes that women should be silent in churches (which must have been shouted at her continually), and, surprisingly, the *Oberlin Quarterly Review* published it. Brown—like many religious feminists before and after her—was under the illusion that if she could just prove that the Bible supported the ministry of women, churches would open ordination to women.

Because of the way she was treated while in school, Brown did not seek ordination through Oberlin and instead asked to be ordained by her church, which, at that time, was Orthodox Congregational. They refused, so she trained herself as a public speaker, lecturing on women's rights, temperance, and abolition. Occasionally a Unitarian minister would invite her to preach at his church. Finally, in 1853, she received a call to the First Congregational Church in Butler and Savannah, Wayne County, New York. It was a tiny congregation that had been unable to secure a male minister, mostly because they only paid a $300-a-year salary. Before they hired Brown, they had employed an African American minister, an unusual arrangement even for an abolitionist congregation. Brown did not only want to be hired by that church, she wanted to be ordained by the denomination, a crucial milestone, she argued, in the fight for women's rights. Most officials in the denomination and even some of Brown's friends were opposed to her ordination because she was a woman. But others, including many members of Brown's congregation, opposed her ordination because they opposed ordination for *anyone,* male or female. As farmer and congregation member George Caudee said, "This church does not believe in the necessity of ordination as a qualification to preach the gospel." In the minds of many congregation members, Brown already had demonstrated her God-given preaching capability; she did not need human endorsement. Nevertheless, the parish voted to ordain Brown even though the powers that be in the denomination were against the decision. She was ordained on September 15, 1853. A storm of criticism followed, and the denomination refused to give her an official certificate.

Despite the congregants' early support of her, Brown and her congregation did not get along. Their difficulties were primarily theological. The Schneiders write, "In contrast to her dour Calvinistic parishioners, she had always insisted on a God of love." The trouble with her congregation and her denomination made her question her abilities as a minister and shook her faith. She left the church and decided never to work in an established church again, writing, "For I cannot breathe there freely." She stayed out of institutional religion until 1875, when she joined the Unitarians—as a minister.

Brown's story sounds eerily similar to those told by the women I interviewed and to the results of the most recent denominational surveys. Churches and seminaries and divinity schools and congregations have been doing the same thing to women for hundreds and hundreds of years. For a long time women have been filling pulpits men do not want in places men refuse to live for salaries men will not accept. Reading about Antoinette Brown I thought to myself, can't churches get a little more creative? And then I thought, if churches have been doing similar things to women for hundreds of years, why do we continue to deny that sexism is a problem? Why do we continue to administer surveys that tell us the same story again and again? Surveys suggest that now that denominations know the truth, they are actively engaged in making the lives of women ministers better, but unless there is an explicit, concrete commitment to remedy what they expose, surveys can be dangerous tools of institutions, allowing us to look like we are paying attention to discrimination without ever really having to do anything to address it.

Just like there are ways to keep people from voting even when the law has granted them the right, there are ways to keep women from getting ordained without ever having to say that is what you are doing. The simple fact that a denomination claims to ordain women does not mean that they actually ordain women, nor does it mean that women have equal access to all levels of the institution. Throughout the ordination process—the denominational requirements for a person who wants to get ordained that begin when a woman experiences a sense of call and end when she finds a job—countless opportunities exist for people with power to tell women who want to be ordained no: No, you do not belong here. No, your theology does not fit here. No, I do not believe you have been called. No, you are not the stuff out of which a minister is made.

In the Episcopal Church, standard process for pursuing ordination looks something like this: Someone feels she is called to be a priest; she tells one of the priests at her church that she thinks she might like to be a priest; the church then becomes her "sponsoring church" and establishes a discernment committee, a group of people in the parish whose task is to determine whether or not she is indeed called to be a priest; and then, usually with the support of the diocese and the church, she attends divinity school or seminary to earn a master's of divinity. The technical term for someone exploring the possibility of ordination is *inquirer.* After you are an inquirer, you become a *postulant,* and then, the final step before ordination, you become a *candidate.* Moving from one stage to the next is an involved and often frightening experience. You meet with the Commission on Ministry, various other committees, and your bishop several times. You are asked all kinds of questions about Jesus and God and your family of origin. And there are multiple hoops through which you must jump—papers to write, divinity school or seminary to attend, internships to complete, biblical languages to learn, psychological evaluations to undergo, general ordination exams to take, hospital patients to visit. The ordination process looks different from denomination to denomination, but, across the board, it's very complicated. How a denomination trains future ministers—what it requires them to do, how it encourages them to think—reveals how that denomination thinks about ministry itself. Is it something that can be learned? Does it require a certain skill set? Is it a profession like any other profession? Is it a job or a way of being? The ordination process initiates would-be ministers into ministry. It is as much about discipline as it is about discernment, as much about teaching you how to be a minister as it is about determining if you are called to that role.

Denominations have developed increasingly standardized procedures for ordination, moving away from the bishop-slaps-you-on-the-back method to straightforward and transparent denominational requirements. Even without backslapping, the process is largely subjective, more ambiguous than clear, and more frightening than supportive. Throughout the process, your task is to convince people that you must be ordained—people on committees, people who are already ordained, people in congregations, people who are part of institutions with histories of shutting women out of ordained ministry for thousands of years, people who, no matter how progressive, still, for the most part, do not picture a woman when they hear the word "priest." The ordination process is not easy for men, either. It is a difficult time no matter what. Rather than simply revealing struggles specific to women, the experiences of women in the ordination process expose a system that is broken, ill equipped to deal with bodies and sex and sexuality and dating and youth and difference and change.

From the moment the women I interviewed felt a pull toward being ministers, they struggled to translate that feeling into institutional processes often designed without them in mind. All through the journey to ordination, beliefs about what a minister should look like, sound like, live like, and think like are laid bare. And these beliefs belong not only to the people women encounter during the process but to the women themselves. Surviving sexism requires women to become experts at being what other people want them to be. The ordination process calls on these highly honed skills of accommodation. Yet, no matter how hard the women I interviewed tried not to rock the boat, their very presence set it rolling. And many denominations, failing to recognize that there was something wrong with the boat and not with the women, threw them overboard.

Chapter One

THE CALL

I once heard the rector of my church in Pasadena quote Frederick Buechner's definition of vocation in a sermon. Vocation, Buechner says, is the place where the world's greatest need and a person's greatest joy meet. Although selfless struggle is seductive, doing the work the world needs—fighting poverty, racism, sexism, imperialism, environmental destruction—is only half of the equation. The work that is yours must also bring you joy.

The word "vocation" comes from the Latin verb *vocare,* which means "to call." Vocation as "calling" has dominated how it is understood in religious contexts. For many who are considering being ordained, the idea of call is something literal: The voice of God speaks, directing the listener to a life of ministry. For others, the idea of call is figurative: It might come as a feeling, a kind of knowing, a crazy idea that won't leave, a sense that this is the work they are meant to do in the world. Sometimes call is understood as the pattern that emerges in a string of events. Other times the voices calling belong to friends and family or to the words on the pages of a book.

The Bible is filled with stories about people who hear the voice of God calling them to a certain kind of work. The plot of most biblical call stories is fairly standard: Someone hears the voice of God; rejects the idea that he or she is the right person for the job by listing all the ways she or he is not up to the task; tries to avoid God's call by running away (remember Jonah?); and, eventually, answers the call, doing what God demands that he or she do. Most often, God calls people by saying their names. "Abraham," God says, and Abraham—or Amos or Isaiah or Sarah—answers, "Here I am." The Hebrew word for "Here I am," *hineini,* can be translated as "ready." God's prophets answer God's call by saying ready, even before they know what they will be asked to do.

For many Christian denominations, believing that you have been called is a central requirement for getting ordained. Whether you believe your call came as the voice of God or as a feeling inside of you, you have to be able to tell your story to others in a way that reveals you have indeed been called to be a minister. The task of the budding minister is to persuade a committee or a priest or a pastor not only that she wants to be ordained but that God intends for her to be ordained.

Call sets ministry apart from all other vocations, constructs being a priest or a pastor as radically different than being a plumber or a teacher or a lawyer. I believe that we are all called to something, that Buechner's idea of vocation is open to everyone, that we all ought to have the freedom to find that place where our deepest joy and the world's greatest need meet. But doctors and architects don't have to prove they have found that place. Ministers do. Even though most of the women I interviewed questioned the category "call," it remained central to the language they used to tell me when they knew they wanted to be ordained. And this language served them more than it got in their way. Claiming your call is an empowering thing to do when other people are telling you that you cannot be a minister because you are gay, or female, or Black, or too political, or too young, or too whatever is outside the dominant version of "minister." Women denied access to ordination—either by their denominations or by individual people in authority—have used their sense of call to sustain them in the struggle. The knowledge that they have been called by God gives them strength to resist oppression, furnishes them with the clarity needed to fight for their vocation and for their rights.

The central idea of Protestantism—that each human being has access to God, unmediated by an institutional hierarchy—has worked in women's favor. Claims of direct communication grant women authority even when their denominations refuse to. Women have understood themselves as ordained by God, if not by the institutional church, and this knowledge has empowered them. At the same time, women's assertions have exposed a fundamental inconsistency in Protestantism: the theological conviction that all human beings are equal before God and the simultaneous belief that some human beings (men, Whites, straight, propertied) are better than others (women, people of color, homosexuals, poor). The professed equality of all human beings has not translated into actual equality.

Many of the women I interviewed knew from a very early age that they wanted to be ministers. Although we sometimes like to believe that they don't, and even hope that they aren't, children pay attention in church and in Sunday school. Most of the women I interviewed attended church as children. They loved church. Some went to church alone, without their parents or siblings. Some worried that when something bad happened to someone they loved it was because they didn't pray hard enough or long enough or because they fell asleep before they finished their prayers. Some held secret communion services in their bedrooms and tree houses, pressing Wonder bread flat between their hands and drinking juice. Some cried, not because they didn't get asked to a dance but because their churches wouldn't let girls be acolytes. When they were teenagers, some went to church on Wednesday nights and Sunday mornings. They listened to sermons, fell in love with liturgy, whispered memorized prayers in their rooms, asked important questions a few adults were brave enough to admit they didn't know the answers to. They craved ritual. They sensed hypocrisy, understood the difference between what happened on Sunday mornings and what happened during the rest of the week, or even what happened in the parking lot right after church. They noticed when they were asked to participate, when they were given responsibility, when someone cared that they were there.

Although many women knew from a young age that they wanted to be ministers, most did not know any female ministers, making it hard for them to imagine themselves as ministers. Because either they did not know any female ministers or they did not know women could be ministers at all, their feeling that they wanted to be ordained sometimes made them feel crazy.

Most of the women I interviewed remember the first time they saw an ordained woman and how this vision opened up their sense of vocation. Jamie Washam, an American Baptist pastor in Milwaukee, grew up Southern Baptist in Texas and didn't see any female pastors. The women she did see in church, women who were shut out of most leadership positions even though they practically ran the church, didn't look like her. "Zipper Bibles, elastic pants, big ol' white sneakers, WHAT WOULD JESUS DO bracelets," she said. "I mean, that's not what I look like."

It might at first seem shallow, the idea that somehow you need to see someone who looks like you, even dresses like you, to be able to imagine yourself doing a certain job, but seeing a minister who looked like them or talked like them or had theology like them signaled to these women that there was a place for them in the church. It was a kind of welcome, and it was only when they felt this welcome that they realized how shut out they had been feeling. When you belong to a group that religions hate and ostracize—or just ignore— you have to be able to imagine what you have not yet seen or heard. This is holy work.

And it is work these women did. Called to be something they had never seen, something their families, their denominations, their churches, and their congregations had never seen, they chose ordained ministry. For every single one of the women I interviewed, it was Buechner's definition that shaped her vocation. I have seen many of them at work. Watching them celebrate weddings, preach sermons, share communion, march in protests, lead congregations in prayer, speak out against injustice, I had no doubt in my mind that they were meant to be ministers. They seemed to glow, as if all the molecules in their bodies had lined up to say yes, this is what I was made to do. This is what brings me alive. This is where the world's greatest need and my deepest joy meet.

Throughout Monica Coleman's fight for ordination in the AME Church, she was confident that she had been called by God, not by the church. "The bishop didn't call me and say, Monica, would you like to be a minister? God bugged the hell out of me until I said, yes, God, I'll do this. And so my first allegiance was and always is to God," she said. "I was also clear that y'all are not the boss of me, to use that expression, and if you don't ordain me, God still called me. I was clear that God had called me, and God was the one I answered to ultimately."

Monica didn't know any ordained women when she was a child. "Preacher wasn't one of the things that was an option for little girls to be," she said. "I never saw female clergy growing up. I never even saw clergy under fifty." Monica didn't see female clergy until she went to college, and it wasn't until her junior year at Harvard that she met ministers who, in her words, weren't old. She was at the Black Women in the Academy conference, which was held at MIT. She couldn't get into the session with Toni Morrison, and, while they were kicking her out, she ended up standing next to a man she thought was cute. It turned out he was a divinity school student at Andover Newton Theological Seminary. He and Monica became friends, and he introduced her to his friends at Andover Newton and Harvard Divinity School. Hanging out with people training to be ministers who were in their twenties and still doing all the regular things that people in their twenties do—dating, drinking, going out to dinner—shifted Monica's perception of the ministry.

About that time, Monica had a friend who began to struggle with her own call to ministry. She was a fifth-generation minister, but the first female, and her family told her she could not preach because she was a woman. "I knew the passages they were quoting her from the Bible. She was having such a hard time personally, continually having to reassert herself and her call to her family, and I was like, wow, you can do it. And then I told her, I am glad it's you and not me." Monica laughed. "I actually said it out loud."

And then, much to her friend's delight, it *was* Monica, too. In college, Monica was in Campus Crusade for Christ, and she was active in a local AME church. Her college fellowship group planned a ski trip, and although Monica doesn't ski, she decided to go, mostly because she looks cute in ski clothes, she told me, laughing. Every day she woke up and did a devotional while the rest of the group went skiing. "One morning, God took me to Amos," she said. "Amos 7. His call story." She read me the passage: "And then Amos said to Amaziah, I am not a prophet, nor a prophet's son; but I am a herdsman and a gatherer of sycamore fruit, and the Lord took me from following the flock and said, 'Go, prophesy to my people Israel.'" The moment Monica read this passage she knew what it meant.

"I was mad about it," she said. "I was just trying to be a student. I wanted to be a scholar, to mind my own business, and God took me and said, go. That's exactly how I heard it." She called her friend and said, "Guess what God had the nerve to tell me this morning." Her friend laughed and laughed.

Although Monica understood that experience with Amos to be a clear message from God—"I mean who just randomly lands in Amos by themselves?" she asked—Monica was not ready to "go" just yet. "I decided I wanted to be as far away from the pulpit as possible but still be in the church," she said. "And so I became an usher. You could find me at the back door."

Later that same year, she attended a conference where Renita Weems—a scholar, writer, and AME minister—was speaking. Throughout the conference, Monica was tortured by her sense of call. She couldn't stop thinking about it. And she couldn't stop thinking about Luke 19. "The part that always stuck out for me was the part where somebody rebukes the crowd for praising Jesus, and he says, if they don't worship me, the rocks will cry out." On the day she was supposed to meet Rev. Dr. Weems, Monica started picturing her dorm room furniture, her books, her couch, and her television set. All the objects in her room had mouths, like Muppets, and they were praising God because she wouldn't. "I had this vision, and I was like, oh my God, I better do this. It was the first time I wasn't scared when I thought about becoming a pastor." Right after this vision, Angela Davis took Monica to meet Rev. Dr. Weems. While she was standing in line to meet her and to ask her to sign copies of her book, Monica started crying. "Renita doesn't know me from Adam, and she is signing books, and I can't stop crying and saying 'I'm going to be a preacher.' And she says, 'Well, good for you. Why don't you sit down and collect yourself and we'll talk about it.'"

Monica was nineteen years old. She returned from the conference and called her mother to tell her she was going to be a preacher. "Great. I knew it," her mother said. "Now you have to start wearing long skirts."

Almost immediately, Monica's call, when heard by others, was filtered through their cultural expectations about ministers. "My mom kind of wanted me to act like I was forty, and I was like, I'm nineteen. I was almost twenty. I was still a kid. I'm young," Monica said. "My perspective on it always was, and still is, that the day before July 3, 1994, I was a Christian trying to do the right thing, and I was the day after. I'm still a Christian trying to do the right thing. I didn't see a radical change that had occurred. I didn't feel like I should have to act any different, or any more holy, or dress different. That's not how I understood it. If it wasn't wrong before, it shouldn't be wrong now." Monica believes that everyone is called to something—"I'd like my doctor to be a called doctor," she said—and she didn't see any reason why a call to ministry should be different than a call to any other vocation.

The pastor of her family's church did not think that Monica was called to be a minister. "I had been active in the church after I graduated from high school, going back and teaching classes, this and that, so they knew who I was," she said. "But the relationship changed drastically once the pastor found out I was called to ministry." Monica was given the task of proving her call. The pastor told her to pray and to fast. "I got sick as a dog fasting and praying. I was anemic. I ended up in the hospital. I really can't fast. I can pray, but I can't fast." Monica understands part of what she was put through as a kind of hazing, the church's way of "making sure you're sure," she said. "Which I think is really silly. It's not like you are going into it for the power, the prestige, and the money. Only God can make you do it."

The pastor's doubt about her call dumbfounded her. Being a minister was not something she had intended to do, and it certainly did not make her life easier. "I mean, I had plans. It put a wrench in my plans. I really felt called to it, but of course, I didn't know exactly what I was called to do." While she was an undergraduate, her advisers were grooming her to get a Ph.D. When her faculty found out she was going to be a minister, they thought it was a mistake. "They thought I was going to 'waste good talent,' so to speak, good academic talent on ministry. That wasn't what they said, but that was definitely how I felt." Her father also wasn't too keen on the ministry idea, either. "I had just gotten him onto the academic plan off the corporate plan," she said. "And he was already mad enough that he was spending Harvard money for me to major in what? You know, African American Studies as opposed to economics and math as I had intended. And so he was like, what's going to happen now?"

Jackie Ballard,* an ordained United Church of Christ (UCC) minister, grew up going to church with her mother. She paid careful attention to sermons from a young age. "I remember leaning in and really listening. I remember looking at the preacher and thinking, how does he know all this stuff? How does he know so much about life and scripture? I remember thinking, that's really cool. I want to be able to know that." Jackie went through her church's confirmation process and began to get involved with the youth group. Because she was preparing for confirmation, she was given more responsibility in the community. She was asked to help tape-record the services every Sunday, and she was also in the bell choir. Seminarians from the local divinity school ran her youth group, and she was fascinated by one in particular, a woman named Susan. She had been a lawyer before she entered seminary, and Jackie, mesmerized, asked her all kinds of questions. "What are you doing in seminary, anyway? Why are you doing this? What does it mean? Those kinds of questions," she said.

Jackie went to confirmation class before church on Sunday mornings, then she attended church and helped tape the service. She stayed after church for youth group activities like afternoon barbecues and went to youth group again on Wednesday nights. "I got really hooked into it," Jackie said. "It felt like a place where I could be myself and explore some of the tougher questions about being a teenager." The day of her confirmation, Jackie was moved to tears. The church was located on the town's green, and after the ceremony, she stood outside on the lawn. "It was a beautiful day," she said. "And I remember looking back at the church and feeling like, I'm going to do this someday. I am going to study theology. I had no idea what theology was. I feel that was clearly the day I was called."

But during and even after college, Jackie rarely went to church. She didn't return until she had a crisis in her late twenties. She was employed at a marketing company and was spending more time than anyone else in the office. "I was working ridiculous hours," Jackie said. "No one else was working those kinds of hours. It was compulsive, overwork kind of stuff, now that I can look back at it: The harder you work, the more you accomplish, the more you are loved, that kind of thing." With her life out of balance, Jackie had a breakdown. "I literally cracked. I woke up one morning, and I was just sitting on the edge of my bed, and I was dressed, and my sister—I lived with my sister at the time—looked at me, and she asked, what's wrong?" When Jackie told me this story, she started to cry. "I said to my sister, I can't do this anymore. I cannot do this anymore. I was weeping, just this awful feeling, how did I get to this point in my life? I had a huge job. I made a lot of money. And I was miserable. Miserable. Single. Lonely." Jackie called work and said she would not be in for the rest of the week.

Some friends directed her to a couple who specialized in career transition retreats. Jackie attended a weekend-long retreat. "I was the youngest one there," Jackie said. "Everyone else was at least fifty-five." Depressed and anxious to find anything that might help her feel better, Jackie turned to books and tapes about the power of positive thinking, some of which were very Christian. "I was at such a low place, I would do anything to try to get out of it," she said. One of the tapes Jackie listened to included guided religious visualizations. "They would say, imagine Jesus at your side with his hand on your shoulder the whole time, and imagine that you have that level of support." Jackie continued to work at the marketing firm through her depression. "I used to walk to work. It was about a half-an-hour walk," she said. "At one point I said, God, it is yours. Take me. It was a conversion experience. I said, take me and use me because I cannot do this alone. And as soon as I did that, things got better."

Jackie went to visit her parents one weekend and returned to the church where she had been an active member of the youth group. There, she met the new associate minister who was a Harvard Divinity School graduate. The associate minister, a woman, told Jackie that they were having a youth retreat near where Jackie lived, and she volunteered to help. "I don't think I knew it at the time, but I wanted to talk to her about what she was doing," Jackie said. "She was yet another woman I felt drawn to. I thought she was really cool and down to earth and interesting." Jackie asked her what divinity school was like, and the minister told her that she thought everyone should go to divinity school. Then she asked, "Why do you want to know? Are you thinking about it?"

"I don't know," Jackie said. "I don't really know what it is."

Jackie began to consider divinity school as a possibility, and she shared her thoughts with one of her best friends who was studying Jewish American History in graduate school. Her friend encouraged her to call divinity schools and seminaries and ask for course catalogs, just to see the kind of classes they offered. Jackie remembers the day the catalogs arrived in the mail. "I started reading the descriptions, and I thought, this is it. It felt like exactly what I wanted to do." She made arrangements to visit a nearby school. After the visit, walking back to her car, Jackie looked over her shoulder at the building. "I turned and looked back at the school and felt this wave of peace, just a wash, and I knew that I had found what I was looking for." She applied to the master's of divinity program, was accepted, and enrolled the following fall. She was on the road to becoming a UCC minister.

When Diana Holbert heard the call to be a minister, she didn't know any women ministers, but she did have a teacher one summer who changed the course of her life. Raised in the church in a small town in Kansas where her father was a doctor and the choir director— "We would have to wait until the babies were delivered before we could sing the anthem!"—Diana knew she was loved. "I knew from the beginning that Jesus loved me, and that Jesus loved all the little children of the world. That was unquestioned," she said. In sixth grade, Diana attended vacation Bible school, and her teacher was named Ms. Irene Paulson. "I don't know what you would call her," Diana said. "A mystic, I guess. And most people in Kansas were not mystics. Some people probably thought she was a little crazy, but thank God they allowed her to teach the sixth graders, the most important age, eleven- and twelve-year-old minds." That summer, Ms. Irene Paulson asked her students to put gold stars on her favorite Bible passages. "She was passing down what was important to her, and telling us it could be important to us," Diana said. "And it was." Ms. Irene Paulson told her class about meeting Jesus on the country roads of Kansas. "My parents were very cosmopolitan, very well educated, world travelers, artsy and all that, but not mystical," Diana said. "She unplugged something in me that was so important. She gave me a language for what I already knew, but it was kind of a preknowing about the spiritual realm, the way the holy spirit works. She gave me this incredibly beautiful gift."

At the end of the summer, Ms. Irene Paulson asked her students to promise their lives to God. Diana said, "I promised in front of God and these witnesses that I would give myself as a missionary to Africa." At that time, the United Methodist Church had only been ordaining women for two years, and Diana didn't know any female ministers, although she had once seen one. "She had on big black shoes, and I thought, she's way too scary for me," Diana said. "When it came my time to promise my life to God, it never, ever would have been to be an ordained minister because I didn't look like her, and I just knew men ministers."

Ignoring all signs that were pointing toward ordained ministry because she didn't really think being a minister was possible for women, Diana misinterpreted her call and decided it belonged to her boyfriend, John, whom she met when she was a freshman in college. They had only been dating for two weeks when Diana knew that she wanted to marry him. John, however, wanted to be an English professor, a vocational desire that did not fit Diana's vision for her life as a missionary. After three months she said, "John, I'm serious about you. I love you. And I want to marry you, but I can't, and it's because you're going to be an English professor. I need you to be a Methodist minister." Diana told me this story laughing. She said, "That was not at all what I needed, but that's the way I translated it because of the culture. That was 1966."

John agreed to switch majors, partly out of a love for Hebrew, partly out of a love for Diana, and partly because the Vietnam War was under way, and his draft number was 13. In that context, Diana said, "The call of God got very loud." John was ordained as a minister, and Diana became a minister's wife.

When they moved to take John's first job as an associate minister, Diana got a phone call. The woman on the other end of the telephone said, "Hello, Diana. I am calling to welcome you. I am the head parsonette."

"What are you talking about?" Diana asked.

"I am the head parsonette," she said again. "Parsonettes are all the ministers' wives in the area."

When Diana told me this, I asked, "Did you get a baton? It sounds like you should be twirling something."

Like a dutiful young pastor's wife with a brand-new baby, Diana did what she thought she was supposed to do and joined the parsonettes. She hated attending the meetings. "It was a bunch of depressed women who probably had been called to be in ordained ministry."

Diana worked on the music staff of the church where her husband was the associate. She was a soloist, directed the children's choirs, and developed a dance ministry. One Sunday, she went with two women to hear one of her friends preach at a different church. When Diana's friend introduced them as visitors, she told the congregation that they were liturgical dancers. Members of the congregation begged them to dance, and so they agreed. They did a short movement response to a psalm. When they finished, people in the congregation had tears in their eyes. After church, the four friends went to lunch at Dairy Queen. Diana complimented her friend on her sermon and told her she thought she should go to seminary and be a minister.

One of the other dancers turned and looked at her. "No, Diana," she said. "You're the one. You need to go to seminary."

At that moment, something shifted for Diana. She said, "It was a weight that actually wasn't lifted from my shoulder, it dropped into my stomach." So in 1988, in March, twenty-two years after she convinced her husband he was the one who ought to be a minister, Diana left the ranks of the parsonettes and entered seminary.

———

In the booth of a Dairy Queen, surrounded by her friends, Diana finally heard her call and claimed it. She needed other women's ears to hear what she needed to hear. Being part of a community that can recognize your call is an essential element no matter what your vocation. And yet, our ability—or inability—to realize our call and the calls of others is shaped by our context and by the limits we put on ourselves and each other. I have always been amazed by women who defy the expectations of what others think women can do— who fly airplanes or sail boats or swim across oceans, who photograph or fight wars, who run underground railroads, who work multiple jobs and raise children, who head corporations and universities. I have also been amazed by women who shatter their own expectations, who realize the life they have constructed does not match their dreams and risk everything to live with integrity— women who go on vacation and decide to stay, who leave high salaries for jobs with meaning, who write or paint or sing or act even though they never thought they could. Discovering something new about yourself is exhilarating; living into that discovery can be terrifying. But as jarring as it can be to realize you are not the person you want to be, it is nothing compared to the sanctions that follow when you are not the person others think you should be, when you defy cultural rules and expectations.

Some of the women I interviewed could not imagine themselves as ministers until they saw ministers who looked like them. Congregations have a similar problem. A 2003 Episcopal survey revealed that congregation members who see an ordained woman in the pulpit and at the altar are significantly more likely to approve of women in all church leadership positions than those who see only men. That doesn't mean things are easy for the first ordained woman who dares to stand in a church's pulpit. But it might be easier for the next woman, and the woman after her, and the woman after her. The presence of ordained women in churches changes everyone, renders what once seemed impossible, possible, the merely imagined, real.

Chapter Two

THE ORDINATION PROCESS

When I first entered the ordination process, the rector of the church where I worked sat me down to explain how to enter the process and come out on the other side as a priest. Every question I would be asked throughout the entire process had a right answer, she told me. Over and over again, she emphasized that the official difference between lay and ordained ministry centered on the Eucharist. "When they ask you why you want to be ordained, there is definitely a correct answer to the question," she explained. "You have to say you want to get ordained in order to be able to celebrate the Eucharist."

She was not exaggerating. The Episcopal Church has been trying to value the ministry of all people ("the priesthood of all believers") while simultaneously articulating what is unique about the ministry of those who are ordained. As a result, a definition of ordained ministry was created that centers on the sacraments. There are two of them in the Episcopal Church, baptism and communion. In this understanding of ordained ministry, priests are like magicians: They are the only ones who can do the correct hand motions, say the right words, and make something happen. This understanding of priests does what the church wants it to do—it broadens the idea of a more general ministry to include the work of all people, not just the ordained, yet still manages to reserve an exclusive and powerful role for priests.

My rector's advice was designed to help me, but it was ironic that she had to encourage this narrow understanding of ordination. It is central to the argument used to bar women from the priesthood.

Most religious institutions have excluded women from ordained ministry using one of two main lines of argument: biblical inerrancy or sacramentalism. Some religious institutions believe the Bible to be the literal word of God, and they use passages in this text to justify their prohibition of women, such as the one found in Paul's letter to Timothy: "I permit no woman to teach or have authority over a man; she is to keep silent." "Proof texting," as it is sometimes known, does not have a good history; the Bible has been used to justify wars, slavery, and all kinds of oppression, discrimination, and exclusion. Those who claim to take the Bible literally often accuse those who don't of treating the Bible like a buffet, accepting what they like and rejecting what they don't. Most biblical literalists, however, do just as much picking and choosing as everyone else—yelling that sodomy is an abomination but not keeping kosher; insisting women should be silent but not visiting the sick or those in prison; claiming only heterosexual couples can marry but not working to abolish poverty.

The sacramental argument against the ordination of women centers on the Eucharist. The communion ritual involves not just *remembering* the last meal Jesus shared with his friends but turning the bread and the wine either into the actual body and blood of Christ (Roman Catholics) or making Jesus present spiritually in them (Episcopalians); the priest is the only one who can do this holy work and, to do it, the priest has to be a man—so the argument goes—because Jesus was a man.

It's hard for me to imagine Jesus would support this argument.

The narrow definition of ordained ministry now championed by the Episcopal Church does not match the richness of the job, nor does it explain why women have fought so hard to get ordained. Being a minister is more than administering the sacraments, and often the most meaningful work ministers do happens outside the walls of the church. The ordination of women provides an opportunity for all denominations to ask fundamental questions about what makes a priest a priest, about what, if anything, makes an ordained person different than a layperson, about the structure of our institutions. But instead of daring to ask these fundamental questions, we have retreated to easy answers, to old and familiar territory. In so doing, we have missed an opportunity to rethink the purpose of ordination, the roles of ministers, the dangers of clericalism, and the revolutionary power of congregations.

Early in the ordination process, prospective ministers have to make a decision: Will they do whatever they need to do and say whatever they need to say to get ordained or will they trust the process and let it work, no matter what the outcome? Most of the women I interviewed decided to tell the truth, no matter what the consequences. "If they are going to ordain me," Jamie Washam said, "they better ordain *me*." Opting to tell the truth means risking the possibility of rejection, of losing your vocation. And the risk is even greater for those who feel called to ordained ministry and are living lives many versions of the church do not sanction—those who are lesbian, gay, queer, or transgender, who are living with the people they love before they are married, who question dogma and doctrine and biblical authority. Many denominations have chosen to follow the military, adopting a version of don't ask, don't tell. Such a policy puts everyone at risk, encouraging dishonesty and secrecy and wreaking havoc on those who don't ask, on those who don't tell, and especially on those who do.

Listening to women's stories, I realized that the ordination process in many denominations assumes things about women's lives that do not fit how they are actually living. The problem for the women I interviewed was not necessarily determining *what* they needed to do to get ordained. The problem was *how* to do it, how to make their complicated life experiences fit into an institutional process that was not made with them in mind. If they deviated at all from what was expected of them—if they had different theology than what was professed by their denominations, if they attended divinity school before they entered the ordination process instead of after, if they chose to go to divinity school instead of seminary, if they entered the ordination process single but then got married, if they grew up in a denomination other than the one in which they wanted to get ordained—things got rough.

As I discussed before, the starting point of the ordination process in the Episcopal Church is finding a sponsoring church. A sponsoring church presents you to the diocese as a possible candidate for ordination and sometimes supports you financially during seminary or divinity school. It is usually understood that you will return to the diocese in which your sponsoring church is located once you are ordained. A sponsoring church can be either the church you currently attend or the church of your childhood. But what if, as in my case, you aren't currently attending a church when you begin the process and you grew up Catholic? I spent my childhood in Dallas, went to college in New Haven, Connecticut, first thought about the priesthood when I lived in Los Angeles, and then moved to Cambridge, Massachusetts, for graduate school. Just where exactly was my home? The expectations that I would be able to find a sponsoring church and that I would want to stay and work in the diocese that ordained me are relics of an earlier time when most Americans, men and women, lived and died in the same place.

Like me, Jessica Mayberry* had trouble fitting her life into the ordination process. She grew up in the South, went to school in the Pacific Northwest, worked in New York City, took another job in the Midwest, and then returned to the East Coast for divinity school. She attended an Episcopal high school, and although the school exposed her to liberal thought, there were also "a lot of sweater sets and pearls and those kind of conservative trappings." Jessica went to a college where people ran around barefoot and wearing tank tops. "It was really exciting, but also confusing." She attended an Episcopal church on and off throughout college, but she usually slept through Sunday morning services.

After college, she moved to New York City. "I graduated from college, and I didn't know what I wanted to do, so I took the LSAT, like everyone else, and moved to New York City." She moved in with two of her best friends and found a job working in a college admissions office. "That year in New York was really powerful for me in terms of my formation, and my sense of…" Jessica stopped. "I actually hate the language of calling. It just sounds so grand," she said. "It implies that we somehow have access to God's mind, and that if I have been called, then the implication is that you have not. I don't like the exclusivity of that, and I don't like the implication that I somehow know what God thinks. I also don't like it because in human terms, it's a conversation stopper. If I say I have been called, then what can people really say to that? I think it prevents people from being responsible in a certain kind of way."

Instead of calling, Jessica prefers to talk about "the deepest desire of our hearts," and it was this that New York City awakened in her. Her two friends worked at New York art galleries. "I would find myself at the Louis Vuitton runway show with somebody's free tickets," Jessica said, laughing. "They were connected women, and it was really fun. It was surreal to be twenty-two and prancing around Manhattan." She paused and then added, "I'm very adaptable. I can move in different kinds of worlds, and so being in New York City was exciting in a way, but I kind of felt soul sick there." During her lunch hour, Jessica would wander to Central Park and lie facedown in the grass. "I would find myself ducking into churches a lot, and I would sit there and just cry," she said. "It wouldn't matter when, what time of day. It could be Sunday morning, or it could be Tuesday at lunch, and I would just sob." She laughed. "I mean, it was really embarrassing. I would sit there and think, I'm such a freak." She began to have a recurring dream about one of her favorite stories from scripture.

"Being a pseudo-cradle Episcopalian I don't know the Bible very well," she said. "But I love the story of Jacob in the Old Testament coming into the river and wrestling with the angel. One of the most powerful aspects of the story for me is that he is injured in the end, and he limps for the rest of his life." Every night, in her dreams, Jessica, like Jacob, struggled with something, or someone. "During the day, I would cry, and then I would go home and have this dream, and my friends would be out in whatever new high heels they had." She decided to move. She got a job in the Midwest at a charter school and left New York on September 5, 2001. Her friends stayed in their apartment, and six days later, on September 11, it was covered in ash.

The charter school was project-based and interdisciplinary, with lots of funding. Jessica was given both support and autonomy. She found the work life-giving and the students incredible, and yet she still felt that something was missing. "The school's money came from tech interests," Jessica said. "And it was real techie, very secular. It worshipped the gods of science." Jessica continued to wander into churches and cry. "I kind of felt like why am I pushing so hard against this? Why do I keep ending up in worlds where there is no room to talk about God?"

She began to make appointments to meet with priests. The city where she lived, however, was part of a conservative Episcopal diocese that did not ordain its first woman priest until the mid-1980s. One of the priests Jessica met with was a woman. "I think she was pretty embittered, and had been beaten up by the process in the church to the point that my experiences with her were really negative," Jessica said. "It was too bad, because I was saying, hey, I'm twenty-three, and I could work at the summer camp, or I could teach this, and I'd like to be more involved, and she was just kind of like, yeah, we don't do that." Feeling as if she had reached a dead end, Jessica did what everyone else she knew was doing: She went to yoga and to the beach.

And then she decided to apply to divinity school. "I knew that I needed to push my discernment—to use a good church word—to a deeper place, and I needed to go someplace where I would be welcome to talk about God or the idea of God or my experiences of church or the whole family of things around that openly." She laughed, and then she said, "I felt like I needed to come out of the closet almost about my sense of faith." Jessica returned to the East Coast to attend divinity school. On her way, she visited the diocesan office in the city where she grew up. She told the bishop that she was going to divinity school, that she was not sure where it might lead, but that, someday, she might like to enter the ordination process in her hometown. "That was very politic," she said. "They appreciated it."

Jessica soon learned that the diocese where her divinity school was located was a hard place to get ordained, but she was not sure where else to turn. "At this point I had lived in so many places, and I really didn't have a home. I didn't have a logical place to enter," she said. "The process is a little crazy that way. I mean, they say they want young priests, and then they make it really hard, I think, for young folks to get in and get through it in any way that makes sense. There was no place I could call home." She decided that the diocese of her childhood might be the path of least resistance. She called and told them she would like to begin discernment with them and work there during the summer. They agreed.

The discernment process went smoothly. Trouble for Jessica did not really emerge until she was in her final year of divinity school. Jessica's sponsoring diocese expected that she would return to her hometown when she finished graduate school and was ordained. At first, this expectation felt okay to her. She couldn't think of any good reasons not to go back. She knew she did not intend to live there forever, but she could imagine working in that diocese for a couple of years. Then she fell in love and got engaged. Her fiancé wasn't enthusiastic about moving south. When they got engaged, Jessica called her bishop to tell him the good news. She told me he said, "In my day, you had to go to the bishop and ask permission first."

Jessica's bishop, a man she describes as fair and smart and kind, but also quite rigid, a rule follower who is very into the institutional church and not open to pushing the limits, called her one Thursday morning—just a week before I interviewed her—to let her know he was in town and would like to meet her fiancé. He suggested the three of them have lunch that afternoon. Jessica started getting nervous. Her fiancé, Jordan, is not Episcopalian, and, in her words, has a lot of theological fire in him. Before the meeting with the bishop, Jessica tried to coach Jordan, asking him not to tell the bishop that they live together. Encouraging this omission infuriated Jordan and didn't sit well with Jessica. When the ordination process first started, she made a promise to herself to be honest, but as time went on, she realized vagueness, not honesty, was sometimes the best policy.

Jessica and Jordan met the bishop for lunch. The bishop entered the café, dropped his suitcase, put his arm around Jordan, and said, "So, Jordan, are you ready to move down south?" Jessica said he then proceeded to explain that he was married to a Yankee and that she agreed to come south with him for a year, just a year, but lo and behold, they have lived there happily for almost thirty years now.

Jessica and Jordan left the meeting feeling coerced, even manipulated. It seemed to them that the bishop had no understanding of their situation. Jordan, like Jessica, has a career path he is trying to follow. Jessica realized after the meeting that she had actually been banking on sexism to help her in that situation. She had hoped the bishop would assume that Jordan had his own vocational desires and that his career mattered more than Jessica's. She thought he would take for granted that she would follow Jordan, not the other way around. The bishop, instead, assumed Jordan would follow Jessica, but not because the bishop is a profeminist, antisexist man. He believed this because he presumed Jessica would follow the rules of the institution, no matter what. Priests are ordained in a diocese, and then they serve in that diocese. And that is that. He thought Jessica would behave the way men before her had behaved, the way he and his wife behaved. That meeting with the bishop forced Jessica to face that the church's hierarchy has not changed although the economic and social climate have. "I think he was counting on me needing or wanting to be ordained so badly that I would kind of roll over," she told me. "But I feel that if there's not a reasonable amount of room in this picture then I am going to go get another job and move on."

Several Episcopal dioceses, recognizing the dearth of young people entering ordained ministry, have developed programs for recruiting and supporting young people who are considering the priesthood as a vocation. The program at my parents' church in Dallas, Pathways to Ministry, offers summer internships to college students and a ten-month internship to recent college graduates. Each year, they also sponsor a national gathering for high school students. The program in Massachusetts is called the Micah Project, a nine-month residential internship during which interns ages twenty-one to thirty live together in community and work in the Boston area in self-selected social service projects while discerning their own vocational calls.

I met Catherine Cooper,* an alumna of one of the Episcopal Church's intern programs and now a priest, at her home, a sweet gray house perched on the top of a hill. She entered the program a year after college. It provided her with a community of people who were engaged in faith, and it made it possible for her to do something she knew she wanted to do but had no idea how to go about doing. She lived with two other interns, one of whom she eventually married—Jesse, who is also an Episcopal priest. Catherine was ordained when she was twenty-four and now, at twenty-seven, she is a solo pastor of a small church in a suburb of a large city. A writer herself, she immediately told me how glad she was that I was writing this book. "I mean the world doesn't know I exist," she said. "No one has any sense that progressive Christianity exists, or that young women are doing this, or that leadership in the church looks like this." She gestured at her corduroy pants, her dyed black hair, and the silver stud in her nose, adding, "I feel sort of messianic about that."

Catherine and Jesse went together to General Seminary, the Episcopal seminary in New York City. While at General, they felt like they had fallen through the cracks in their home diocese. Catherine ended up finding out about requirements for ordination from her classmates. General, to Catherine, seemed stuck in the model of education of the 1940s and 1950s, assuming that every new student was a twenty-two-year-old White man who had just graduated from college. The student body today, however, is much more diverse and includes people who have already had careers, people who are really interested in being in school, and people who hate school and are only going to seminary because it is required. "Everyone's got such different goals and motivations," she said. "But we all get poured into this one model—this is how your education is going to be, and this is how you're going to be formed as a priest."

Nevertheless, by the end of her program, Catherine deeply believed General was where she was called to be, and, even more, that she came out of General a better priest than she would have been had she gone somewhere else. Surprisingly, General showed her how radical Christianity can be. "I learned that being a Christian and being a priest is not about making people feel better about their lives so that they can become consumers of objects and live in the suburbs and have heterosexual families, which I think is what passes for the most part as Christianity, in pop culture, at least," she told me. Even though she has tattoos and piercings, even though she used to shave her head in college, even though she protests wars and the president and supports a woman's right to choose, Catherine believes becoming an Episcopal priest is the most radical thing she has ever done.

In addition to emphasizing the importance of presiding at communion, the rector of my church told me that to be ordained I would have to say I wanted to be a parish priest—not a professor at a divinity school, not a chaplain at a hospital or a college or a prison, but a priest who works in a church. At least for a few years. Apparently newly ordained priests in the Episcopal Church are sometimes required to work in parish ministry for a period of time before they are allowed to do ministerial work in other settings. Although the construction of parish ministry as a requirement reveals something about the job of the parish priest—it is sometimes hard, usually draining, and often lonely—this view of parish ministry primarily results from the narrowed understanding of ordained ministry. If ordination centers on the sacraments, if I have to say I want to be a priest because I want to celebrate Communion, then it would be a contradiction for me to want to be a professor, a writer, or a prison chaplain. Most of the work I would do in a university, at my desk, or in a prison I could do without being ordained. If that is true, then why seek ordination to the priesthood? This is a question that has returned to me again and again, and, although in my case I decided I did not need to be ordained to do the work I wanted to do in the world, the question is perhaps the wrong one to ask. It betrays the need to broaden our concepts of ministry, both ordained and lay. A better question, I think, would be: How would ordination transform the work I feel called to do?

Claudia Highbaugh knew she wanted to be ordained when she was eight years old. "For the very first time I saw a woman in the lectern," she said. "But in my mind as a third grader, the priest talked to the children only from the lectern. When I saw my first woman up there, and it was an Episcopal nun, I remember a voice saying in my head, this is where you are going to be. It never occurred to me that I would be a nun, but, oh, I'll be speaking to the people, and that is what I thought when I was eight." Although the voice was clear, Claudia didn't pay attention to it and pursued a career in education instead. Claudia was in kindergarten when Rosa Parks refused to give up her seat on the bus, and she grew up in Chicago highly aware of the civil rights movement going on around her. "I am not really sure how this happened, but my consciousness was that, if you would say it in third-grade parlance, if the people could learn, the people could grow. So I was always into education and asking questions and questioning authority, so I went all the way through school wanting to be in education." After college she enrolled in graduate school to study education, but she hated it. "After six weeks I knew it wasn't the place for me. I switched to seminary, with the idea that I would do pastoral care and counseling, but I didn't like that, either," Claudia said. In the 1970s, pastoral counseling was dominated by White men. "For somebody like me to try to do pastoral counseling, it just wasn't going to happen," she said. "But being in young adult development, I could do that."

In seminary, Claudia began earning a doctorate and entered the ordination process in the Christian Church (Disciples of Christ) in Southern California, where she worked in a church for two years. "It was horrible. They were mean to me," she said. "It was a small White suburban church, and they weren't mean to me as a young adult, they were mean to me as a woman." Disheartened, she returned to seminary and was the head resident at a nearby college while she finished her last two years of school. "And of course I loved that. I love the environment of higher education much more than the church. It is just more flexible." She went through the rest of the ordination process intending to be a chaplain on a college campus. She was active in the denomination, on boards and committees, running youth camps and women's events. The process went smoothly until her final interview. "This is when the manure hit the air-conditioning," she said. "They asked me this question: Could you see yourself as a minister in the church? And I said, no, could you? And they said, well, we can't ordain you if you cannot imagine yourself in a pastoral job. And I froze. Because it never occurred to me that they would do this. It is the last hour, the last minute, my ordination interview, and the committee is saying, if you cannot sit here and tell us that you can see yourself as a minister in the pulpit, then we can't ordain you." Claudia reminded them that her background was in education and that she had been clear throughout the ordination process that she felt called to work in higher education. Nothing she said stopped them from asking her whether she was willing to serve in a parish. "I finally said, well, I tell you what. If you can give me an example of one Black woman that you know who has graduated from seminary and has gotten ordained and has a church, then I can consider it. And they said, maybe you will be the first. And I said, God did not call me to that. And that was the end of the interview." Fortunately for Claudia, two people with power in the denomination intervened on her behalf and forced the committee to approve her ordination. "So it was pretty hard. From that moment on, I have never had any help from the church."

What happens when you feel called to be a minister but your church does not ordain women?

Jamie Washam grew up in a faithful Southern Baptist family that was always going to church. "My brother and I were like, just because they unlocked the church we don't have to be in there," she said, laughing. Each morning at breakfast, they shared a devotional as a family, and they prayed before every meal. Jamie's closest friends were from church, not school. She had amazing Sunday school teachers who were not afraid of her questions. "They didn't just give me a pat answer," Jamie said. "If they didn't know, they would say they didn't know, and they'd come back the next week with a lot of scriptures and say, go read these and we'll talk about it next time." She felt the church community had made an investment in her. "They gave me the tools I still use, and I would encourage other people to use," she said.

After college, Jamie attended Harvard Divinity School, but not because she thought she wanted to get ordained. She intended to get a Ph.D. "I didn't see anyone like me doing this, or at least not doing it in the way that I am, and so it didn't even really occur to me," she said. Women in Jamie's church worked with children and directed music, which remain the only positions open to them.

During her second year of divinity school, Jamie began to feel what she calls a kind of "gnawing, a nudging that wouldn't go away." She said, "It was a feeling that I needed to be ordained, and I was not

really interested. I thought they had the wrong gal. Thank you, no."
But the feeling was insistent, "dripping like a leaking faucet"—be
ordained, be ordained, be ordained, be ordained. "Finally I said,
okay, let me see what that would look like," Jamie said. "I started
talking to everyone I knew who was ordained but who was doing
something else—being professors, running nonprofits, leading children's homes, doing community activism—and I thought, okay, I
can get ordained, but really do something else." Jamie began to work
at an American Baptist church near her divinity school just to see
what that might be like, and it radically opened her sense of what ordained ministry could look like. "The people there really just blew
the hinges off for me," she said. "I couldn't even understand them for
a while. I was teaching Christian Education, and I was like, what
holds you people together? How are you a church? They were just so
different than anything I had ever known, racially and theologically
diverse." She paused, and then she said, "They were patient and loving and supportive, and I was able to reconstruct the temple that I
needed, I suppose, but from raw materials of my old one that had
been shattered and blown apart."

Jamie credits the faith of her childhood for supporting her during a time when that very faith was being questioned, critiqued, shattered, and remade, both in divinity school and at the church. "It was
a piece of work to let go of my assumptions and images of what
church could be and what pastors look like and how they operate,
and to give myself the permission to reform that. That's an ongoing
process," she said. "It can be scary at first when you are in free fall, but
then I realized that my universe didn't fall apart when I questioned the
fundamentals of it." Jamie compares possible approaches to faith to
different ways a person might choose to live in a house on stilts. One
stilt dweller might have such absolute trust in the stilts' power to hold
up her house that she does not feel the need to test it. Another might
show her trust in the house's ability to withstand all kinds of movement by shaking its foundation. This person might say, "I have so

much faith that I can hit it, beat it, kick it, saw at it, try to pull a leg out from underneath it. I can test it like that, and it will show me that it won't fall." Jamie said, "Those are both faith. It's just odd that we use the same word for them, but I think that God accepts both."

When Jamie eventually decided that she would heed the leaking faucet and pursue ordination, she returned to her home church, a Southern Baptist church, and asked to be licensed as a preacher, the first stage in the ordination process. Jamie had seen people licensed to preach all her life, usually teenage boys. They would come back from youth camp and say they felt God's call and were ready to give their lives to the Lord. They would be licensed during the Sunday altar call when people were also baptized or rededicated.

Jamie was not a teenage boy when she asked to be licensed. She was a woman in her twenties who had already spent almost two years in divinity school. She asked the pastor of her church to license her, and instead of simply saying yes as he had to all those teenage boys, he told her he would have to take the issue—whether or not the church could license a woman to preach—to the board of deacons, all men. (Although the Southern Baptist Convention theoretically ordains women, individual churches are free not to. As Jamie said, "The Southern Baptist Convention does ordain women. However, good luck finding a job.") When the pastor of the church spoke to the deacons, he did not ask if they would license Jamie, whom they had known her whole life. He asked, instead, if they would agree, theoretically, to license a woman. The deacons were split. "Some of them were like, yeah, what year is this? 1999? We have to get on with it. We can't turn our back on half the population," Jamie said. "Others shook their finger in the pastor's face and said, you're wrong for even asking." The deacons said no.

Jamie determined their decision wouldn't hold her back. The American Baptist church where she worked had already agreed to license her. Jamie only returned to her home church to ask to be licensed because she *wanted* their blessing, not because she *needed* it.

She decided she would simply let go of their refusal and move on. "That's not a fight I need to fight," she said. "I would rather be fighting about war and injustice and equal rights for all kinds of people, not just for my particular subset in this one county, you know. I have other fish to fry." She worries, however, about other women from her community who might feel called to be pastors. "It is just too bad that someone else may get hung up and never do this."

Working at an American Baptist church gave Jamie "room enough to follow God the way I hear God leading." Nevertheless, the road to ordination was still a grueling one. She describes the ordination process as "a series of flaming hoops you have to leap through and then turn around and douse." She was required to write an ordination paper in which she shared her spiritual history and outlined her theology. She then had to defend the paper in front of a committee of local Baptists. Her meeting lasted three and a half hours. "I was really ready for it because this is stuff I have been thinking about for years and years and years," she said. "They don't lob you little easy slow balls. Some of my congregation members were throwing me some serious curves." Jamie realized she could have told them exactly what they wanted to hear and been ordained easily, but she chose, instead, to tell them what she actually believed. When they finished questioning her, they sent her out of the room to deliberate about ordaining her. They voted in favor of ordaining her, although the vote was not unanimous. The members of the committee who were unsure she should be ordained were most troubled by her resistance to the idea that human beings are saved by the blood of Christ. "I didn't give them the whole I'm-saved-by-the-blood-of-the-lamb theology," she said. "I am discomforted by that."

After the meeting, the dissenters approached Jamie. "Some people said, I want you to know I'm very concerned about your theology and I'm praying for you," she said. "And I was just like, thank you, sister. I'm praying for you, too."

The blood-of-the-lamb theology that makes Jamie uncomfortable centers on Jesus's death. A version of atonement theology, it compares the blood of Jesus to the blood of the Paschal Lamb marked on the doors of the Israelites as a signal to the angel of death to pass over their homes. In Christianity, atonement theology is the understanding that the death of Jesus on the cross, like the blood of the lamb, saves human beings, making possible new life, the forgiveness of sins, and the reconciliation between God and human beings. Atonement—or at-one-ment, as some theologians and preachers like to say—restores the human-divine relationship. According to this theology, God required, even demanded, the death of Jesus to save the world.

Jamie is not alone in her reservations about this theology. A long line of theologians has critiqued it, arguing that atonement theology sanctions violence. In divinity school and seminary, students, like Jamie, learn doctrinal theory; read patristic, feminist, womanist, and liberation theology; and discover the history of Christianity. Being exposed to alternative ways of understanding the dominant symbols of their traditions allows students to claim new ways of understanding them. For example, what we now know as atonement theology did not emerge in Christianity until the eleventh century, articulated by a man named Anselm, archbishop of Canterbury, just as the first crusade was beginning, leading many theologians to ask whether there is a connection between the "sacred" violence of the crusades and the "sacred" violence of atonement theology.

One of the challenges faced by recent divinity school graduates— and the communities they serve—is the disjunction between the theology they learn in school and the theology being preached in and professed by churches. There is a vast difference between what denominations claim as official doctrine and what students learn in graduate school. In many master's programs, students are encouraged to think to the edge of things, to question fundamental beliefs, to critique theological concepts, to recognize the effects of their theological constructs, to challenge the symbols and stories of their traditions. This critical work is understood as part of faith, not separate from it. Many church communities have not been encouraged to do the same. With lazy preaching and simplistic adult and children's education programs, we have done our congregations a disservice. Most congregations can handle—in fact they crave—complicated, challenging theology. This is not easy work. Challenging people's long-held beliefs—and having one's own challenged—can be frightening, uncomfortable, even devastating. What's more, exposing people to a variety of beliefs means making room for people to have a variety of beliefs and raises questions about what makes a community a community: What would a faith community look like that celebrated difference? What is essential? What holds us together? How do we make meaning?

I attended Jamie's ordination. She sat in a chair at the front of the sanctuary flanked by two children she had taught in Sunday school, Autumn Grace and Luke. Autumn Grace sat very still, attentive throughout the service. Her brother Luke, whom Jamie describes as "a little hurricane with bright red hair," was beside himself with excitement. He spent half the time hiding under his chair and the other half climbing on Jamie's lap to whisper in her ear again and again, "Jamie, Jamie, Jamie, I love you." At one point during the service, members of the congregation—a gathering of Jamie's family, partner, friends, and people from the church where she worked—were invited, one at a time, to lay hands on Jamie's head and bless her. "In some traditions, only ordained people do this," Jamie said. "But we believe in a priesthood of all believers, that everybody's a minister." Jamie knelt, and all of us who were gathered there stood in a line that wrapped its way around the sanctuary, waiting our turn. When they reached her, some stood with their hands on Jamie's shoulders, silent. Others, like me, followed Luke's model. We leaned in, whispering blessings of love and hope in her ear.

Chapter Three

MENTORS

The support of the rector at the church where I worked helped get me started on the ordination track. I never could have entered the process without her. She bent rules for me, sped things up, introduced me to the bishop, and did anything else that would move my process along. Being her special case worked for me for almost a year, but then, when she stopped supporting me, things fell apart.

Many of the women I interviewed made it through the ordination process in their denominations as special cases. Someone in a position of power helped them—gave them jobs, put them on the fast track, allowed them to skip parts of the process, let them do things out of order, wrote letters to people with even more power. But, almost every time, being a special case eventually backfired. If surviving an institutional process requires special attention, then there is probably something wrong with the process. If you have to depend on a person with power to navigate institutional structures and he or she ever changes his or her mind, the institutional structures won't support you.

I know the rector at my church took me under her wing with the best intentions. I think she liked me. I believe she thought I would be a great priest. But then things changed. I felt she expected me to do what she wanted me to do, to be the kind of priest she wanted me to be—a priest like her. And I wasn't. Although I doubt many mentors would admit this, most are not interested in helping their mentees become their own kind of minister. They want to help their protégés become ministers like them. Some mentors take anything done differently as a personal insult: You don't like the way I preach? My liturgy isn't good enough for you? You think I'm a bad priest?

Many of the women I interviewed were supported by women, but just as many suffered at the hands of other women. Sometimes the most ruthless and bitter opposition they encountered came from women, ordained and not ordained, congregation members and colleagues. Some of the mistreatment seemed to result from resentment: women wanting other women to play by the same rules they had to play by, to give up the same things they had to give up, to suffer the same way they had to suffer. Some of these women were good girls for ten or twenty or fifty years and were angry that someone else didn't have to be. Other trouble was caused by women who wanted to get ordained but were never given the opportunity, either because they grew up when women were not allowed to be ordained or because other life circumstances kept them from pursuing that path. Some of the abuse was perpetrated by women who were the heroes of those they treated badly. The very women the next generation worships are sometimes maddeningly cruel as mentors.

One of the signs of a good leader is that he or she is surrounded by competent people. Insecure people, however, are threatened by competent people. Others' aptitude reveals their own ineptitude. Most of the women I interviewed seemed to have mentors who were threatened by them, and these mentors acted out their insecurity. Some ministers who have been working in parish ministry for decades are exhausted and burned out. They are simply surviving, going through the motions, trying to make it to retirement. New ideas, new theology, new rituals, new energy threaten to expose this tired state of affairs. Any change must be shut down.

Mentor relationships are inherently unbalanced—one person has institutional power and the other person doesn't—making the relationship ripe for abuse of all kinds. Being offended personally often leads mentors, male and female, to do things that damage their mentees personally and professionally. When the relationship falls apart, the best-case scenario is that the mentor stops being a mentor, breaks the relationship, and leaves the mentee to fend for herself. The worst-case scenario is that the mentor takes the mentee down in whatever way possible. In both cases, the person who pays the highest price, who suffers most of the consequences, is the mentee.

Because mentors are often essential players in the ordination process, denominations ought to institutionalize the mentor relationship, making it transparent, training mentors in how to be mentors, holding mentors accountable, and giving them the support they need to be effective. Instead of mentors choosing their mentees because they like them or because they see potential in them or because the mentees remind them of themselves when they were their age, a mentor should be assigned to every person entering the ordination process. Institutional oversight, procedural transparency, and support groups for mentors and mentees could transform a volatile process into an encouraging one.

A few transition-into-ministry programs exist that attempt to create an institutionalized, transparent, and supportive mentoring program for recent seminary and divinity school graduates. They are designed to assist new pastors in making the critical transition from student to full-time minister. Three women I interviewed participated in congregation-based residency programs that follow the medical school model of placing "residents" in a teaching congregation before they assume leadership of their own church. Not one of the women was satisfied with her experience. "They emphasized the program's professional integrity and commitment to the importance of education, dialogue, collegiality, and diversity so that one would not go into the ministry feeling burned out and underresourced but rather well equipped and well connected," one woman said. "And it failed on all fronts."

Because such programs are often well-respected and the residencies are competitive, hosting ministers-in-training (most of whom come from big-name divinity schools and seminaries) brings status to the church communities—and money. The residents are usually paid by the programs. Although they often welcomed the free labor, ministers at the churches are not quite sure what to do with the residents once they are there. "There was very little thinking about how our presence might affect the churches. We had no job description. We had no office in the church," one resident said. "I think that the senior ministers who were supposed to be our mentors had no idea how to be mentors or supervisors. To be honest, I think they had problems dealing with women. Many had issues with sexism."

The male resident one woman worked with received more support from the senior minister than she did. "He just got more attention," she said. "The senior minister would go to his funerals, give him advice and suggestions on sermons, invite him to go to the movies or to hang out with him, and there was none of this given to me or to my female colleague." She spoke to the senior minister about the imbalance in treatment, and he called her "petty and childish." She said, "It did not go well. He said I was acting like one of his children trying to get as much as the other siblings."

The senior minister at the smaller church where she also worked was, initially, supportive. He seemed, in her words, "sensitive, in touch with the issues, very open and liberal." As her difficulties with the other minister became more pronounced, she confided in him. "I didn't expect that he would support me against the other minister," she said. "I approached him as a sounding board, a listening ear." During the first year of her residency, a family at the larger church demanded that her male colleague perform their child's baptism, even though she was the one scheduled to lead worship that day. "They didn't know him any better than they knew me because we were both new." She went to see the minister at the smaller church to ask for his advice. When she pointed out that she thought the family was making a choice based on her sex—that they wanted a male minister to perform the baptism, not a female—her mentor exploded. "He said, this is your problem, your fault. You have obviously been hurt by sexism, and you are bringing it into the situation," she said. "It was devastating."

Most programs do not prepare congregations and ministers for working with young female ministers-in-training. A successful mentoring program requires not just oversight but intimate knowledge of the particular challenges faced by female ministers and the congregations that host them. The transition from school to ministry is hard for everyone, men and women, but the fact that most mentors and congregations are not used to working with female ministers compounds the problems faced by recent graduates who are women. Being mentors for young women is an opportunity for church communities to face their fears about hiring women, to learn about sexism in the church, their particular congregation, and the world, and to become advocates for women ministers.

I first met Eve Belisle,* an ordained UCC minister, when I went to see a friend preach who was working at Eve's church several years ago. Standing and leading us in prayer, Eve seemed to be lit from within. I can still picture her glowing, arms spread wide to send us out at the end of the service to do good work in the world.

In college, Eve worked on a daily paper as an editor and a columnist, and she started her own feminist newspaper. She wanted to be a journalist, a foreign correspondent, but her experience at summer camp changed her mind. The imagined glamorous life of travel and reporting couldn't compete with the pure joy she felt in her everyday life as a counselor eating grilled-cheese sandwiches, helping sixteen year olds recover from bulimia, learning how to live in a loving intentional community, and singing "Kumbaya." She was sold. She knew she wanted to do that kind of work for the rest of her life. "I think fundamentally, for me, ministry is being with people at these very precious, most vulnerable moments of their lives, really as a stranger more or less, being invited into these very intimate spaces with them," Eve said. "It is such a privilege—birth, death, marriage, those are the highlights, but all kinds of other ways, the hospital bed, all of it. It's very real. It is real life."

Her mentor, one of the chaplains on staff at the camp and a parish minister, recognized Eve's passion for the work and dared her to go to seminary. "He knew how to get to me," she told me laughing. "He preyed on my contrarian nature." The minister told her he could get her into seminary in the fall and, challenged, she told him she could get herself into seminary. She did.

At seminary, she worked for the local paper, and, although she loved the work, she realized that she didn't have the cutthroat mentality required to make it as a journalist. "I always fell in love with the people I was interviewing, whose stories I was learning," she said. "But of course when you are done writing the story and it is published, you move on, and you don't have relationships with them anymore." Working at summer camp, she discovered that ministry, like journalism, involved listening to people's stories and telling them in a way that is meaningful to others. "You do that in sermons, you do that in newsletter articles, you do that in pastoral counseling sessions. You are putting people's stories into the service of other people's stories. To me that is what ministry is about," Eve said. "It is gospel. It is what Jesus did. He told stories."

Although Eve knew fairly early on that she was interested in urban ministry, she worked for two years in her mentor's suburban church while she was a student. His congregation was a template for many UCC churches—big, White, middle to upper class, mainline, mainstream. While she worked at the church, she was also a full-time student and a waitress at night. During that time, she was sexually assaulted.

Eve was traumatized, exhausted, and overwhelmed, and, for a while, that dynamic strengthened her relationship with her mentor. He seemed to like being needed. But when she got stronger and healthier, emotionally and spiritually, and began to have her own ideas, she pulled away from him. She didn't need him to be her pastor anymore. Eve said, "I think that really hurt his feelings. I think he really wanted me to go serve a big middle-class church. He was grooming me to be him, maybe to be his replacement. But I wanted to go work with underprivileged youth, and I think he thought I was squandering my gifts."

She decided to leave her job with him, and during her last year in seminary, she worked at an inner-city Lutheran church. It was mostly a church of youth and children because parents were often either working jobs on weekends to support their families or had completely come apart at the seams, drug addicted or absent for one reason or another. Eve thrived at the church. She had always felt between worlds: She's White, but she has lived in integrated communities; she grew up on welfare, but she went to an Ivy League college and graduate school. She said, "This work was really calling me back, reminding me that this is part of my development, too."

When she graduated, she and her boyfriend decided to defer their student loans and live in voluntary poverty for a year in Bolivia working in an orphanage. Before they went to Bolivia, she went back to her mentor's church—what she considered to be her home church—and asked them to call her, officially, to work at the orphanage. In the UCC, this official call from her congregation would allow her to get ordained before she went to Bolivia. They would ordain her to do missionary work.

She met with the committee at her church for two hours. They drilled her with questions, and then they said no. Although she has no way of knowing if this is true, she is convinced her mentor persuaded them to say no. Eve went to Bolivia, anyway.

When she came back, she got a call to work at a church in a suburb of Boston, and she took it. Because she had a call from another church, her home church could not refuse to ordain her. Her ordination service, as is traditional in the UCC, was held at her mentor's church. He halfheartedly welcomed people to the service and didn't participate in her ordination in any other way. Out of a 900-member congregation, only one person attended Eve's ordination.

———

Much like the feeling of being called, a mentor can create the sense that you are special, chosen. Investing time and energy in you, mentors believe in you and in what you might become. They seem to see your best self, and being seen can be healing, even intoxicating. People are drawn to ministry for different reasons, but sometimes, some of those reasons emerge from the places we have been badly hurt, the places in us that are needy, broken, wounded, desperate to be loved. In this context, mentor relationships can take a dangerous turn. Without clear boundaries and oversight, the intimacy of mentor-mentee relationships—like the intimacy of minister-congregant relationships—can become sexualized, manipulative, and dangerous.

Adah Reed* met a priest in college, Jonathan, who became her mentor and used the idea that Adah was called to be a priest—his idea, not hers—to abuse and manipulate her, sexually and emotionally. Her freshman year in college, Adah went on an outreach trip to Mexico, and Jonathan was one of the adult supervisors for the trip. During a meeting before they left for the trip, Jonathan asked if anyone could speak Spanish. Only Adah raised her hand. Jonathan approached her at the end of the meeting. He was wearing a clerical collar. Ironically, the first sentence he spoke to her had to do with boundaries. He said, "You are going to have to figure out how close I can be to you that's comfortable for you because I'm going to be at your side the whole time that we are in Mexico."

When they returned from Mexico, Adah started to see Jonathan as a therapist. He was not a licensed therapist or counselor, although he counseled other girls and women at the school. Adah went to see him because she was having problems with alcohol, and Jonathan had been very public about his status as a recovering alcoholic. "I thought it would be a nonjudgmental, safe space for my issues," she said. Knowing from their counseling sessions that she was suffering from low self-esteem, he showered her with attention, told her she was sexy and that he was crazy about her, that he wanted to go running through the streets screaming about how amazing she was. Jonathan began to push her into the priesthood. Although Adah did not want to be a priest, she wanted to see herself the way Jonathan saw her. He made jokes about ordination, gave her the *Book of Common Prayer* in Spanish, asked her to help him lead morning services. And then he started knitting her a scarf.

Adah and Jonathan often took walks together in the woods, and on one of the walks, he led her to a bridge over a stream. While they stood on the bridge, he took the scarf that he had knitted for her out of his bag. "It was extremely long, too long for a scarf, especially since it was so wide. It was more like a stole, and it felt like he was calling me to ministry," she said. Jonathan wrapped it around her and quoted something from Second Kings, the passage when the prophet Elijah calls Elisha to succeed him by passing on his mantle.

After he gave her the scarf, Jonathan started talking in ways that implied they would eventually live together in Mexico. And then he started coming on to her sexually, with massages, hugs that lasted too long, and kisses on her forehead.

Jonathan isolated Adah, cutting her off from any support other than his. She had very few friends besides Jonathan's daughter and spent most of her time with Jonathan's family. Adah sensed something was wrong with their relationship, and she tried to establish some boundaries, but Jonathan tried to get her to break them down so she might really "heal." He insisted she talk to him about sex, telling her that to help her recover, he needed to hear about the destructive sexual behavior she sometimes engaged in when she was drunk. Sensing their relationship was heading toward, if not already in, dangerous territory, Adah asked Jonathan to promise that he would never have sex with her. "I can't promise you that," he said. Adah ended the relationship.

When I first met Adah, she was still traumatized, and her body bore witness—anxiety, stomachaches, sleeplessness, dizziness. "I still can't see men in collars, you know the white collars, and not have him pop into my mind and all of the complicated feelings and experiences that he represents for me now," she said. Adah was beginning to sort out what impact Jonathan had on her sense of vocation, her understanding of God, and her belief in unconditional love. She was training to be a teacher, not a priest. "What was most wounding about his behavior was the way he unearthed my psychological and spiritual vulnerabilities not to help me heal them but to take advantage of them," she said. "Not only did my counseling with him not lead to any healing, it drove those wounds deeper and made it more difficult for me to trust myself, others, and God."

Several months after our interview, Adah contacted me to share that she had reported Jonathan to his diocese. Working with an advocate experienced with church abuse cases and a spiritual director, Adah is beginning to heal.

When news of the sexual abuse scandal in the Catholic Church finally broke, I was not surprised. Leaders of religious communities of all kinds have used their positions to abuse people for a long time, and the institutions to which these leaders belong have covered up such abuse again and again. The cocktail of spiritual intimacy, power, fear of sex, culture of secrecy, and denigration of women is a lethal one.

In the only course I was required to take during my master's program in divinity school, we were taught about clergy sexual misconduct and were warned—as future clergy—about the intoxication of power. We were told that sexual relationships between ministers and their congregants (of any age) are not okay, and that if we were ever to fall in love with one of our congregants and wanted to pursue the relationship, then there were aboveboard options for handling the situation. Many ministers and congregants have fallen in love. Pursuing a consensual relationship between adults is not the problem. Keeping the relationship secret is. What I remember most about that class is not the outdated video we watched about a manipulative pastor who slept with practically every woman in his congregation but my professor's warning about secrets. He told us that we each needed at least one person in our lives to whom we told the whole truth.

This person could not be our significant other, our spouse, our partner (although he encouraged us to tell them the truth, too). It had to be someone outside of our family—a pastoral counselor, a friend, a therapist. If there was something about our lives that we could not say out loud to this person, then we had a real problem.

Adah's mentor kept the nature of their relationship secret, and he encouraged Adah to do the same. When I listened to her story, I wondered how Jonathan was able to counsel women at the university without any official oversight, and then I realized that this lack of oversight is exactly what allows mentors to mistreat their mentees. What happened to Eve during her relationship with her mentor is not as traumatic as what happened to Adah, but both are symptoms of a system that is not working. Mentees need their mentors. They need them for employment, to negotiate the ordination process, for recommendations, and for money. Often they cannot afford—professionally or financially—to report the abuse to the authorities. And, even more troubling, the authorities are often friends of the mentor. In most cases, the abuse is so insidious—subtle, confusing, crazy-making—that it feels impossible to name. If you did decide to report it, what exactly would you say? My mentor told a committee to ask me hard questions about Jesus? My mentor did not welcome people to my ordination very warmly? I think my mentor had fantasies about a sexual relationship with me? My mentor thinks I am wasting my gifts?

Mentor-mentee relationships during the ordination process in many denominations—and probably in most professions—often function as vestiges of the old-boy network, when ordination or promotion was something that happened in back rooms, on golf courses, or in bars. Having a person who can help you claim your vocation and train you professionally is not inherently bad or wrong or dangerous. Sometimes, perhaps even the majority of the time, mentor-mentee relationships work beautifully. The women I interviewed who had positive experiences with mentors were usually not the first women their mentors or congregations had worked with. Another contributing factor to successful mentor-mentee relationships was having more than one mentor at the same church. Before she was ordained, Jackie Ballard had consistently helpful experiences with mentors. In divinity school, she worked at the university's church and facilitated a youth group for college students with the associate minister. Encouraged by that mentor to try parish ministry, she worked at a UCC church in a suburb near her school. There she had two mentors, a male minister and a female minister. Both were extremely supportive. "Right from the get-go I had enormous responsibility," Jackie said. "I led worship almost every single weekend, which meant I did everything except for speaking the invocation, preaching, and doing the benediction. I did all the prayers. I did the offering. I read scripture." Guided and empowered by two mentors, Jackie discovered that leading worship was central to her call. Jackie worked closely with the other woman on staff. "We worked with the youth group, and we did a lot of women's ministry," she said. "It was great to work with her because she gave me room to try new things. I learned a lot just watching her. She has tremendous depth and spirit, that combination of being really smart, really spiritual, and a great leader."

Like Jackie, Abby Cook,* now a Unitarian Universalist (UU) minister, had two mentors when she worked at a church during her field education placement: a woman in her forties and a man in his late sixties. "I trusted my supervisors. They looked out for my well-being," she said. Two elements are essential to her positive experience: She was not the first female intern and her denomination is used to change. Unlike many mainline Protestant denominations that have set, traditional liturgies—some members of my own tradition, the Episcopal Church, still fight over whether to use the 1928 prayer book or the "newly" revised 1979 version—parts of UU services change from week to week. "I had a lot of freedom," Abby said. "There is room for creativity." A church used to liturgical change can accept other kinds of changes more readily. If the words and rituals used each week to express faith, to communicate what is important, are always in flux, then flux is normal, not threatening. And when change is not seen as threatening, women often aren't, either.

Chapter Four

THE JOB SEARCH

When Sharon Zimmerman Rader, a retired United Methodist bishop, went to seminary, there were less than ten other women enrolled with her, and of those ten, Sharon was the only female student who was married with children. Male students and professors confronted her constantly. She said, "There would be questions in class from men like, why aren't you home taking care of your husband and children? Another question was, why do you want my job?"

When Sharon graduated from seminary and was ready for her first appointment as a minister, her bishop assigned her to a church in Chicago. When she went to the introductory meeting at the church, her husband—as spouses were expected to do—went with her. She was also accompanied by the district superintendent of her conference. The committee at the church had not been told that a woman was interviewing for the position. They assumed Sharon was the wife of the prospective pastor, not the pastor who had been assigned to their church, and so they addressed the first few interview questions to her husband. He soon interrupted them and told them they ought to be talking to his wife because she was the person who had been appointed to work there. Sharon said, "There was dead silence. It was a short and very, very difficult introductory meeting, and at the end of the introduction time my husband and I were sent to another room of the church to wait while the district superintendent talked to the committee." They waited in that room for an hour and a half. Then, the district superintendent told Sharon that he had determined that the committee didn't want to have her as their pastor, but since the only reason they could provide for their refusal was the fact that she was a woman, he was going to go forward with the appointment.

Sharon and her husband returned to the room where the rest of the committee was waiting. Nobody would look at her. The district superintendent said, "This is your pastor, and she'll be here on the first of July." Two days later, on Easter Sunday right after the sunrise service, the committee reconvened itself, without the superintendent or Sharon, and decided they would refuse to take her. Pastors in nearby churches formed a group to protest her appointment and to support the committee's stance. The bishop was furious. He worked for a month to try to get the church to accept her as their pastor, with no luck. He called Sharon and asked for her advice. "I told him this was my first appointment, and I didn't make my own appointments, but that I thought he really needed to reconsider it, given the fact that it was a church that was in great transition right in the city and probably needed to be making decisions about its ministry, not about whether or not it would have a woman." The church won. The bishop withdrew the appointment.

There was only one other congregation the bishop had to offer her. When the district superintendent discussed the church Sharon told me he said, "We don't know if this congregation is going to live or die. You will have to help them figure that out. And if they need to have a funeral, well, then help them have a good funeral. Good luck."

This time, Sharon went to the introductory meeting without her husband, determined that the church know they were going to have to deal with her. She asked the committee point-blank what they thought about having a woman as a pastor. "One of the members of the committee was a man by the name of John Nelson who was about seventy-six years of age at that point. He leaned back in his chair, and he said, 'Let me tell you something, Sharon. Given everything else that has happened to this congregation, you couldn't be any worse.'" Sharon welcomed his honesty and took the job. On her first Sunday, there were twelve people in worship. Under her leadership, they became the fastest growing congregation percentagewise in the conference.

I wish that I could write that things have changed, that congregations actively seek women priests, that women are sent to thriving churches, but I can't. We may have changed the rules, but we haven't changed people's minds. In his article, "The Stained Glass Ceiling: Career Attainment for Women Clergy," Paul Sullins shows that resistance to the ministry of women is undiminished over the past twenty years and that this unchanging resistance is found primarily at the congregational level, not in the decisions of the church hierarchy or other clergy. The discrimination women face results from the embedded values of individual members of congregations. Although several mainline Protestant denominations are now celebrating decades of ordaining women, putting on display the few women who have made it to bishop, desperately wanting to believe things have changed, statistics tell otherwise. Across denominations, women's job searches are longer than men's, and are even longer when they are women of color. This should come as no surprise. Survey after survey shows that congregations remain resistant to female ministers. And congregations who are resistant to female ministers are, of course, not willing to hire them.

A survey administered in 1995 for the celebration of the twenty-fifth anniversary of the ordination of women in the Evangelical Lutheran Church in America revealed that women waited more than three months longer than men for their first job offer from a church. A 2003 Presbyterian study on "Clergywomen's Experiences in Ministry" found that 76 percent of women experienced gender-based discrimination in the call process and 55 percent of women thought racism was a problem. The study also disclosed that while 42 percent of women are associate pastors, only 15 percent are solo or copastors. The same trend is apparent in most mainline denominations. Women are far more likely to be hired as associates and assistants than they are to be hired as rectors, solo pastors, or priests-in-charge. A study conducted by Delores Carpenter of Howard University looked at the career paths of more than 800 Black men and women who earned divinity degrees from sixty-one seminaries covering eighteen denominations from 1972 through 1998. While half of the men went on to positions as senior pastors, barely one-fifth of the women did. Some of the women in the study had to shift to more theologically liberal denominations—for example, from Baptist to United Methodist or Presbyterian—to increase their odds of landing a job. The 1993 United Methodist Clergywomen Retention Study exposed that even when churches are willing to hire women, they will pay them less than they would a man. The 2003 Episcopal survey documented that the larger the membership of the congregation—which usually translates into a bigger, more powerful, wealthier church—the less willing the respondents were, personally, to have a woman as their rector. That 2003 survey confirmed that male priests are nine times more likely to be hired as rectors than female priests (and that this disproportion increases nearly exponentially with congregation size); that men are far more likely than women to be senior pastors of larger, wealthier congregations; and that the higher the position in the hierarchy, the less enthusiastic people are to have a woman fill it. And as if that is not bad news enough, congregations that say they support women offer a caveat: Their support is contingent on the woman not being a lesbian and on whether she will give her full attention to the church (meaning they don't really want her to have young children).

Catherine and Jesse got married during their second year at General Theological Seminary. The following year, they graduated and started to look for jobs. It would be nearly impossible to design a better experiment for revealing sexism in the Episcopal Church than their job search. I have heard of groups that submit identical résumés for the same jobs. Some résumés are marked with stereotypically African American names, others with stereotypically Anglo names. Again and again, the Anglo name résumés solicit 50 percent more callbacks. Catherine and Jesse lived this experiment not in terms of race but in terms of gender.

Catherine and Jesse applied for fifteen jobs. Some they both applied to; some only one of them applied to. In the cover letter that accompanied their applications they were up-front about the fact that they were both in the job search. If they applied for the same position at the same church, they told the church that they were married, that they were in good communication, and that there would be no hard feelings if the church chose one of them and not the other.

The rector from one of the churches in Chicago called Catherine to set up an interview. Although Jesse had applied to this job, too, he was not initially chosen for an interview. When the rector discovered that Catherine was married to another applicant for the position, and that Jesse would be traveling with Catherine to Chicago, the caller suggested that the church interview Jesse as well.

Catherine tells the story without a trace of bitterness in her voice. "We both went out to Chicago to interview. Jesse had an interview at another parish, and I had an interview at another parish, and then there was this third one that we now shared." The third church interviewed them at the same time, in the same room. At the end of the process, they returned home. Jesse got two job offers. Catherine got none. The rector who initially brought Catherine out to interview, adding Jesse as an afterthought, called and said, "Well, we'd like to hire Jesse, but if Jesse can't come, then we'd like Catherine." They both refused.

It wasn't just that Jesse got more job offers than Catherine. The entire experience was radically different for each of them. They would compare letters and e-mails they received from churches, putting them on their dining room table, side by side. Catherine would get a one-line e-mail asking her to send her résumé, while the e-mail addressed to Jesse would be two pages long, single-spaced. Jesse came into the kitchen while Catherine was telling me this part of their story and joined in. "Even for situations where it was pretty clear they wanted to hire a woman, still it was like the father, or rector, or priest was just so into connecting with me," he said. "It was really bizarre."

When all was said and done, Jesse got half a dozen job offers, and Catherine didn't get a single one. They decided Jesse would turn down both jobs in Chicago and take the position he was offered in their home diocese, hoping Catherine would have a better chance at employment there. Catherine taught English as a Second Language over the summer.

Catherine credits the difficulty of her search not only to sexism but also to ageism. "No one had ever seen a young woman priest before, and nobody was willing to touch me with a ten-foot pole," she said. She was the youngest ordained woman she knew. Most of Catherine's women friends from seminary were in their late twenties when they started school, or else ministry was their second career, which they were beginning in their forties and fifties. Catherine was in her early twenties.

Congregations are continually shocked when they see a female minister in her twenties or early thirties, even though that is the age men have been getting ordained for centuries. The women I interviewed who were in this age range insisted that age played a part in the discrimination they experienced as ministers. Being perceived as "young" compounded the difficulties they had being recognized, by themselves and by others, as people with authority. In addition, many of the women I interviewed who began their ministries as young women were single. Being single and young seemed to magnify the perception of these women as sexual and embodied. Even though young single men, like young single women, date, go out to bars, and have sex, this behavior, because of the cultural double standard, remains more acceptable for men than it is for women, especially for women in ministry.

Being ordained and not having a church felt terrible to Catherine. Then things started looking up. A priest at a local church decided he wanted to hire an assistant who would work part-time. Catherine met with him, and they hit it off. He set up an interview with a group of people from the church, during which he told them that Catherine was the person he wanted to hire for the job. Hired initially for a half-time position, Catherine was promised full-time work and pay by the following September.

The church was an exciting place for her to be—liberal, political, intellectual—but her relationship with the priest who hired her was odd from the beginning. When she first interviewed for the job, he said he was going to leave the church in five years. Once she started working there, the five years shrank to two. By the time she had been there six months, he told her he would leave before the end of the year. It soon became clear that the parish was in financial trouble. There was talk about the fact that they would never be able to afford to hire Catherine full-time, even though the assistant priest who preceded her, an older woman, had been hired for full-time work. Even if they could have afforded to hire Catherine, it seemed to her that the priest made sure that they wouldn't, undercutting her attempts to transition to full-time ministry. She also felt he denied her all forms of support, shutting off her access to lay leadership in the church. "He wanted to be this happy-go-lucky guy with this cool young assistant priest. She's so cool. I'm so cool. Look, we're colleagues," Catherine said. "We were so not colleagues. He wanted to have all the power, and not admit it, basically."

Once she realized she would never get full-time work at that church—that the people there were too alarmed by her age to consider hiring her as a replacement for the priest who was leaving and that the priest who was leaving was too threatened by her to put her in a position of authority—she began conversations with the diocese about finding another job. She was not given a solid job offer until she was offered a job in another diocese. After that, a possibility surfaced. A church in a nearby suburb was looking for a priest. The church was recovering from a terrible experience with a priest-in-charge, who had replaced a priest who had been there for thirty years and had caused lots of trouble in his own right. He told anyone who had an ear at the diocese how completely messed up the congregation was, and the powers that be in the diocese believed him, never bothering to talk to the church on their own. Catherine was told that she was placed at that church because there was nothing to lose. Catherine said, "They sort of thought, if this interim priest with twenty-some years of experience can't fix those people, then what else are we going to do? Why don't we put Catherine there?" She told me the bishop said to her, "It's really important that you succeed there because it will show people that young people can do things." Not only did she have to prove that women could be priests (she was that congregation's first female), she also had to prove her whole generation could be priests. Pissed, she took the job.

And then she had to fight for her salary. The Episcopal diocese where she works has a set procedure for determining how much a church can pay its priest. The salary the diocese calculated that her new church could pay was $61,000 a year for a full-time priest working and living in an area with such a high cost of living. The minimum salary for a priest in the diocese at that time was $53,000. Catherine arrived at her salary negotiation knowing they were in financial trouble, so she was willing to split the difference between the minimum salary and the salary determined by the diocese. She planned to use the difference in salary to negotiate for extra vacation and continuing education time.

They offered her $45,000.

Catherine told them she could not accept that salary, and that, in fact, she knew the diocese would not let her accept it. "And they were sort of stunned by that," she said. The members of the hiring committee sent her out of the room so they could discuss whether they were willing to offer her the diocesan minimum. They eventually did.

Although she is proud that she stood up for herself from the very beginning, Catherine remains frustrated with their original offer. She told me that she has seen paperwork that confirms they had been told by the diocese that they should pay a full-time priest $61,000. They knew, and yet they offered her far below not only the suggested amount but below the diocesan minimum. They also did not, at first, pay her health insurance costs. Her husband's church did.

Despite the initial resistance and low salary offer, Catherine's church loves her. They have claimed her as their priest. Soon after her arrival, one of the matriarchs of the church died, and Catherine performed the funeral. The congregation's response was positive. "When I did that funeral I really felt like I was auditioning to do every person there's funeral," she said. "It was like, if she can bury her, then she can probably bury me." Although their acceptance means a lot to her, Catherine acknowledges that they have accepted her because they have to. The church has been ignored, even abandoned, by the diocese, suffering under a difficult priest for thirty years and then under a priest-in-charge who talked about them like they were trash. Catherine said, "I'm the priest they've got, and they can either accept me and let me be their priest, or, you know, that's it. There's a certain level at which I am accepted as a woman priest in this working-class, marginalized parish because I have to be."

In her job search, what Marion Reeves* knew all along was confirmed: Congregations in her Protestant denomination don't imagine a Black woman when they hear the word "priest." She said, "They talk a big game, but what they really want is somebody who reflects the best of what they want to think about themselves, that is, a White man in his early to midfifties."

Marion is a lifelong member of her denomination. To disguise her identity, I can't tell you which denomination. Out of all of the ordained people in her denomination—and they number in the tens of thousands—fewer than 200 are Black women. And out of those Black women, fewer than ten of them are under forty.

Marion has been in leadership roles in her denomination since she was a teenager. She has worked for almost every part of the denomination, writing curriculum for the national level and editing policy statements. Immediately after graduating from divinity school, Marion participated in a transition into ministry internship program. Designed to support new ministers and help them get off to a good start, it allows interns to spend time working in congregations before assuming leadership of their own churches. When she went on the job market, she already had two years of work experience at a church in the Midwest.

In Marion's denomination, the average amount of time for a man to find a job is six to nine months. For women, that time grows to a year. For Black women, a year and a half. When she told me that, I asked, "How are you supposed to afford to live during that period of time?"

"Good question," she said.

The people running the internship program couldn't imagine that after her internship Marion would have any trouble finding a job. They assumed churches would line up to hire her. The two male residents Marion worked with found jobs fairly easily. Despite the fact that Marion began looking for a job well before her internship ended, she still didn't have one at the end of the program.

Several churches to which she had applied for jobs had invited her to interview, including one church in a city she loved. She had a conference call with them that she describes as going magically well, and they then flew her out for a face-to-face interview. By and large things went smoothly. Except for one thing: The search committee took her to a restaurant that she found, to put it mildly, a bit odd—a biker bar and restaurant where, every week, they have "smut 'n eggs Tuesday" when they serve eggs and show porn on the big-screen television screens above the bar. Fortunately, her interview was not on a Tuesday.

Nevertheless, Marion still wanted to work at that church. It was a big church in a city, and the size and location lured her despite her misgivings. At the end of the smut 'n eggs brunch they offered her a job—at least hypothetically. They told her they were really impressed with her and planned to e-mail her an offer right away. Look at it, they said, see if it seems reasonable, and then let us know what you think. Marion returned home and received an e-mail outlining a hypothetical position and salary. She called and asked a few clarification questions, which they answered. Satisfied, she said everything looked great and that she was pleased with the offer. They told her they would contact her in a week.

A week came and went. Then two weeks. Finally, at the end of a month of waiting to hear from them, she called the chair of the search committee. "He told me they had decided to go with somebody else, somebody who was more of a fit." And then he hung up.

Marion contacted both the office on ministry at the national level of her denomination and its local office in the city where she interviewed. She told them about smut 'n eggs and that she had been misled and given a hypothetical offer to consider. Marion said, "The person I spoke with on the phone said, what are you bitching and moaning about? This has nothing to do with race."

But for Marion it did have something to do with race. After several similar experiences, Marion figured out exactly what was going on. In her denomination—and this is the case for most denominations—the only level at which anyone is held accountable for equal opportunity is at the interview stage: Each search committee calls several candidates to interview, makes sure at least one of them is Black, and then can say they looked at a diverse group of people. "They use people of color to diversify their applicant pools. They have no intention of considering them seriously. That's what was happening to me. I was diversifying their applicant pool. I was not being considered seriously," Marion said. "They were curious. They get dazzled. They are interested to see what an Ivy League Yankee Negro looks like. They are like, 'Bring her in!' and that satisfies their curiosity."

Her hunch was confirmed when she learned about what happened to an African American friend of hers. Her friend was interviewing for a position at a mixed-race church with a White pastor in an urban center in the Midwest. The search committee had identified her as their top choice and planned to issue her a call. On the day that she was to preach a sermon for the congregation (the final stage of the interview process, after which the congregation would vote on whether or not they wanted to call her to work at the church), the pastor called the whole thing off. He told the search committee, "This just won't work." When Marion learned about this, she asked herself, "Why play this game anymore?"

In some instances, Marion was not sure the churches knew she was African American until she showed up in person. That created a different problem, but the results—no job offer—were the same. Soon, Marion stopped beating around the bush when she got interview calls from churches. "I lay it out right up front," she said. "Are you aware that I am a Black woman? Because if you are, and you are interested in talking with me, let's talk. If you aren't, then let's just walk away right now, no harm, no foul, because this is ridiculous."

After searching for well over a year with no luck, Marion broadened her search and started to apply for jobs in places she hadn't considered before, including the South. Soon she got a phone call from a congregation in the Deep South. She liked the man on the other end of the phone immediately, liked his demeanor, the way he talked about the church, and how many nice things he had to say about her qualifications. Before she could start to feel too hopeful, Marion interrupted him. She said, "I beg you to excuse my ignorance, but I grew up in New England, and I have spent a little time in the Midwest, but I know nothing about the South. Are you aware that I am an African American female?"

There was a long pause. Then the man started to laugh. "Are you aware that I am an African American male?" he asked. He was the first Black person on any search committee she had ever spoken with. He and Marion set up a time for an official phone interview, and, following the phone interview, Marion was asked to send tapes of her sermons. After listening to her sermons, the search committee flew her down to make her an official offer in person. She took the job.

Chapter Five

ASSISTANT MINISTERS

Newly ordained ministers arrive at their first jobs all fired up, stimulated by course work, excited by new ideas for liturgy, eager to develop education programs and small groups, and reveling in what might be possible for church communities of the twenty-first century. Ministers fresh from divinity school or seminary often confront a reality that bears little resemblance to what they imagined. Suddenly, what they took for granted in school—inclusive language, acceptance of female ministers, freedom to try new prayers and ideas and clothing—seems radical, strange, rebellious. Some land in congregations averse to change. Others work under senior ministers terrified of it. Most confront church communities that are not ready for them.

Like most first jobs, a new minister's first placement in a church affects her sense of herself as a professional and often determines what the rest of her career will look like. Will she stay in parish ministry? Will she leave the church to work in the academy? Will she leave the church altogether?

As is the case for most mentor relationships, there is little official oversight of relationships between senior ministers and their associates, which is usually the position a newly ordained minister will be offered. The women I interviewed suffered as associate ministers. Over and over again, I heard the same kinds of stories from assistant ministers, and soon, a pattern emerged. Senior ministers—male and female—undermine their female associates. They undermine the associate's ministerial authority by humiliating her in public and cutting her out of pastoral and sacramental duties. They undermine the associate's confidence by criticizing her constantly, often with no rhyme or reason or evidence. They undermine the associate's support structure by denying her access to support inside and outside the church.

Although some of the women I interviewed sought help from people in positions in authority in their denominations (and received none), many of the women I interviewed never told anyone in any official position or in their congregations about their experiences. Sometimes they did not report the behavior of the senior ministers where they worked because they feared they would be marked as troublemakers who were difficult to work with. They worried that if word got around the denomination, they would never be offered another job. Although these concerns played a large role in their decisions not to pursue formal avenues of complaint, the dominant reason they kept their stories to themselves was a pastoral one: They wanted to protect their parishioners. They refused to let what they understood as "personal problems" affect their parishioners' lives of faith. Again and again they put the congregation's needs first. Knowing that exposing the congregation's leader—who had often been at that church for years and years—as abusive, manipulative, or outright mean would be devastating for the community, they refused to force their congregations to choose between them and the senior minister. Even when their situations were so bad that they had to leave the church, they shaped the telling of their stories in order not to implicate anyone.

Congregations also played a role in such myth making. Like their ministers, congregations overwhelmingly erred on the side of keeping the peace. They much preferred smoothing over problems to confronting them, a preference that often led to massaging the truth or to outright denial. Sometimes, because the woman had done such a good job hiding what was going on behind closed doors, people at the church had no idea what had happened and were left hurt and confused as they watched the minister they loved disappear, wondering what in the world had gone wrong.

Although choosing not to tell the congregation the whole story emerges out of a desire to take care of your church members, it does more harm than good in the long term. Because people do not know why their minister left, they are bound to feel abandoned and hurt, and might even be distrustful of the next minister who comes to take her place, wary of getting too close to someone who might also leave quickly. If the woman who leaves without an explanation is the first woman ever hired by that congregation, the congregation might be hesitant to hire another. As Jamie said, "The same thing happens with anybody who becomes a minority or a token. Everyone places the whole categorization of the group upon you."

Most of the women I interviewed who left positions as assistant ministers never received a phone call from someone in the denomination asking about their experience. No one followed up. No one investigated the church or the senior minister, even when that church or that senior minister had a history of assistant ministers who left the job soon after they were hired. It was easier to let the woman leave in disgrace than to disgrace a senior minister or a wealthy congregation. The women I interviewed who struggled with their senior ministers are powerful women, with clear senses of vocation and real gifts for ministry. They are smart, strong, and capable, and they are good at what they do—good preachers, pastoral counselors, and ritual creators. They have each crafted a life that makes visible the commitment in their hearts—a commitment to the belief that another world is possible, a world where we might live in ways that nourish and sustain the earth and all living beings. And yet, each woman worked under a senior minister who eventually drove her from the church that first called her to ministry. And, in every case, the only person who had to bear the consequences of the senior minister's destructive, threatening, manipulative, and abusive behavior was the woman. In general, there were no consequences for the senior minister—no questioning, no inquiry, no formal process, no exit interviews, not even a slap on the wrist. Nothing. Women became scapegoats, sacrificed to avoid having to look at the system as a whole and see its dysfunction. No one—not the woman, not her congregation, not the senior minister—was either held accountable or taken care of. When the canary in the coal mine stopped singing, they simply looked for another to put in the same cage in the same mine.

When Marion showed up for her job as an associate pastor, she was greeted with everything short of a parade. She began her ministry in late 2003, and her mother drove out with her and stayed for a week to help her get situated. They didn't have to cook for days because members of the search committee brought dinner every night. The local newspaper wrote articles about her. There were parties and celebrations of all kinds.

Nevertheless, in retrospect, Marion can see there were warning signs from the beginning. When she arrived, she asked the hiring committee about their expectations, what they hoped she would accomplish during her first year on the job. Marion said, "The first answer from somebody was, oh, just to get to know us, know who we are, know our names."

"In a year?" I asked. "That's all they wanted you to do in a year?"

"That's what they said they would expect, which is not the answer you want to hear," she said. Marion wanted to hear clear, concrete expectations, things like expanding the adult education program or increasing people's satisfaction with pastoral care. Although she asked for a written job description, she was not given one until 2006, almost a year and a half after she started working there. The lack of a job description did not stop her from doing great work. She expanded the pastoral care program; created young adult ministry programs; started weekly Bible studies, a meditation series, and an adult education lecture series; and empowered lay leaders to minister to one another. People loved her. That is, everyone except the head pastor, Jefferson.

Jefferson treated Marion like she was not an ordained minister, and he talked to her like she was his hired help. Marion felt he withheld important pastoral care information from her, rarely let her preach, and often tried to humiliate her publicly. Everyone at the church called the pastors by their first names: Jefferson was Jefferson; Marion was Marion. Whenever Jefferson would refer to Marion at staff meetings or in worship services he would call her, in a patronizing singsongy voice, "the Reverend Miss Marion Reeves." Other people noticed and asked why he always called her "the Reverend Miss." When a staff member finally brought it to his attention, he stopped.

It was clear to Marion from the beginning that Jefferson expected her to keep her opinions to herself and agree with him about everything. At committee meetings he would act as if she had not even spoken. During one of the first meetings Marion attended, a parishioner asked Marion what she thought about a controversial issue, and Marion shared her opinion. She recalled, "I could tell, it was written all over Jefferson's face, that the correct answer was not actually to think about the question and answer it. I was supposed to act like I didn't know anything and walk on. He was almost apoplectic that I actually had something to say." After she spoke, Marion recalled that Jefferson made a comment that suggested to everyone seated around the table that Marion had no idea what she was talking about.

During Sunday worship services, Marion's job was to emcee the service—a role Marion refers to as "the cruise ship captain." She welcomed people, made announcements, and helped things go smoothly. For Marion to make sure she knew everything she needed to know for announcements, she suggested that she and Jefferson have weekly meetings. Jefferson refused. Each week, Marion had to track him down to ask if there was any information she needed. Almost every week, it seemed Jefferson omitted something crucial when they talked about what she should announce in church. On Sunday mornings, Marion would begin the announcements, and Jefferson would interrupt her to tell everyone in the congregation what Marion had "forgotten" to tell them.

After three months of not being given information for the announcements, Marion asked yet again if they could have weekly meetings with each other. Jefferson agreed to biweekly meetings, which turned into his biweekly "bitch sessions," his time to complain about the denomination, other staff members, or people in the congregation. Marion felt he continued to neglect to share important pastoral issues with her.

One evening, Marion's phone rang. It was a parishioner asking about another parishioner who had died suddenly, early that morning. Marion had no idea what the parishioner was talking about, which made the conversation awkward and painful. That very afternoon she had knocked on Jefferson's office door—well after Jefferson knew the parishioner had died—and asked if there was anything she needed to know. Jefferson said no. The next morning she confronted him, demanding to know when he was going to get around to telling her about the parishioner's death. Marion told me Jefferson said to her, "Stop. You are behaving like a child."

At first, Marion tried to rationalize such incidents. The church had been without an associate minister for a long time, and she recognized that it must have been hard for Jefferson to share authority. She had compassion for him, understood that it would be difficult, even painful, to have the congregation so excited about her arrival. Jefferson made it really hard for her compassion to last.

Marion's installation service—the service during which she was ritually and officially recognized as a minister on staff—was held in January. Right before she was hired, her grandmother, one of the women who helped raise her and shape her vocation, passed away. On the back of the bulletin for her installation, Marion dedicated the service to the memory of her grandmother.

Jefferson confronted Marion in the hallway one morning after he saw the program. "He said, 'We don't dedicate worship to anyone. Worship is dedicated to God,'" Marion told me. "'You need to get rid of that dedication.'"

Being an Episcopalian, I am used to people dedicating all kinds of things: worship services, brass crosses that get paraded down aisles, benches outside churches, pews inside churches, trees, altars, bricks on the sidewalk, stained-glass windows, kneelers. Chances are, if you look closely in many Episcopal churches, most of the big-ticket items will have someone's name on them. We aren't shy about putting the names of people who give money on sacramental objects. Marion's denomination isn't as dedication-happy as mine, but they do dedicate things in churches, so Marion's desire to acknowledge her grandmother was not out of the ordinary. The most common dedication in Sunday bulletins at her church was for flowers: "These flowers are dedicated to the glory of God and are given in honor of _____." If Jefferson felt so upset by the dedication of the service to Marion's grandmother, a better approach would have been to suggest she model the dedication on the language used for flowers. To try to soothe Jefferson, Marion made the change herself.

Jefferson realized that criticizing Marion's dedication to her grandmother was out of line, and he eventually apologized, but after the apology, things between Marion and Jefferson went rapidly downhill. "That was the beginning of the end," Marion said. "He was forced to acknowledge that he had done something in poor taste and wrong, and he had to tell me, his little underling, that he messed up."

Soon after the apology, Marion began to feel bullied by him, in private, behind closed doors. During one meeting in his office when no one else was present, Marion recalled him saying, "I don't like the way you're using your time." Although Marion was almost never late, kept longer hours than Jefferson, and was practically running most programs at the church, Jefferson insisted lateness was a problem for her. While Marion was on time for all meetings, Jefferson was notoriously late, so his accusation was almost laughable. Marion suggested she keep track of all her hours and what she did with her time. She turned in a written document at the end of each week. There was no follow-up or feedback.

After months of private accusations, harassment, and intimidation, Marion approached the personnel committee to ask for help. The committee met with Marion and Jefferson separately, and then together. Marion described the whole process as "useless." The personnel committee assigned a subcommittee to work with Marion and Jefferson, a subcommittee that had been handpicked by Jefferson. In the spirit of southern hospitality, the subcommittee recommended Marion and Jefferson try to be "extra sweet and tenderhearted to one another."

Throughout her tenure at the church, Marion felt she was doing all the work. It seemed to her that when he was actually in his office, Jefferson spent his time sitting in front of his computer; he rarely went to youth events, attended parish outreach functions, visited people in the hospital or in their homes, or ran Bible studies or adult education programs. He did, however, preach almost every single Sunday at all the services. "He preached inane, inept sermons," Marion said. "He regurgitated the same information with a different title every Sunday." He usually only scheduled Marion to preach when he was going to be out of town.

Jefferson allowed Marion to preach on September 29, 2005, just weeks after Hurricane Katrina. The congregation had decided to donate $50,000 to the relief effort. The parishioners were proud of their financial donation, but they wanted to do more than simply give money. Marion organized the church's response. She gathered information, made sure it was on the church's Web site, kept track of donations, coordinated volunteer days, and worked with other local churches.

One of the readings for that Sunday was Exodus 16, when the people of Israel are hungry and thirsty, wandering in the wilderness, what Marion calls the "did-you-take-us-out-of-Egypt-only-to-starve-us?" text. When Marion discovered what the lectionary reading was, she remembered an e-mail she had received written by people trapped in a hotel in New Orleans. Although they had not seen any news or television, they wrote that they could imagine what was being broadcast across the country: images of Black people the media will insist are looting stores and rioting. The e-mail writers wanted to contradict this false image. The e-mail, single-spaced and multiple pages, documented the heroic actions of people in New Orleans: electricians who stayed up all night working, construction workers who fashioned makeshift boats to rescue elderly people, nurses who manually administered oxygen. These heroes, the e-mail said, were the desperate people, the people without food or water or shelter. The e-mail also documented how the police had treated residents. Marion said, "It was horrendous, and I was like, wow. This is it. This is the Israelites in the wilderness. This is what it means to be in this plight."

That Sunday, Marion delivered the first prophetic sermon she ever preached at that church. She talked about suffering: "On the one hand, there is this narrative that we know as good church people, about God providing for the Israelites, taking them out of the danger of the Red Sea. They had just encountered this miracle. How dare they complain of their hunger and thirst? These griping, complaining whiners, how dare they judge God? On the other hand, there is a different narrative. They were almost deluged in the Red Sea, but they made it across just in time. They had almost been captured by the Israelites, but at the last minute the waters fell. They almost died, and then manna fell from the sky." Marion suggested that although the story in the biblical text and the story being lived out in New Orleans were years apart, hunger is hunger, thirst is thirst, and desperation and dislocation are desperation and dislocation. The story in Exodus, she claimed, is a story about radical abundance. God doesn't discriminate. God gives to all in need. We choose the God we serve, Marion preached, and she challenged the congregation to ask themselves whether they served a God of scarcity or a God of radical abundance.

During the pastoral prayer that followed, Marion talked about one of the workdays she had organized for the church. Marion brought a group of parishioners to a relief distribution center. They sorted items that had been donated. Marion was asked to organize women's lingerie. She spent the afternoon sorting women's underwear, and she was appalled to discover that people had donated previously worn underwear. More than half of what Marion sorted was preowned and preused and had often not even been laundered. She learned from the people running the distribution center that this was not unusual. During the prayer, Marion commended the generosity of the congregation. She complimented their thoughtfulness and ability to empathize as reflected in the quality and quantity of their gifts. She went on to say that this was not the case everywhere, and shared what she had discovered while working at the relief center. Marion asked the congregation to encourage friends and family to be mindful of the integrity of their gifts, to be sure to give out of a sense of empathy, and to try to identify with the suffering of others.

The next week, Marion was immediately summoned to Jefferson's office. At the appointed time, she walked into Jefferson's office and found him sitting with the chair of the personnel committee. Jefferson handed her a document titled EMPLOYEE WARNING FORM. Marion started laughing when she told me that part of the story. She said, "Let me tell you what is wrong with the employee warning form. Jefferson does not have the authority to create that kind of document given how our denomination functions and how that particular congregation operates. He subverted the protocol outlined in the personnel handbook and created a form that didn't exist. He created the document out of the blue and without any accountability."

Marion described the warning form to me. It listed three complaints. First item: lack of respect for the reverence of worship. Jefferson insisted he received multiple phone calls, e-mails, and personal visits from members of the congregation about her mean-spirited, angry, and un-gospel-like message on Sunday. "Jefferson refused to quantify the number of complaints," Marion said. "And when I offered to give him a list of people who had come up to me after that service to tell me how powerful they thought my sermon was—even the name of a man who told me it was the best sermon he had ever heard—he was not interested." Jefferson told her that her sermon did not "share the good news." People want to be lifted up, he said. They don't want to hear bad news on Sunday mornings, not to mention how inappropriate it was for her to mention dirty underwear in worship. He also pointed out that she had not worn her robe while she preached, which was against regulations. Marion had never been told that she was required to wear a robe, and that Sunday, like Sundays before, she had chosen not to wear the robe to create a sense of intimacy between herself and the congregation while she preached what she knew would be an affecting sermon.

Second item: failure to represent the church appropriately in public. Here, Jefferson was referring to a casual conversation between Marion and another African American member of the congregation. Jefferson took the conversation out of context and accused Marion of representing the church poorly in public, citing this interaction as evidence. Later, when the man Marion had been talking to discovered Jefferson used him to do his dirty work, he left the church.

Third item: gossip. Jefferson accused Marion of spreading a rumor that he was looking for a job at another church. This was a simple misunderstanding based on a congregation member who misheard a conversation Marion was having with another person. Once she explained what she actually said, Jefferson agreed to drop that third point.

Beneath the three items of complaint, the form listed steps Marion would be required to take to remedy the situation: Robes are to be worn at all times. All sermons will be proofread and approved by the pastor. You will write a letter of apology to any whom you have offended. Below the list of steps there was a place for Jefferson to sign, for Marion to sign, and for the head of personnel to sign. Because signing the form would signal she agreed with all the accusations, Marion refused to sign. "He was outraged, and he said,

'Obviously this isn't working. You need to dust off your résumé and find another job, and you better start looking soon,'" Marion said.

Marion told Jefferson that she would not sign anything until she had a conversation with the head of the regional governing body. "Jefferson said, 'What do you need to talk to him for? This isn't a denominational issue. This is a staff issue,'" Marion said. Marion felt pressured by Jefferson not to tell anyone what was happening or the contents of the employee warning form. Despite his threats, Marion followed protocol and went immediately to the head of the regional governing body and the chair of the commission on ministry (of which Jefferson was a member) and told them what happened. While they acknowledged that there were "significant issues" to be addressed, they were reluctant to pursue disciplinary action against the head pastor. They discouraged her from filing a formal complaint. "They said it would hurt me and it would hurt the congregation. They instructed me to take the moral high road and get out of a sick situation," she said. "These are people who are peers, and often it is very difficult to discipline other peers. Their fear over addressing this particular situation won out over holding people accountable."

Marion started looking for another job. She soon found one in higher education. She took the position. Despite her disappointment with how they handled (or did not handle) her situation with Jefferson, she continues to have a positive relationship with the regional governing body and the commission on ministry. She is regularly invited to preach and lead workshops throughout the area. "Since the beginning, I have received such affirmation of my gifts and of my call," she said. "I was surprised that they let me go so easily."

I visited Marion during her last two weeks working at the church. I attended a church event with her, and, throughout the evening, people kept coming up to me to tell me how much they loved her. They grabbed onto me and looked right in my eyes. "We love Marion so much," they would say. "We are really going to miss her, but we knew she was a shooting star when we hired her. We knew someone else would be quick to snatch her away from us!"

Although many people in the congregation knew Marion was leaving because of repeated abuse from Jefferson, they decided to tell themselves and me a different story about her departure. It seemed to me they could not afford to acknowledge what happened to Marion and hold Jefferson accountable for his behavior because it would require real change for them and for their church. Instead, they sacrificed Marion to maintain peace. It was easier for them to let her go than to examine what really happened, to look carefully at the fact that their White pastor drove an African American female out of their southern town. Instead, they told themselves she left because she was off to bigger and better places, told themselves they were lucky to have had such a star in their midst even for a short time. The price of keeping the peace was a high one. They lost the one person who was breathing life back into their congregation and their community.

After Marion announced she was leaving, Jefferson tried to eliminate the associate minister position altogether. Marion told me that during one of the last meetings she attended, Jefferson proposed a change to the staff structure in which he would be the only called and installed pastor on staff. Instead of hiring another ordained minister, Jefferson proposed they have "parish associates." Jefferson listed several retired clergy in the congregation whom he would ask to work, on a volunteer basis, at the church. They were all White, mostly male, and the median age was seventy. The rest of the staff, Jefferson proposed, would be made up of "directors" of various ministries— children, youth, music—and they would not be ordained.

Jefferson's desire to nix the associate position and the experiences of other women I interviewed expose not only the difficulties faced by women who are associate ministers but problems with the associate position itself. It is rife with power struggles and is often not well enough defined or supervised to avoid them. The troubles associates have and the failure of churches to address them also reveal a system not willing to hold itself accountable. Churches seem unwilling to police their older, more senior members, and often the committees responsible for such policing are peopled, at least in part, by those causing the problems and by their friends.

But the difficulties of the position are compounded when the person filling it is a woman. Part of what makes the experiences of female associates different than their male counterparts is that women get disproportionately stuck in that position. For most men, the associate position is a stepping-stone to something else: solo pastor, senior minister of a multistaff church, or rector. Few ordained women go on to be hired by churches as senior ministers. When women are hired as senior or solo ministers, it is usually by smaller, underfunded communities. Becoming a solo pastor if you are a woman often means accepting a salary well below what you could make as an associate.

In addition, some congregations' difficulties with associate ministers stem from cultural expectations of women more generally. In many churches, the associate minister is assigned the caretaking, relational work often known as "pink-collar ministry"—pastoral care, children's ministry, education programs. Our relational requirements for women are far tougher than they are for men. We expect women to be caring, available, nurturing, and selfless, and while these qualities are expected of all ministers regardless of their gender, they are demanded even more of women. When a man demonstrates an inability or an unwillingness to exhibit these qualities, he confirms the gendered relational expectations we have of men, and so his behavior is often excused. When a woman fails to meet these expectations, she fails not only in her role as minister but in her role as *woman*.

I have heard more members of congregations than I can count complain about the fact that their ministers won't "let them in." Many want to be friends with their ministers, and when they discover that their relationships with their ministers have limits, they feel betrayed and disappointed. We don't do a good job showing congregations and ministers what healthy relationships look like.

Ministerial intimacy is often mistaken for friendship, but ministerial intimacy is not the same as relational intimacy. The relationship between a parishioner and her minister is, in some ways, artificial, constructed: The minister is employed by the parishioner to play a specific kind of role, and this role, like the role of a therapist or a doctor, is an intimate one. Ministers, by profession, are present at major life events—birth, death, divorce, marriage, rehab, pregnancy. They are paid to listen, and sometimes parishioners share things with their ministers that they might not share with anyone else. Often neither ministers nor congregants understand the dynamics of their relationship. Some ministers thrive on the intimacy they share with the members of their congregations. The minister is the authority figure, the one in the robe, the one wearing the collar, the one with the office. While many ministers may struggle in personal relationships with friends or family, they can, in some ways, be in control of relationships with parishioners.

But these relationships are also taxing. People need things from their ministers constantly, and if ministers do not have sources of support outside of their church communities, they can become exhausted, burned out, and drained. When people in churches—both ministers and congregants—do not understand the nature of ministerial relationships, when they do not understand what healthy relationships look like, when they do not admit what each is projecting onto the other, what each expects of the other, what each needs from the other, or how each might be using the other, they get confused and hurt.

Jocelyn Jones,* an ordained UCC minister, worked as an associate in a wealthy, large New England church. Like Jefferson, her senior minister, David, rarely let her preach. He didn't allow her to do funerals and only let her do weddings if he was going to be out of town. David also seemed to neglect to give Jocelyn important information about the church and parishioners. In fact, he hardly ever spoke to her at all.

One Sunday, Jocelyn and the youth group put on a play during the worship service. A parent of one of the kids in the group, Jen, worked closely with Jocelyn and the group, but she told Jocelyn that she really did not want to be thanked publicly. She reminded Jocelyn and David that she didn't want any public acknowledgment several times weeks before the performance. Right before the service, Jen stopped Jocelyn in the hallway and told her, again, that she wanted the play to be about the kids, not about her. Jocelyn immediately went into the office to remind the parish secretary that Jen didn't want public recognition. David came out of his office and said that he had bought flowers for her. Jocelyn suggested he give them to her after the service instead, since Jen did not want to be recognized during church.

After the performance, Jocelyn stood to lead the applause. David rushed in front of her, flowers in hand. Jocelyn recalled that he said, "I want to invite Jen to come up so we can recognize her." Jocelyn couldn't see Jen's face from where she was standing, but she said Jen must have looked aghast because she remembers that David then said, "I know you didn't want to be recognized, but we have these flowers for you, and I wouldn't have done this if Jocelyn had told me more than five minutes before the service that you didn't want to come up."

What bothered Jocelyn most was the fact that David blatantly lied in front of the entire congregation to make Jocelyn look irresponsible. Monday morning Jocelyn talked with him. She told him she could not believe he said things he knew were not true. "His response was, 'I guess I should be more careful with my words,'" Jocelyn said. "And that was it."

It wasn't the last time David said something untrue during worship that made her look incompetent. "It wasn't like he was outright saying, gee, our associate is a loser, but it was subtle. He said things you don't say in worship about your colleague."

Because David didn't treat Jocelyn as a colleague or as an ordained minister, the rest of the staff didn't either. Jocelyn's office was next door to the parish secretary, and she could overhear conversations between the secretary and people who came into the office. Sometimes someone would ask to speak to a minister, and the secretary would say, "He isn't here right now. Would you like to leave a message?" Committees at the church also acted like Jocelyn wasn't one of the ministers in the room. "I would be working with one of the committees I was in charge of, and if there would be a decision to make, I would offer my opinion, and it would be as if I had said nothing. They would say, well, we'll ask David about that." Jocelyn grew accustomed to the fact that her opinion had no weight and wondered why she bothered to attend meetings at all.

After three years of David's silent treatments, of being ignored in meetings and humiliated in worship, Jocelyn decided to look for another job. She found one as a solo pastor of a small church in a suburb outside a neighboring city. When the congregation learned she was leaving, many said to her, "Now you can be a real minister." Their statements confirmed that although Jocelyn was already an ordained "real" minister, she hadn't been perceived as one. "Is that because I was the associate?" she asked. "Probably. But, you know, it has got to have something to do with the fact that I was a young woman, too. I think each one is a further layer of not being taken seriously."

Jocelyn wasn't taken seriously as a minister in the church, and she wasn't taken seriously as a minister outside the church, either. When she met people in the community, at local meetings or events, they would always ask her if she was a seminarian. Now that she is head pastor at a different church, people think she is an associate minister, not a head pastor. Jocelyn said, "There is an immediate assumption that my position is less than whatever it is, which is just bizarre. Do I look like an associate? Do you think that a woman couldn't be a solo pastor? Do you think I am too young to be a solo pastor? Clearly I don't look like what I'm supposed to look like for people to recognize me as the minister of a church! It really drives me crazy."

The assumptions about Jocelyn's position are, in and of themselves, fairly innocent. Young women and men often have to listen to people say things like, "You look way too young to be a minister." Jocelyn's reaction to such comments, however, suggests something about what it is like to be a woman minister. Because she already experiences not being taken seriously as a professional, because her senior pastor ignores her and humiliates her in public, because her congregation often acts like she is not in the room, seemingly innocuous comments smack of sexism, adding insult to injury. What Jocelyn hears is that she does not look the part, that there is something wrong with her.

Unlike Marion, Jocelyn never got into any outright "trouble." David never yelled at her or delivered any "employee warning forms" or harassed her. "I think it was almost worse than getting in trouble," she said. "There was no engagement at all. So in a sense I guess I could have done anything. Sometimes I wonder what would have happened if I had just been like, screw it, I am going to do a sermon as a biblical character and dress up and roam the aisles of the church." Jocelyn never roamed the aisles of the church in costume. Instead she kept herself in check—her politics, her preaching style, her clothing. No one ever sat her down and gave her a list of rules, but she knew there was a list and that it was her job to try to guess what rules were on it. She said, "I wanted to figure out where the box was so I could get into it. I wanted them to like me. I wanted to fit in. I wanted to keep the job."

Now that she is a solo pastor, Jocelyn cannot imagine going back to being an associate. "Working with a male senior minister was so hellish," she said. "I'm sure there are some good ones out there, but it is generally a messed-up dynamic, especially having an older man in power with a younger woman as an associate. Hello! I am your eager assistant. There is no way for the woman to avoid looking like a little helper."

At the end of the interview, I asked Jocelyn if there was anything she would like to add, anything she wanted to tell me that I had not asked her about. She said, "It's funny, because when I think about being a woman in ministry, I feel like I have been really lucky. My first experience was awful, but that could have happened to a young man. Maybe not. But, in so many ways I feel lucky. I had really good field education experiences. I had no problem in the ordination process, and so many people had a hard time. I found that first job before graduation with no problem. I got this job with no problem, and it is wonderful. Here I am, a young, unmarried woman living with my boyfriend, the first woman pastor that they have had here, and they have completely accepted me and are allowing me to be myself."

Jocelyn lives with her boyfriend of several years, James, in a house they bought together. Although she feels she can be herself at her new church—her goofy, inclusive-language-using, nose-ring-wearing self—only some members of the congregation know she lives with James. Before her final meeting with the search committee, she met with her spiritual director, who asked her what she would do if the committee were to be upset that she lived with James. Jocelyn said, "I won't take the church. I'm not going to let the damn stuck-in-the-1950s church run my life. Everybody lives with their boyfriend before they get married, 50 percent of people now, and I am sure it is more like 95 percent where I live." Even thinking about the possibility that the search committee might give her a hard time infuriated Jocelyn. "Luckily the search committee was totally supportive and fine," she said.

Although they were personally supportive of her living arrangements, the members of the search committee advised her not to tell the congregation. The committee's insistence that she not tell them suggested to Jocelyn that there might be people in the congregation who would be upset by the fact that she lived with James. "But then, at the same time, I'm like, my grandmother would probably be upset with it if she knew," she said, laughing.

When I first contacted Jocelyn to see if she would like to be interviewed for the book, she said she would love to talk to me, but she was afraid that she had nothing "juicy" to tell me. Her experience seemed tame compared to other women she knows who have had "awful experiences"—lesbians who have been kicked out of the ordination process or fired from jobs, women who have had to endure demeaning comments. She went on to say that in her new position, she hardly thinks about sexism at all. "I don't think about it that much, and when I get together with some of my friends who have been fired from churches, I think, oh my God, I have been so lucky. They have really accepted me here, which is amazing. I just wanted to say that. I realize how lucky I am, and often I forget that it still is a huge problem."

Like Jocelyn, many of the women I interviewed insisted that they had been "lucky." Some almost seemed embarrassed that they had been, in their words, complaining to me about their experiences. Compared to what other women had experienced, they had it relatively easy, they said. After sharing their stories, many women began a campaign of minimization, trying to convince me that what happened to them was minor, almost apologizing for taking up my time. To survive a sexist world, women have had to develop heightened capacities for empathy. While this contributes to their ability to be effective ministers, it often impedes their ability to advocate for themselves. Ever aware of what other people are thinking or feeling, women often do what is necessary to placate those who have power over them.

Jocelyn's story lends itself easily to minimization. What did David really do to her? So he gave someone flowers to thank her for putting on a play? So he didn't talk to her much when they passed in the hall? What's the big deal, really?

The big deal is that David made Jocelyn doubt her vocation, her sense of self, her body, and her behavior, all the while looking like he was doing nothing, like he was Reverend Mr. Nice Guy. That is how sexism works in Protestant churches. It is insidious, almost impossible to point out, difficult to prove. But the fact that Jocelyn used the word "lucky" betrays her. You are only "lucky" when something good happens to you if there is a real possibility that something bad could have happened to you. Her use of "lucky" reveals the terrible weight of knowing what has happened to other women and believing there is a high chance it will happen to you. Other women's stories—stories of sexual harassment, silent treatments, pay cuts, being defrocked, run out of town, called names, fired—discipline the women who hear them. Keep in line, or there will be real consequences, these stories remind them. And even if you do keep in line, you'll need "luck" to avoid these consequences. Rather than empowering women to know that what is happening to them is not an isolated incident but part of sexism, these stories threaten women. When women use the word "lucky" when they talk to me, I realize how afraid they are. Sometimes they even knock on wood. By belittling their own experiences as lucky (or unlucky), women get to feel shame instead of anger, and for many good Protestant girls, shame is much more comfortable and familiar than fury.

I interviewed Jocelyn in her office in her new church, where she is the solo pastor. Driving up to the church I saw the signboard with her name on it and felt the pang I sometimes get when I wish I were ordained. When I walked into the church offices, she was in the middle of trying to figure out where one of her congregants left the check to pay the consultant they have hired to help them launch a new capital campaign. I explored the building while I waited for her to find the check, and I noticed posters about domestic violence, news about upcoming bake sales, and even a big pile of free tampons in the bathroom. When Jocelyn finished looking for the check, she invited me into her office, a small room with big windows looking out to a yard filled with trees. It was devoid of all knickknacks and flowery couches, no footprints posters or framed cheesy poems, just a sleek modern couch, a small table, and a white candle. I felt a kind of peace I have not felt in church for a long time.

Jackie—the former marketing executive turned minister—got her first job as an ordained UCC minister at a big church called Faith

Church, in a wealthy suburb on the East Coast. After she graduated from divinity school, she had several job offers and chose Faith because she liked the people on the search committee and the way her job would be structured: 50 percent youth ministry and 50 percent developing the spiritual life of the community. Jackie understands developing the spiritual life of a community as a fundamental part of her vocation: crafting rituals, leading a community in worship, and creating spaces in which transformation might happen. The fact that this would be 50 percent of her job exhilarated her. She was also excited to be part of a large staff. In her final interview for the job, the senior minister, Nelson, spent most of the time talking about the fact that the staff worked as a team. Jackie chose a big church instead of a smaller one where she would be the only pastor because she was afraid of being swallowed up by her work. She wanted the luxury of having other staff to lean on. She wanted colleagues.

Jackie realized, early on, that she was going to have trouble with Nelson. When she was negotiating her contract, Nelson assured her there was no reason to put what she was asking for—vacation time, continuing education opportunities, defined work hours—in writing. She told me he talked her out of almost everything she wanted to include.

The staff met every week, and once a month they worked with a pastoral counselor who helped them make sure they were working well together. The meetings were also a time for them to take a break from the business of running the church and talk instead about their spiritual journeys. While Nelson's commitment to the staff's development influenced Jackie's decision to work at that church, it turned out to be a charade. "He wanted everything to appear as if the 'team' was healthy and well cared for. He knows how to talk the talk," she said. "I know he genuinely believes in the importance of discussing group dynamics, but he often insisted on facilitating the meetings and used up most of the time to talk about himself. Ironically, we spent our meeting time taking care of him instead of each other."

During one of those meetings, the conversation turned to the possibility of making changes in the structure of the worship service. Because part of Jackie's job was to support and develop the spiritual life of the community, she spoke up during the conversation, echoing some of the deacons' suggestions for changes and offering some of her own. Nelson didn't say anything. About a week later, he approached Jackie. "I met with the deacons," she recalled he said. "We have decided that we are not going to change anything. We're just going to leave it the way it is." Jackie believes that Nelson wanted to keep the format of the worship service the same because, in its current state, the entire service led up to his sermon. Rather than the service revolving around the word or communion, everything revolved around him.

During her first month at Faith Church, Jackie took the youth group on their annual retreat. When she accepted the position at Faith, she had been told that most of the retreat had been planned already, but when she arrived, Jackie discovered nothing was in place. Nevertheless, she pulled it off. Nelson's daughter was in the youth group, and the cabin to which she had been assigned was not, in her view, the "cool" one. The group returned in time to go to church on Sunday morning. Jackie was in her office getting ready when Nelson walked in.

"How did it go?" he asked her.

"It went really well," Jackie said. "I feel positive about it. The other leaders feel positive about it. The kids seemed to have a great time."

"My daughter didn't have a very good time. She didn't like what cabin she was in," he said, and then Nelson turned and walked away.

Jackie felt Nelson strategically cut her off from any support in the church. In the UCC, it is recommended that each minister have a pastoral-parish relations committee (PPR), which is typically a two- to three-person committee a minister selects to support him or her. It is a place where pastors can share their struggles, whether they are with the senior minister, the youth, the congregation, or with pastoral care. Rather than create his own committee, Nelson took over the group of deacons in the church as his PPR committee. As a result, he refused to allow Jackie to attend deacons' meetings, even though that group was partly charged, like Jackie, with overseeing the spiritual life of the church. When Jackie asked if she could form her own PPR committee, Nelson told her she could have the buildings and grounds committee. PPR committees are formed for the sole purpose of supporting ministers; the buildings and grounds committee is charged with taking care of the infrastructure of the church, not its minister.

Jackie felt criticized by Nelson constantly. He would find her on Sunday mornings before she was supposed to preach and tell her things she felt were intended to throw her off balance. Like Marion's and Jocelyn's senior ministers, Nelson humiliated her in public, often saying things that were not true to do so. Jackie was away one Sunday, an absence she had arranged weeks in advance. Some members of the congregation told Jackie that even though he knew she was out of town, Nelson stood up in church and said, "Where is Jackie? I guess she must have overslept. If she shows up, let's welcome her like nothing happened."

Jackie said, "He made it look like I had not lived up to my responsibilities. And that was not the only time. He continually undermined my pastoral authority with the community, even though people were desperate for me. In fact, they crafted my job because they weren't getting from him what they wanted in church."

Nelson barely let Jackie participate in the worship service. He refused to let her do baptisms, turning them into a strange kind of popularity contest. "He told me that as people got to know me, they'd feel comfortable asking me to baptize their children," she said. "But he added that right now, most of the people would come to him because they knew him." He assigned Jackie the same small parts in the service week after week. She was allowed to do the pastoral prayer, the offering blessing, and, if Nelson was feeling generous, the benediction. If it was a communion service, she was allowed to administer the cup, never the bread. "It was stifling," Jackie said. "I felt so pigeonholed."

In the beginning, Jackie expressed her feelings to Nelson. She asked to be given more responsibility in worship. She pleaded with him to take her seriously as a minister, to let her use her gifts. She told him how isolated she felt, how she needed more support in the church, and that the multiple late-night meetings she had every week were making it hard for her to maintain a life outside of work. She remembers that Nelson told her that if she would just accept that Faith Church was her only community and stop trying to keep friends on the outside, Jackie would probably feel more comfortable.

Being a minister—no matter your age or your gender—can be an isolating experience. You are surrounded by people all the time, but the people who surround you are not your friends. They are your parishioners, your congregants. For young ministers, the isolation of parish ministry can be devastating. From the social world of divinity school or seminary, newly ordained ministers are thrust into suburban or rural communities where, sometimes, they are the only single people without children. A minister's schedule is not conducive to having an active social life. Late-night meetings and working every single weekend mean that you are often not free when your friends are. Saturday nights find you home alone working on the sermon that you have to preach at the crack of dawn on Sunday morning. This isolation is also what allows senior ministers to get away with abusing their associates. Disoriented, unsure about just what they are experiencing, associates often duck their heads, keep their mouths shut, and endure. To combat this isolation, some ministers form clergy support groups—ministers who come together regularly to support one another. Ministers need the support of other ministers who understand what they are going through, who can reflect back to them that what is happening to them is not healthy or normal, or who can simply laugh and drink margaritas.

Even though Nelson didn't support her at all, Jackie still tried to see him as a colleague, even as a mentor. She often asked for his advice or opinion. When she began to officiate at weddings, she consulted him about how she ought to proceed. Jackie said, "When I asked him about weddings, his response was literally like he was an old burned out pastor who searched for the wedding recording in his brain and pushed PLAY. He would say the same thing over and over again, telling me the exact same stories multiple times." He seemed to be on autopilot, terrified to engage anything new.

Then, right before Easter, Nelson had a heart attack. Suddenly, with Nelson incapacitated and in the hospital, Jackie became the head pastor. It was a defining moment for her. She led the church for a month before Nelson returned. She did baptisms. She preached. She handled all the Easter services. During that time period, Jackie worked primarily with two other women on staff. She said, "The three of us were the epitome of feminine power, energy, creativity, and collaboration. We shared leadership, and it worked incredibly well."

When Nelson was well enough, he started attending church. He sat in the front row and whispered commands to her, mouthing the words of the prayers like an elementary school teacher helping students remember their lines in a school play. Jackie knew almost immediately that she was in trouble. "Things had changed so much for me—it was like, I am woman, hear me roar, and there was no turning back," she said. "You think you are going to put me back in the corner, but baby ain't going in the corner."

When he returned to work, Nelson seemed to want things to return to the way they had been before he got sick. "The logical step was for me to be removed," Jackie said. Nelson tried to squeeze her back into the tiny space he had allowed for her before he had a heart attack. "He tried to make my job really narrow, and the more narrow it was, the less creativity I had, and the harder it got for me to stay," Jackie said. "At a certain point, it is a soul death." Jackie was not seeking an unusual level of responsibility for an associate. She was not trying to take over Nelson's job. She simply wanted to be allowed to do the job she was hired to do. It seemed to Jackie that the more she tried to live into her own sense of ministry, the angrier Nelson got, and the more often his anger surfaced in public.

In the UCC, ministers are ordained at their sponsoring parish, but when they get a job, there is an installation service at the church where they work. Installations are generally done within the first six months that a person arrives at a new call. Because of Nelson's heart attack, Jackie's installation was delayed. By the time her service was scheduled, Jackie was already questioning whether she would be able to continue to work at that church.

I attended Jackie's installation, and Nelson's behavior was so inappropriate I almost crawled over the pews in front of me to tackle him. Nelson preached a sermon during which he told a story about a woman with smallpox. She was so sick and disfigured that she could not leave her bedroom. She hated herself, he said. She was ugly. She was weak. Her husband sat by her side every day and eventually convinced her that, even though she was ugly, she should come out and be part of the world. Seriously. That was his sermon. And it convinced Jackie she needed to leave. She called the area minister and arranged a meeting with him and Nelson. She knew she needed a witness.

The area minister, like almost everyone in a position of authority in the denomination, was a good friend of Nelson's. Jackie not only had no support in the church, she had no real support outside the church, either. Jackie knew Nelson would show up early so he could shape the story before she arrived. "So I got there earlier than he did," Jackie said. "When he walked in he was surprised to see me because he was fifteen minutes early. I was half an hour early."

Jackie shared her version of events. She told the area minister she had tried to work as part of a team. She said that she understood worship as central to her call, and that she had repeatedly tried to negotiate with Nelson to include her in the service in new ways. The area minister was no help at all.

Jackie decided to leave the church. When one of her older parishioners learned Jackie was leaving, she found Jackie after worship one

Sunday morning and gave her a small wrapped box. Inside the box was an ivory cross that had belonged to the woman's grandmother. "I want you to have it," she said.

Several months after she left that job, Jackie met with the area minister again. Having taken an official leave of absence from ministry to heal from the trauma of her experience with Nelson, Jackie was trying to figure out what to do next. She knew she was not ready or willing to work as an associate pastor. "I was pretty anxious about what to do. I went to him needing pragmatic advice and pastoral support. As the area minister, he is charged with being my pastor." She shared her struggle to try to determine whether parish ministry was for her. In particular, she wondered whether she would be able to make a sustainable living doing that work. "Most women who aren't associate ministers end up having to be solo pastors in small churches where you don't get paid nearly as much as you would elsewhere," she said. "I was talking about how women get shafted in this whole deal, and he didn't want to hear it." When she asked him what to do, she told me he said, "Maybe you should go into sales."

Despite the fact that Jackie left her position ten months after she started, despite the fact that she had been identified as a rising star in the denomination, no one in any position of authority in the denomination called to find out what happened. "You would think that someone who had three job offers when they graduated from divinity school, and then works in a church where it doesn't work out in just ten months, should raise some red flags, that there would be some sort of process," she said. After Jackie left the church, she scheduled meetings on her own with various people in her denomination to try to figure out what to do next. She even met with a leader at the state denominational level. Jackie shared her story, and when she finished, the woman said, "Why are you here? What did you expect?" She then compared Jackie's experience to the sex abuse scandal that was happening in the Catholic Church. "It could be worse," Jackie remembers she said. Jackie had meeting after meeting like this with people she hoped might help her. "It's like when you are feeling low anyway, and then someone kicks you in the ass, and then they kick you in the gut, and then they kick you again," Jackie said. "That's what it was like. It was repeated. There was nobody to help me, none of the leaders in the denominational structure."

Jackie eventually met with one woman who was hired to help support newly ordained pastors. After Jackie shared her story, the woman apologized on behalf of the church. Jackie was relieved.

But I'm not. What good, really, is a private apology? So some woman in some office in the denomination said she was sorry about what happened to Jackie. She did not start an official investigation to look at what was going on at Faith Church. She did not hold Nelson accountable for his treatment of Jackie. She did not help Jackie find another job where she could live out her vocation as a minister. She did not start a task force to look at the way women are being treated in the denomination. She apologized, Jackie left the office, and that was that. Private apologies, while they may help the women feel better temporarily and may acknowledge that something happened that deserves an apology, do not fix sexism. They cover it up. Much like Marion's subcommittee that encouraged Marion and Jefferson to be kind and tenderhearted, such apologies render sexist abuse personal and private, a matter of right relationship between two people as opposed to a political, intellectual, theological conflict where much is at stake. The hope, I think, is that after the apology, the woman will never bring up what happened again.

While Marion's church told themselves Marion left because she was a superstar, Jackie heard that Nelson told people Jackie left because she couldn't hack it. This was the story people in the denomination seemed to believe. They blamed her, and they just wanted her to disappear. In a way, Jackie made it possible for this myth to persist. To get people to listen to her, Jackie told her story in a way that didn't implicate Nelson. She took care of him, just like his congregation took care of him even though they saw the way he treated her. She said, "It's like daddy-god is hurt so everybody is trying to protect him." The congregation and the denomination circled the wagons to keep one of their own safe, and they left Jackie on the outside to fend for herself.

Marion found another job at a university, and she could not be more pleased. Jocelyn is a solo pastor at a church that she loves. Jackie has not been able to return to ordained ministry in a parish. She does not attend church. The thought makes her feel like she is going to throw up. She is a director at a nonprofit. Even in their new positions, Marion, Jocelyn, and Jackie, like many other women I interviewed, carry the scars of their experiences as associate ministers. Some suffer depression. Some anxiety. Others stomachaches and migraines and sleeplessness. The church, meanwhile, goes on as if nothing has happened.

But it goes on having undermined itself. By underusing the talents of ordained women, by abusing and isolating young women, by ignoring and devaluing and shaming the very women who could revitalize the church, by failing to hold themselves accountable, by refusing to reform, congregations are harming themselves. For every woman whose story I heard—who suffered in the ordination process or in the job search or as an associate or as a senior minister—there are countless others, men and women, who simply walked out the door never to return. Perhaps numbering more than those who walk out the door are those who never dared walk in the door in the first place.

The blame for associate ministers' difficult tenures cannot be placed only at the feet of senior ministers. The position leaves associates vulnerable, and many a congregation is known for eating up associate ministers and spitting them back out. Assistants are often more vulnerable to attack than senior ministers. Usually younger, less experienced, or female, they are easy targets. Church communities often operate like family systems. Like a family that externalizes its dysfunction by blaming an individual member of the family rather than looking critically at the system as a whole, congregations scapegoat assistant ministers. Made to bear the weight of a system that is not working, assistant ministers sometimes literally hold the pain in their bodies.

Although Claudia Highbaugh wanted to work on a college campus, she first spent some time working in a church in Orange County, California. "And it was the worst three years of my life," she said. "I was paid half the senior minister's salary even though we were only four years apart in age." The congregation, proud of themselves for hiring a Black woman to work at their church, shut her down at every possible opportunity. "They completely obliterated my identity by saying things to me like, we don't want to hear anything about you, where you come from, or your background when you preach from this pulpit. You are better than your story."

"What the hell does that mean?" I asked.

"It means they don't want to hear anything about how I grew up on the south side of Chicago or in the ghetto. They didn't want to hear anything about me. They said, we don't want to hear another word about you in your sermon because you're better than that. And we have met our demand of being diverse by hiring you. The very fact that you are here means we are open-minded and liberal. We don't want to hear that stuff."

For three years, Claudia was sick every single day. "I was sick and sick and sick. Nervous, crying, throwing up," she said. She developed a serious intestinal problem. The minute she left her job at the church—for a position as a chaplain at Yale—her body was healed. "I went from there to Yale, and I felt like I had been released from prison."

When Eve returned from her year in Bolivia living in voluntary poverty, she was called to work as an associate at a big, middle-class, White, suburban UCC church, much like her mentor's church. She had been looking for a job for eight months, and although this kind of church was not what she had in mind, she took the position they offered her as an associate pastor. She was twenty-seven years old. "Having grown up on welfare and having been the recipient and beneficiary of a lot of systems of power, I had a chip on my shoulder," Eve said. "I really needed to learn how to love upper-middle-class White people and pastor to them. And I did. I really think I did. It was a hard lesson to learn, but it was a good one."

A few years after starting to work there, Eve became pregnant with her first child. During the eighth month of her pregnancy, twelve members of the congregation circulated a petition demanding a congregational meeting about Eve. She and the senior minister sat down with the dozen petitioners to figure out what was driving them. Everyone had a different reason he or she was upset with Eve. The church was changing, and, although Eve was not the only person changing the church, some of the changes had resulted from her leadership. The petitioners were scared. And they blamed Eve.

One of the main complaints they voiced was their anger about the fact that they thought Eve was trying to bring the church through the "open and affirming" process in the UCC, an official process that results in churches making public statements welcoming people of all sexual orientations and gender identities into full congregational life and ministry. When they raised this point, Eve challenged them, asking if she had ever brought up the open and affirming process. They said, no, they didn't think she had. She asked, "Have I ever done anything other than state my own position? Have I ever done anything other than be clear when preaching and praying what my personal position on homosexuality and homosexual identity is?" Again they said no.

Although their fear of all things gay was the first issue they raised, Eve knows that homophobia was simply a subject they wanted to hide behind. She said, "The whole gay issue is a red herring. It's really about change in the church. It is about losing power and control. And it's about sexuality, which is very taboo." The petition was circulated in 2001 right after September 11, a time when people in the church wanted to, in Eve's words, "batten down the hatches." She said, "It was like, let's get back to tradition, let's kick those Afghan asses. I mean, people didn't say that in church, but that is certainly how they were feeling. They wanted to find the culprit. They wanted to feel safe." Whatever congregations may think of the individual women ministers they know, they tend to view being female as code for having liberal views and hiring a female minister as a sign of progressivism. And so they targeted Eve, with her growing belly and her politics.

In addition to the petitioners' homophobia, three other issues surfaced. First, they didn't like what they called Eve's "political activism" in the community, meaning they did not like that Eve stood on a street corner with Catholic nuns and Quakers holding a candle and singing "This Little Light of Mine" on Sunday evenings to protest the war in Afghanistan. They thought she was "too political," and they didn't want other people thinking Eve represented their church. Eve told them, "I represent myself as a Christian, and I do believe I represent the gospel of Jesus Christ, but, no, I don't represent this particular church. I'm not punching the clock at that time." Protesting the war was what she felt she had to do to follow the gospel. "This is how I hear the gospel, and this is how I have to live it out," she told them. "I do not want to face Jesus at the end of my days and hear him say, you were ashamed of my word, and so I am ashamed of you." Then she laughed and said to me, "They didn't like that."

The second issue had to do with a sermon Eve preached a year and a half earlier in which she had questioned the historicity of the birth narrative of Jesus, something that has been questioned for decades by historians and biblical scholars who have argued that both Mary's virginity and the notion that her pregnancy resulted from divine intervention (the Holy Spirit) are literary devices, not historical facts. A mortal woman becoming pregnant by supernatural forces signaled that the child who resulted from that pregnancy would possess special powers, such as the ability to perform miracles. Rather than a literal fact, the virginity of Mary is a rhetorical device intended to demonstrate the significance of Jesus. "I was basically taking away their happy second-grade Christian theology," Eve said.

The third issue had to do with her maternity leave. She planned to take a couple of weeks completely off, and then return half-time for six months, after which she would return to full-time work at the church. She made this decision with the personnel committee and the entire staff. The fact that the petitioners questioned her maternity leave confirmed for Eve that her pregnancy threatened them and made them uncomfortable, forcing them to face that when she became a mother she would not be *their* mother anymore. "The fact that there was a big conflict that happened around the time of the birth of my child is not a coincidence. I was eight months pregnant when the shit hit the fan. It was Christmas, the middle of winter. We were living in the parsonage. I mean, where were we going to go? Here I am, pregnant, I must be having sex with my husband," she said, and laughed. "Surprise. Surprise."

"You didn't say, no, I'm a virgin?" I asked.

"It's Christmas! It's happened again! A friend of mine made this incredible theological connection. He said, Eve, you are Mary and they are telling you there is no room at the inn."

Eve later learned that the church had targeted associate pastors for years, especially when the associates were women. Outspoken women didn't last long. The church moderator told Eve it was as if all associates had signs on their backs that said KICK ME. Although Eve's senior minister supported her in private, in public he was very careful. He didn't join the petitioners' efforts to get rid of Eve, but he didn't make clear statements supporting her and condemning their behavior, either. Eve said, "He could have asked them to be more specific. He could have depersonalized it. He could have told them this is not the way we handle conflicts in our church. We don't write a petition to remove people from their positions. We speak one on one." None of the petitioners had ever come to Eve to voice his or her concerns directly. When Eve pointed this out to them, they told her she was too intimidating. "I suggested that maybe it was their opinions that were intimidating them and not my presence. Maybe in your heart of hearts you know that you're full of shit," she said, laughing. "I didn't say that, but I thought it. That was what I really wanted to say. I knew that they knew that if they came to me I would undermine their beliefs, and their beliefs were all they had."

All three complaints the petitioners voiced against Eve had to do with change—theological change, political change, and relational change. They wanted change to stop, so they needed the person they perceived as engineering it to leave. The petitioners' strong reaction reveals a common fear in church communities—the fear that if you let go of one part of your faith everything will begin to unravel. Eve challenged some of her congregation members' beliefs, like the historicity of Jesus's birth narrative, but she offered something else back, a kind of faith that demanded something of them. Hers is belief that is not about simply accepting certain facts or creeds but involves being challenged, being uncomfortable. "God likes to keep us guessing, keep us a little off-kilter," she said. "I think that is the point. God's job is to shake us out of our preconceptions and out of our self-righteousness." Because ordained women already symbolize change for many congregations, when women question even the smallest part of faith or tradition, some people are afraid that their deepest fear—the loss of what they hold most dear, their faith, their God—will be realized.

Even though the senior minister did not support her publicly, Eve had amazing mentors in the denomination who helped her survive the conflict, including the area minister and her in-care adviser where she was ordained. Although she was angry, she worked hard to follow her mentors' advice to depersonalize the conflict. One debunked the good-girl myth for her. He said, "You can't say, if they really knew you, they would know what a great person you are." He reminded her they were acting out of their own sense of loss, grief, anger, and fear. He encouraged her to go out with friends for beers (she could have herbal tea) and blow off steam.

The petitioners eventually came to realize that despite the fact that they tried to speak for the whole church, they really did not represent the whole. It became clear that more and more people did not share their feelings, and this realization undermined their confidence. Surprisingly—or maybe not surprisingly at all—most of the petitioners were people Eve had supported pastorally in crisis moments in their lives, bereavement, illness, loss, divorce. Eventually their desire for relationship with her won out over their desire for power and their desire to be right. She spent a lot of time with them, and, before the petition, she really trusted them. "I don't really trust anyone in the church anymore," Eve said. "You can love them, but you can't trust your parishioners."

Eve describes the church as "divine decisions in the hands of mere mortals." She said, "I think people get very disappointed when the church does reveal itself as utterly, utterly human, and yet, if we're made in the image of God, then there has got to be some divinity even in the midst of that humanness." The highlight of Eve's week is Sunday morning at 10:15 when she looks out into the congregation and sees the people gathered there. "I look out and see all these faces. I know people's stories. I know how different they are. I know that these people would never be in relationship with each other in any other network, in any other place that they go, work, socially. It's only church where they come together, and they are willing to share things they would never share in the outside world, sides of themselves, stories, tears, activism." Eve told me that people always say the church is twenty years behind the culture, but she thinks it is the other way around. "I am really proud of the UCC for ordaining women 150 years ago or ordaining a gay man 35 years ago or standing up, standing with, falling down beside Black civil rights leaders in the South," she said. "I love the church. I love the church in different ways than I love God because it is fallible, but I am very proud of it. But then you get into deacons or vestry meetings where all they can talk about is whose turn it is to wash the little plastic cups, and it's like, is this where you are going to get stuck? Is this really what we're going to spend our energy on when there is so much crying need in our world?"

Part Two

INCARNATION

THE BODY

I desire, then, that in every place the men should pray,
lifting up holy hands without anger or argument; also that
the women should dress themselves modestly and decently in
suitable clothing, not with their hair braided, or with gold,
pearls, or expensive clothes, but with good works, as is
proper for women who profess reverence for God. Let a
woman learn in silence with full submission. I permit no
woman to preach or have authority over a man; she is to
keep silent.

—I TIMOTHY 2:8–12

During the summer of 2006, Bishop Katharine Jefferts Schori was elected presiding bishop of the Episcopal Church USA. The presiding bishop leads the entire Episcopal communion in the United States for a single nine-year term. Bishop Jefferts Schori is the first woman to hold that office.

Rev. H. W. Herrmann, rector of St. John's Episcopal Church in Quincy, Illinois—one of three dioceses in the American Episcopal Church that still refuses to ordain women—told the *New York Times* that the new bishop would not be welcome in his diocese. "Just like we can't use grape juice and saltines for Communion, because it isn't the right matter, we do not believe that the right matter is being offered here," he said.

I interviewed Katharine Jefferts Schori, and I asked her about Herrmann's grape juice and saltines quote. "Well, that's his opinion," she said. "We have been wrestling with that question for much more than thirty years." While she reads texts like the gospels and Acts and finds evidence of women exercising public leadership—"Mary Magdalene is understood as the apostle to the apostles. She is the one who brings news of the resurrection"—Herrmann finds evidence that some human beings are appropriate and others are not. "It comes out of that strand that says that mind and spirit are okay, and matter is not, and some traditional understandings have understood women to be more material than men," she said.

Biological sex is one of the most fundamental ways we sort people. The labels "male" and "female" are essential to how we navigate the world. The moment a child takes a first breath—sometimes even before that first breath, when the fetus is still in the womb—biological sex is announced. I know a woman who asked that her obstetrician not tell her right away whether her child was a boy or a girl. She wanted to have a few moments immediately after the birth with her baby not as a girl or as a boy but simply as a human life, wet and new, lying on her chest. Given how hard she had to fight for this simple request, you would have thought she had asked her doctor to let her give birth on the moon.

Because biological sex has become so fundamental for sorting and labeling people, you might assume that the designation male, female, or intersex (displaying biological characteristics of both sexes) is straightforward, obvious, clear-cut, "scientific." However, this is not the case. Scientists and theorists of all kinds continue to debate what, if anything, determines biological sex, and new evidence constantly throws into question theories that used to be taken as fact.

Gender, as distinct from biological sex, is the set of characteristics that identify the social behavior of women and men. Shaped by history, culture, race, religion, ethnicity, and class, it is what professor of psychology Suzanne J. Kessler means when she insists that we decide whether someone is male or female without ever seeing their genitals or their chromosomes. We identify people as women or men by the way they look—what they wear, how they talk, how they move through the world.

Although biological sex and gender are not the same, it is hard to draw a definite line between them. When a doctor declares, "It's a girl," she assigns biological sex *and* gender. "It's a girl" signals both that your baby's biological sex (as far as the doctor can tell) is female and that she is destined to be wrapped in a pink blanket and brought to a room full of pink balloons. Although indisputable scientific evidence has revealed that there are more than two biological sexes, biological sex and gender in the United States are most often understood as binaries: male or female, man or woman. "Man" is defined against "woman": Man is spiritual; woman is embodied. Man is violent; woman is nurturing. Man is intellectual; woman is physical.

Man is rational; woman is emotional. Man is strong; woman is weak. Man is protector; woman needs protection. Man is active; woman is passive. The list of opposites goes on and on and on and on.

Many people mistakenly understand biological sex and gender as identical, believing that chromosomes or genitals or hormones exclusively determine behavior, that we become men or women because of nature, not nurture. I am not arguing that there are no differences between men and women, nor am I arguing that biology plays no role in gender differentiation, but I am suggesting that the reasons for these differences are difficult to tease out. Many of the differences we think are shaped by biology have been shaped just as much (if not more) by culture. Girls and boys get strong messages about what is appropriate behavior for their sex and what is not, and they are usually punished when they fail to conform. Many of the behaviors we associate with women are learned, not instinctual. And it is not simply the differences between men and women that are problematic; it is the way these differences are valued and devalued—the way, for example, we reward aggressiveness in males and demonize it in females, or the way we celebrate strength (a masculine trait) and fear weakness (a feminine trait). And what concerns me even more than the value ascribed to gender differences are the consequences that await those of us who dare to step out of line—whether that line has been drawn by biology or by culture. Collapsing the difference between biological sex and gender makes it seem that those who violate gender norms violate society as a whole.

Christianity has played a huge role in collapsing the difference between biological sex and gender. Many Christians insist that the differences between men and women are part of the created order, blessed and ordained by God. Adherents to this line of thinking point to the creation story in Genesis—usually ignoring that there are, in fact, two creation stories. In the first creation story, found in the first chapter of Genesis, God says things like let there be light, and there is light, let the waters bring forth swarms of living creatures, and the waters bring forth swarms of living creatures. When it is time to make human beings, God says, "Let us make humankind in our image, according to our likeness," and then the story tells us that "God created humankind in his image, in the image of God he created them; male and female he created them." Those who like to emphasize the essential difference between men and women point to this story to prove that from the beginning there are two sexes and, although both might be in the image of God, they are different or complementary. To blur the difference between male and female is to mess with the divine order of creation.

During the second creation story, which can be found in the second chapter of Genesis, God makes the Earth and the heavens, and before there are any plants, God forms a man from the dust and breathes into his nostrils, and the man, with this breath, becomes a living being. Then God plants a garden in Eden and grows "every tree that is pleasant to sight" and puts the man in the garden and tells him that he may eat of every tree but the tree of the knowledge of good and evil. Then God decides that it is not good for the man to be alone, and so God makes him a "helper as his partner." First God makes animals of all kinds and calls on the man to name them. Then God causes the man to fall into a deep sleep, takes one of his ribs, and from this rib makes a woman whom the man calls "bone of my bones, and flesh of my flesh." Those who insist that marriage should be exclusively for heterosexual couples and that woman is supposed to be man's "helper" point to this version of the creation story.

In both cases, the stories are used to insist that gender difference is ordained by God—to contradict gender roles, then, is to contradict the way God intended the world to be. As an example of this sort of argument, consider a statement issued by the Vatican in 2004 entitled "Letter to the Bishops of the Catholic Church on the Collaboration of Men and Women in the Church and in the World." The letter was authored by Cardinal Ratzinger (now Pope Benedict). In addition to claiming that women who demand equal rights "make themselves the adversaries of men" and destroy the family, the document is adamant that women's "natural" role is the *feminine* role:

"listening, welcoming, humility, faithfulness, praise and waiting." Ratzinger writes, "While these traits should be characteristic of every baptized person, women in fact live them with particular intensity and naturalness." The Church did not make this up, the letter argues, God did, and, therefore, through no fault of the Church, which is simply following the will of God, women cannot be priests.

Ratzinger could have saved himself and his readers a lot of time if he had simply quoted one of Paul's passages about women, calling on them to be subordinate, telling them it is shameful to speak, urging them to be silent and submissive. Quoting Paul to women is quite similar to quoting Deuteronomy to homosexual people. Paul's words and Ratzinger's words about women might seem less violent than the biblical passages yelled by homophobes to people who are gay or lesbian—being told to be silent or to wait or to have humility or to listen sounds a *little* better than being called an abomination—but the biblical passages hurled at women and at homosexual folks have similar effects: God becomes a cultural tool, wielded to keep people playing by the rules human beings have made, rules that give power to some and take power from others. Or, as the Vatican likes to insist whenever it is fighting against equal rights for homosexuals or women, "the law of man cannot undo the law of God." Such a bold reversal! It is no accident that God happens to exhibit the qualities ascribed to "man" (spiritual, intellectual, rational, strong) and human beings happen to exhibit the qualities ascribed to "woman" (embodied, physical, emotional, weak), no accident that God is called "He." From the beginning, men created a god to do the work they needed him to do.

This version of god is too small for God.

Even though most professions have been open to women for some time—military, medical, political—there is still cultural resistance to women in certain occupations. In many professions, the gender-exclusive history is written right into the name of the job itself: *mailman, fireman, policeman, chairman, congressman, waitress, stewardess.* For others, such history is not as visible or audibly obvious.

Although "man" is not tacked onto the end of *doctor, soldier, lawyer, banker, scientist, professor,* or *president,* the underlying assumption for many people is still that the doctor or president or professor is a man. This is arguably even more the case for *priest, pastor,* and *minister.*

Katharine Jefferts Schori is no stranger to breaking professional gender norms. In addition to being the first female presiding bishop of the Episcopal Church, she is a pilot and a scientist. In the mid-1970s, she was the chief scientist on a research cruise, and the captain of the ship refused to talk to her because she was a woman. "It was just kind of flabbergasting," she said. "I hadn't run into that overt kind of sexism—certainly lots of subtle sexism—but not anything quite that blatant." Katharine solved the problem by "working around it," she said. "He talked to somebody else who would talk to me. It was kind of funny in retrospect." More than thirty years later, the Anglican Communion (the name for the worldwide group of Anglican churches, including the Episcopal Church) looks eerily similar to that 1970s ship. In February of 2007, Jefferts Schori attended a five-day meeting in Tanzania during which members of the Anglican Communion delivered an ultimatum to the Episcopal Church: Stop blessing same-sex unions and forbid gay men and lesbians to become bishops—or get kicked out of the Anglican Communion. To signal their disapproval of Jefferts Schori's support of equal rights for gays and lesbians, seven conservative archbishops refused communion rather than celebrate the Eucharist with her. (What would Jesus do? Probably not that.) Conservative bishops in the United States have demanded alternative oversight, refusing to report to her and aligning themselves with conservative Anglican bishops. Some churches in the United States have gone so far as to secede. Not incidentally, most bishops who oppose same-sex unions and the ordination of gays and lesbians also oppose the ordination of women as priests, not to mention as bishops.

Having women in the pulpit—African American women, Latina women, Hispanic women, Chinese American women, White women, Native American women—exposes the assumptions that have been made about ministers and about women, assumptions that have been so much taken for granted that no other possibilities have occurred to us. It is only when we see something other than what we expected that we are able to realize what we have been expecting. An ordained woman reveals both our expectations about *ministers* and our expectations about *women,* and she often conforms to neither. When "minister" and "woman" collide, it is a kind of explosion, and, as in any explosion, the person standing closest gets most of the shrapnel lodged in her body.

Jamie Washam, the American Baptist minister whose Southern Baptist church refused to ordain her, recently decided to build a small house in a neighborhood close to the church where she works as the solo pastor. New to the area, Jamie is still meeting her neighbors. One afternoon, she stood in her front yard talking to the builder of her home. After the builder left, her next-door neighbor came over to introduce himself.

"Is that your husband?" he asked, pointing to the man driving off in the truck.

"No," Jamie said. "He's the builder."

"Where is your husband?" he asked.

"I'm not married. It's just me," Jamie said.

"Oh, well, that's funny," he said. "They told me a pastor was going to move in here."

"I am a pastor," Jamie said.

Flustered, the man said, "Oh, I mean they said a man pastor was going to move in."

Jamie, never one to mince words, looked right at him and said, "Why don't we start out by not lying to each other. No one says man pastor. They say pastor, and you assume that means a man."

When women choose to be ordained, their vocation frequently becomes provocation. Jamie's neighbor expected to see a "man pastor" and instead saw a woman—a blond, five-foot-ten, young, blue-eyed woman. When congregations expect to see a man (whether or not they realize they held such expectations) and instead see a woman, when congregations expect to see a straight person and instead see a gay person, when congregations expect to see a White person and instead see a person of color, suddenly everything they presumed about ministers is up for grabs. And, like Jamie's neighbor, they get flustered, embarrassed, even a little angry. Moments like the one on Jamie's front lawn happen to women ministers all the time. Over and over again they come up against people's expectations about ministers and are reminded, sometimes subtly and sometimes not so subtly, that they do not meet them.

The women I interviewed endured relentless comments about their clothing, their bodies, their dating lives, their sexuality, and their appearance. They were incessantly told that they did not look professional or ministerial or appropriate—all ways of saying they did not look like "ministers." "You're the minister?" people asked them when they walked into hospital rooms or sanctuaries or town meetings. "You don't look like a minister." Faced with continual reminders that they, somehow, did not look the part, they had to reassert their identities as ministers, over and over again. They had to believe—no matter what anyone else said—that they were the "right matter." "God called all of me," they told me. "And that includes my body."

The stories that follow are full of contradictions, and that is because the experiences of women who are ministers throw into relief the conflicting cultural messages we carry about women. We are a Puritan culture obsessed with pornography; we constantly display women's bodies as sex objects but insist women cover up so they don't distract us; we are sexual beings but are ashamed of our sexual needs; we need our bodies to live but deny we have them. The women I interviewed unearth these confusing messages: They want to be seen, yet not constantly looked at; they long for their whole selves to be accepted, including their bodies, yet they do not want to be reduced to a body; they demand to be taken seriously, yet don't want to have to be desexualized for this to happen; they want to celebrate human sexuality, yet don't want to be sex objects; they want to be celebrated as women ministers, yet not seen only as *women* ministers. No wonder having a woman in the pulpit is hard for all of us to navigate.

We don't know what to do with women's bodies in the pulpit, and that is largely because we don't know what to do with bodies in most forms of Christianity. The body—and in particular, the female body—has been denigrated, feared, understood as sinful, shameful, something to be covered up, tamed, and mastered. There is something ferocious about our fear of bodies in churches. And yet, at the heart of Christianity are stories about incarnation, about a God that dwells in a human body, a God that makes bodies and breathes life into them.

Chapter Six

LANGUAGE

Seeing a woman in the pulpit not only brings us up against our implicit or explicit assumptions about the categories "minister" and "woman," it also challenges how we think about God. In many denominations, the minister is understood as a kind of stand-in for God or for Jesus. Priest as proxy is one of the fundamental arguments against the ordination of women of the Roman Catholic Church: Jesus was male, therefore priests must be male.

Most liturgical language refers to God as male—God is called "He," "Lord," "Father," "King"—and prayers in many churches use the pronoun "he" or the words "man" or "mankind" to refer to human beings. When pressed, proponents of this kind of male-only, exclusive language insist that "men" is a generic, gender-neutral term. "Men" does not mean biological males, they argue, it means all of us, men and women. But "men" has never meant all of us. Just think back to the Declaration of Independence and the phrase "all men are created equal." The authors did not mean all of us when they wrote "men"; they meant White, property-owning men over the age of twenty-one. And they did not need to be explicit about this. Everyone already knew what "men" meant, knew who was included and who was not, who was considered human and who was not. Insisting that "men" means everyone is a kind of double-talk: "Men" means all of us, but only men can get ordained.

Proponents of male-only language for God also try to justify their exclusion by insisting calling God "He" is metaphorical, not literal. "We know God is not actually a *man*," they say. But all you need to do is look at Christian art throughout most of history to know this is not the case. When God appears in paintings, God looks like a White man. And, usually, so does Jesus (even though given where Jesus was born and when he lived, we know he was Black, not White). Children all over the United States are being taught that God is a White man who sits high up in the sky and watches over them. The prayers they say before bed, the stained-glass windows lining the walls of their churches, the biblical texts they hear read from the pulpit construct this image of God. And although their Sunday school teachers and their ministers and their parents might never actually say that God is White and male, ask any kid to draw God and I bet they will draw a person who looks a whole lot like Santa.

The impact of carrying around in our heads this image of God cannot be underestimated. It was only when I heard a prayer that said "she" instead of "he," when I heard God called "Mother" instead of "Father," that I realized how much translating I had to do when I sat in church, how much energy I spent wondering if I was included, how much I longed for theological language I could see myself in.

A survey administered by the Episcopal Church in 2003 demonstrates that support has increased for using inclusive language when referring to human beings. It also reveals, though, that inclusive language referring to *God* is less acceptable than ever. The authors report that even though ordained women personally prefer inclusive language, church worship services are no more likely to use inclusive language for God than they were in the 1970s. Given the stories I heard from women in all different denominations, I would say the same goes for worship services in 2008. One woman told me that sometimes, when she is standing at the altar leading worship, she feels that if she hears "he" or "him" one more time she will stand up and yell "pussy!"

Stacey King,* a newly ordained Episcopal priest, works in a church that is taking steps toward inclusive language, moving some "Father" language out and some "Creator" language in. She struggles, however, with what to do when she preaches. Writing does not come easily to her, and trying to use inclusive language only makes writing sermons more difficult. Many proponents of inclusive language do not use any pronouns to talk about God. Instead of saying "He" or "She," they simply say "God" over and over again. Not using pronouns for God creates some grammatically awkward sentences. Stacey said, "I could use Redeemer and Creator, but at some point, you want to have a paragraph that doesn't continue to say God-God-God. You wind up needing a pronoun." The pronoun Stacey chooses is "He," not "She." She continued, "I don't know if you run into this when you are preaching, but it is very hard if you ever want to use a pronoun for God and you try not to use 'He.' Using 'She' to me is just as jarring as the 'He,' and so, as a writer, you rape the language to try to avoid using 'He.'" She paused, and then she said, "I have finally, I confess, given up, because it is so stifling for me."

When I listened to the recording of my interview with Stacey, I was struck by her choice of the word "rape." I rewound that part of the recording several times and listened again to make sure I had heard her correctly. You rape the language to try to avoid using "he."

I don't blame Stacey. As a newly ordained female priest on the staff of a large church, the pressure on her is intense. Stacey was also not the only woman I interviewed who insisted that it was the God-God-Godself-God-Godself-God grammatical phenomenon of inclusive language that was the problem and not sexism. She was not the only woman—and not even the only feminist woman—who tried to explain to me that it just made more sense to call God "He," even when she personally believes that God is not a man.

What's stifling isn't trying to talk about God without calling God a man. What's stifling is the fact that male-only theological language has so powerfully shaped—or misshaped—our understandings of God that it is practically out of the question for many preachers and pastors and parishioners to call God anything other than He. Even feminists like Stacey. Male language for God runs so deep that it seems impossible for people to think or write or imagine their way out of this kind of thinking. Oh, I know God's not a man, people say to me, but He definitely isn't a woman.

When Laurie Brock, an Episcopal priest in Alabama, preaches, she never uses male pronouns for God. She always uses "God," which makes for some interesting and awkwardly structured sentences. "I use the female pronoun for spirit," she said. "And that is always fun, because then the rector of the church has to get a few phone calls the next day."

In a casual conversation, Laurie once asked the bishop of her diocese to talk to priests and congregations about using inclusive language. She suggested that he write a letter officially telling clergy that inclusive language is permitted. He didn't think that was such a good idea.

"We all know that 'men' is inclusive," he said.

"If 'men' means everybody, then let's all start using the men's bathroom," Laurie quipped.

She finds the struggle for inclusive language in the Episcopal Church frustrating. "We are better than that," she said. "I wish sometimes that men could feel how hard it is to stand there at the altar and say 'he' all the time. Do we not exist at all?"

Laurie says she will continue to bring up the issue of inclusive language until things change. "I know there are people who are like, does she ever shut up?" Laurie said. "No, I don't. I am one of eight women in my entire diocese, so, no, I am not going to be quiet. I am going to keep banging that drum until somebody pays attention to us."

Like Laurie, many of the women I interviewed were committed to helping their congregations think in new, creative, and liberative ways about God. Shannon Davis* was one of these women, and she lost her job because of it.

After working at Planned Parenthood, Shannon got her first church job as a solo pastor at a UCC church. Before she accepted the job, Shannon asked a minister in a leadership position in her denomination if the church had any history she needed to know about. "She told me they were the healthiest church in the conference."

Although Shannon said several times during the multiple interviews of the hiring process that she used inclusive language, once she arrived at the church and actually started using inclusive language, people in the church went crazy. They wrote nasty e-mails about her. They told her they hated her children's messages. They called secret meetings to complain about her.

Shannon was surprised, not by her congregation's actions—she knew friends who had had similar experiences—but by the fact that people were acting this way so soon. Usually ministers enjoy a honeymoon period of at least six months with their new congregations. People started criticizing Shannon immediately.

Because things were going so badly at the church, Shannon did some research about the church on her own, and she soon found out that the minister she had replaced, also a woman, allegedly had an affair with a parishioner, regularly got drunk during church hours, and neglected to keep confidentiality. The church hated her, and the minister took a leave of absence and never returned.

"Did the minister who called the church the healthiest in the conference blatantly lie to you before you took the job?" I asked.

"She didn't lie," Shannon said. "She just didn't know anything about the church, and so she made things up." Given everything Shannon's parishioners eventually said about her, Shannon now wonders if what they said about the previous minister is even true.

Shannon went again to meet with the minister to ask for advice and help, but Shannon received no support from her at all. "She totally blew me off," Shannon said. "She said things like, you're young, it will be fine, don't worry about it." And then she spent the rest of the meeting talking about herself and her own bad experiences working in churches.

Shannon suggested her congregation seek outside help, and they agreed. And then they changed their minds. First they protested working with the outside consulting group Shannon hired, and then they protested working with Shannon. The day before she was supposed to go on her first vacation, they called her in to a meeting planned without her and told her there was a petition going around the church to fire her. "I didn't know what to do," Shannon said. "I decided to go on vacation and to see it as a test. If the church has a strong enough countermovement to this kind of b.s., then it might be worth staying. If not, then I'm not going to deal with this." When she got back from vacation, nothing much had happened. Shannon called her local conference and asked them to come work with her and her church. Everyone in the conference told her to leave.

"Inclusive language became the rallying cry for all of these people who hated me," she said. And then paused and corrected herself. "Well, I don't think they really hated me. They hated the 'minister.'" The changes Shannon made at the church were very minimal, and before each change—even if that change was one word in a prayer—she explained everything she was doing and invited members of the congregation to discuss the changes and to be part of the process. "I think language was an easy target because it had nothing to do with them," Shannon said. Focusing on inclusive language as the problem meant they did not need to look at their own behavior or take responsibility for it.

Just a few months after starting the job, Shannon left, and like Marion's church and Jackie's church and Jocelyn's church, her church went on as if nothing ever happened. "There were no ramifications for the church," Shannon said. "It's amazing to me. Ministers are brought up on review for doing bad things; why shouldn't churches be brought up on review for doing bad things?"

When I interviewed Shannon, she was pregnant with her first child. Her husband, also a minister, is a solo pastor at a church, and they are in discussions with his church about becoming copastors there. Her husband, Joel, has been at the church for three years, and it was his positive experience that revealed to her how bad her experience was. "Joel could come in and change everything completely, and his church was fine with it," Shannon said. "But a woman comes in and changes anything, with lots of process, with lots of explanation, and she gets crucified."

Even though Shannon left her job and was devastated by her experience, she knows what happened was not about her. "Things were so bad that it made it kind of obvious that it wasn't about me," she said. "I can't go into a church and cause that much strife and craziness. I am just not that powerful of a person. That helped in a weird way because I knew it couldn't be me," she said. Then she laughed and added, "And I should probably say my faith in God did, too."

"How did your faith help you?" I asked.

"I think my belief in the mother God sustained me. There was strength in that. God is not gendered. God is not some male, White, bearded man in the sky. That is a fundamentally important part of how I view faith and my relationship with God."

Jocelyn, in her new role as solo pastor, has ushered her church into using inclusive language, and no one seems to mind. When she first started working there, she experienced an enormous tension between her personal understandings of God and the language she was required to use in the liturgy, tension between the words she feels comfortable using during worship and the words her congregation expects her to use. Often she does not mind meeting their liturgical expectations. "Sometimes I can feel okay using certain language, for example calling Jesus the son of God," she said. "I can say that because I understand it in a metaphorical sort of way, even though I know there are people sitting in the pews who understand it in a completely different way." But there are other things she won't say, no matter what the congregation's expectations. "For communion, I will not say body and blood."

"What do you say?" I asked.

"Bread of heaven and the cup of blessing," she said.

Jocelyn recently had an experience in prayer that moved her to push her congregation toward more inclusive language. "It felt like I was being told, you know who I am. You don't have to apologize for that. Say what you believe." Since she does not believe in a God who is a being who talks to people, she continues to struggle with how to make sense of hearing what seemed to be the voice of God during prayer. "The experience came out of me thinking about the Lord's Prayer. So the next Sunday I changed it," she said. "Now the bulletin says Our Father/Creator, and I just say Creator."

"Has anyone said anything to you?" I asked.

"The only comments I have gotten have been positive, including from a couple elderly people, which really blew me away," she said. Jocelyn was shaking when she introduced the prayer for the first time after she had changed the words to Our Father/Our Creator. "It's just a word," she said. "Everybody knows God isn't a man, and yet I was up there shaking because it's the Lord's Prayer, and I have heard of other women getting a lot of crap when they have messed with the Lord's Prayer."

Jocelyn was ready to accept the consequences and, luckily for her, there weren't any negative ones. She has been an ordained minister for five years, and it took her all five of them to risk changing one word in the Lord's Prayer, and she only did it then because she had a religious experience that told her to. "It's so weird that my political convictions didn't give me the courage to do it, but feeling like God was telling me it was okay, even though I don't believe that is possible, made me feel like I had to do this, that this is about God."

I sometimes imagine a Phantom Gourmet equivalent for churches. Instead of reviewing food and service and decor in restaurants while pretending to be a regular customer, this phantom—let's call her the Phantom Priest—would review theology and liturgy in area churches disguised as a regular parishioner. She would have a checklist with different categories to evaluate: inclusive language, theology, gay-friendly, racial diversity, class diversity, dress code, sermon, music, justice work, solidarity, children's programs. She would grade the church she visited and then use that report card to write reviews about the church. I like to imagine how such a review, even just the possibility of such a review, would change what churches serve on Sunday mornings. Would the fear of being publicly called out on sexism or racism or homophobia transform people? Would the possibility of reading in the paper that the sermon delivered that Sunday was boring or offensive alter the kinds of sermons given? Would ministers imagine a different audience for their songs and liturgies? Would congregations think about the people who would come to their church when they read a positive review published in the newspaper and realize they might be welcome?

The dominant religious discourse in the mainstream media creates the sense that the majority of Christians are against homosexuality, against so-called liberal positions of all kinds. Believing that the opinions of the religious right reflect those of most Christians generates fear in congregations that might otherwise be willing to speak out against this discourse. What if they aren't actually the minority?

Many ministers worry so much about the people they will upset if they change the language of the liturgy to inclusive language that they forget about the people who are upset because they don't use inclusive language. So harassed are they by the people who call to complain that the Holy Spirit was called a "She" or the Lord's Prayer called God "Creator" instead of "Father" that they don't have time or energy to think about the people who visit their churches and decide never to come back because they heard God called a man again and again and again. Refusing to use inclusive language, refusing to be creative about the metaphors we use to talk about God, sells our congregations short. And it sells God short.

When Jackie left the church where she was the associate minister a few months after the senior minister had a heart attack, she went on a retreat at a meditation center. The combination of her father's death when she was in divinity school and her experience at her church forced her to rethink her ideas about God and to realize that she had been holding on to an image of God as an all-powerful man who was going to take care of her. At the meditation center, she participated in a group exercise called a hands meditation. She sat in a circle of people with her eyes closed and was instructed to move her hands very slowly. After a period of silence and slow movement, she was told to imagine she was holding a golden ball of light and energy. "I felt this intense magnetic field, and it was so powerful that I was like, holy shit," she said. "I started to get really scared, which started to bring me out of the meditation, and then I went back and said, just stay with it and see what happens. I could have stayed like that forever." At the end of the meditation, the facilitator looked right at Jackie. He seemed to know that something powerful had happened for her. After the session, she went to talk to him. She was wearing a cross around her neck, and when he saw it, he asked her if she participated in other spiritual practices.

"I'm a minister," Jackie said.

He said, "Some people equate what you experienced with the Holy Spirit."

Jackie looked at him and said, "This is way bigger than the Holy Spirit. Those words do not fit what I just experienced."

Jackie told me about holding an imagined ball of golden light in her hands. "I felt that universal, beneficent rhythm and energy of the world, which to me now is God," she said. "But the word God— I couldn't use the word 'God' for a long time because it didn't even fit. It was..." She paused trying to find the right words. "It was too small. Does that make sense? Just too small."

Inclusive language—language that does not exclude or demean on the basis of gender, race, religion, ability, age, sexual orientation, or any other factor—does not mean that churches stop calling God "He" and start calling God "She." Replacing one form of gender-exclusive language with another does not solve the problem. Inclusive language is more expansive than that. It requires that we use multiple images, metaphors, and analogies for talking about God. It requires that we believe God is bigger than anything we can say about God. God is not only Father, Lord, or King. God is Mother. God is breath. God is rock and tree and wind. God is mystery. God is creativity. God is light. And God is darkness, deep and infinite.

Although I know changing the language we use for God does not eliminate sexism—that it might even hide sexism, making it seem to have disappeared when it has merely been covered up—shifting metaphors is like pulling on a single loose thread in a sweater. Pretty soon, the whole thing will unravel. Such unraveling can be frightening. We will have to grieve.

To many people, inclusive language seems silly, a small matter, simply about pronouns. But congregational and institutional resistance suggests otherwise. Resisters are right to be afraid. Changing the language we use to talk about God will change how we think about God, pray to God, and worship God. Changing theological language will transform our church services, our songs, and our stories. We will have to believe that exclusive language is not so fundamental to how God has been understood that without it there will be nothing left. We will have to trust that God is bigger than anything we can say or write or sing about God. We will have to have faith in God.

Chapter Seven

CLOTHING

One Sunday, five minutes before church was about to begin, I was gathered with everyone in the narthex—acolytes, lectors, the choir, and the rector. I was the scheduled preacher, and I was already sweating under the big black burlap sack of a robe I was required to wear over my clothes.

"The Lord be with you," the rector said.

"And also with you."

We bowed our heads. I looked at the floor. The rector looked at my shoes.

"Oh my God, Sarah," she said. "You can't wear those shoes!"

"Excuse me?" I asked.

"You can't wear those shoes when you preach!"

I looked at my shoes. They were black with two-inch heels. The lining of the shoes was pink. My toes were visible. I had just had a pedicure. "Oh," I said. "Why?"

"Open-toed shoes are not appropriate," she said.

"I didn't bring any other shoes with me, so it's these or barefoot," I said.

I think she seriously considered asking me to go barefoot, but then her fear of germs must have trumped her fear of open-toed shoes in the pulpit. "You can wear those this morning," she whispered. "Just think more about what you are wearing when you preach next time."

The Tuesday after the open-toed-shoes incident, the rector pulled me into her office for a chat while I was walking down the hall to use the restroom. "Can we talk for a second, Sarah?" she asked.

"Sure," I said.

"This is a little awkward," she began. "Don't you know what those shoes you wore are called?"

"Slides?" I asked.

She shook her head.

"Mules?" I tried again.

"No," she said. "They're called fuck-me shoes."

"Oh," I said. "My mom gave them to me."

She just looked at me, and then she said, "I know you don't have very much money, and I imagine you don't have any other shoes that would be more appropriate than the ones you wore last Sunday."

"Are boots appropriate?" I asked. I owned several pairs of boots.

"It's a little hot for boots," she said. She was right. It was the middle of the summer and the sanctuary was not air-conditioned.

"Here's my suggestion," she said. "I will write you a check out of my discretionary fund, and you can buy some new shoes."

"You're going to give me money to buy shoes?" I asked.

"Yes," she said. "But not just any shoes. Nice, sensible shoes. Shoes you can wear to church. I don't want to see your toes or any other part of your feet. People really do not like to see feet when they take Communion."

She took out her checkbook and began to write a check. She ripped it out of the book, folded it, and ceremoniously handed it to me. I was about to refuse her charity, but then I thought better of it. I might as well get paid for being publicly humiliated.

"Have fun shopping," she said.

"Thanks," I said.

I waited until I left her office to look at the check. I walked slowly down the hallway to the bathroom. I put the lid down and sat on the toilet next to the fake plant. I took a deep breath. I wondered how much she thought a good pair of shoes cost. I opened the check. Fifty dollars.

After work I went home and dug through my closet. In the back, I found a black pair of shoes I bought a few years before. They would work. Small heel. Full foot coverage. I called my boyfriend Eric and asked if he wanted to grab a bite to eat. I walked out of my apartment and deposited the check in the ATM at the end of my street. I took Eric to dinner using the $50. We drank beer.

I read an article in the *New York Times* titled, "When Young Doctors Strut Too Much of Their Stuff." Accompanying the article were six photographs of the same woman. In none of the photos was her face visible, just body parts: a bare leg crossed over another bare leg; two long legs wearing high-heeled black strappy shoes; a bare midriff; a low-cut dress revealing cleavage; a short black skirt with a slit up the side; bright red lipstick on the lips of a woman with long red hair. In all six images, the photographed woman wore a white doctor's coat. Although the article purported to be about the fact that young doctors and residents don't dress "professionally," it was really about the fact that *female* doctors and residents don't dress "professionally." The article referred to one male student who showed up to class unshaven, but the rest of the people cited for wearing inappropriate attire were women: sunbathing on the grass in view of a patient's window, wearing low-cut dresses, plunging necklines, and open-toed shoes. By "professional attire," the author of the article (a woman) really meant men wearing white coats. Anything else makes the patients and other doctors uncomfortable.

While the article chastised women for wearing skimpy, sexy clothing when working in a hospital, the photographs reveled in that fact. This was a woman to be looked at, lusted after; she was the stuff of heterosexual male fantasies, the protagonist of a pornographic tale about a visit to the doctor's office. Although the article suggested these photographs were hospital "don'ts," the images themselves looked like a hospital "do." Young female doctors are being blamed for wearing certain kinds of clothing, and, at the same time, a young female doctor is photographed wearing that very clothing and portrayed as a sex object. What renders young female doctors unprofessional is not the clothes they wear but the bodies they wear those clothes on—female bodies. In a sexist culture where many people still think "man" when they hear the word "doctor," it is the simple fact that they are *women* that makes people uncomfortable, not what they wear.

The article could easily have been written about women working in churches. The photographs would have looked much the same, except instead of a white doctor's coat, the woman would be pictured wearing a clerical robe over her "inappropriate" clothes. And, if you were to read the article carefully, you would see that what renders women ministers inappropriate is the fact that they are *women,* that they have women's bodies.

During my doctoral program, I was awarded a three-year fellowship by an Episcopal foundation. I was one of five students across the country in theology selected, the only woman. The foundation asked me to send a photograph of myself that they could post on their Web site and use in their publications. I sent one taken at my aunt and uncle's wedding, a ceremony I officiated with my godfather, an Episcopal priest. In the photograph, I am wearing a floor-length dress with spaghetti straps. Soon after sending the photo, I received a newsletter from the foundation announcing the winners of the fellowship. Under a headline that read "Five Fellows Chosen" (a headline my friend later altered to say "Four Fellows and a Girl"), my photograph appeared, flanked by four men wearing clerical collars or coats and ties. Something looked strange to me right away, although I couldn't figure out what was wrong for a few minutes. Then it hit me. They had Photoshopped my picture, wrapping me in a shawl, covering my shoulders with a dark, velvet-looking cloak. No longer was I wearing a dress with spaghetti straps. Instead I looked like I was in a shroud.

Clothing was an issue for every single woman I interviewed. They wrestled with what to put on their bodies. They acknowledged clothing's power to communicate, and they struggled with which message to broadcast, with how to be authentic, with how much they needed to change to conform to what was expected of them, with wanting to be taken seriously as ministers and yet wanting to express themselves in that role. When I asked the question, "What do you wear?" many laughed and laughed. And then they asked, "How much time do you have?"

Almost all of them endured continual comments about their clothing and their bodies. They were told they dressed inappropriately for work, or stood too provocatively in the pulpit, or needed to stop flirting with the congregation during sermons. Parishioners criticized haircuts, nail polish color, skirt lengths, and shoes, and they also showered ministers with compliments about different haircuts, nail polish color, skirt lengths, and shoes. They noticed new earrings, new pants, and new lipstick. Parishioners pointed out when ministers lost or gained weight and whether they looked prettier with short or long hair.

Although most of the women I interviewed suffered relentless commentary about their appearance, the men they worked with, or for, did not. Women's appearance is scrutinized and is an object of discussion in a way that men's isn't. This difference, however, does not mean male ministers are free from the gaze of their congregations. It is just a different gaze when it lands on women.

I sympathize with parishioners who talk to ministers about their appearance. I know most mean no harm. Some comments about clothes or hair or lipstick reflect how pleased many parishioners are to have a woman minister, but other comments do not, and it is often difficult for women to tell the difference. Regardless of the intention of those sharing observations about women ministers' clothing (or hair or makeup or body), the impact is to remind women that they are being watched, judged, surveyed, objectified. Even if meant as simple kindness, comments about a female minister's appearance let them know that no matter what they do—whether they play up their sexuality or cover it up—people are taking note. I asked some of the women I interviewed whether they ever told parishioners how uncomfortable continual comments about their appearance made them feel. Most had not. "What would I say?" one asked. "Don't tell me I look pretty?" Together we tried to imagine what parishioners might say if we told them not to tell us to wear our hair down when we preach. "Hey, settle down," they might say. "Why the big reaction? I just made a comment about your hairstyle. I was trying to be nice."

Most often, congregations' expectations about what women ministers should wear are unstated. Ministers are not handed a list outlining what clothing is appropriate and what clothing is not. Women in sexist cultures have been trained to be cultural chameleons, and, as is the case for chameleons, changing their outer appearance to match the surrounding environment is a matter of self-protection. Meeting expectations for how ministers ought to look, dress, and act is a way to keep themselves safe, under the radar, loved. The women I interviewed intuited what was expected of them, and, like good girls, they met these expectations. When they did not—whether by wearing blue toenail polish or hip-hugger jeans—someone always let them know. And often there were consequences.

In some Christian traditions (including the Roman Catholic, Episcopal, and Lutheran churches), priests and ministers are required to wear clerical collars, a white band around their necks. In other denominations, ministers can choose to wear the collar or not. Most often these collars are worn with black shirts. The collar is detachable, and it buttons onto a (usually) black clergy shirt. The clerical collar is a uniform of sorts, much like a firefighter's or police officer's. It's supposed to be an outward and visible sign of a priest's commitment to God. Basically, the collar is designed to separate the ordained from the nonordained. A letter urging Roman Catholic priests to wear the collar compares it to a wedding ring. (Following that analogy, priests are married to God, and if they believe that God is male and only males can be priests, then this sounds an awful lot like gay marriage to me.) The collar "identifies bishops and priests...and manifests their proximity to the Divine Master." The letter goes on to say that its purpose is not only spiritual but utilitarian; the collar prevents "mixed messages." "Let's say," the letter reads, "that a priest is required to make pastoral visits to different apartment houses in an area where drug dealing or prostitution is prevalent. The Roman collar sends a clear message to everyone that the priest has come to minister to the sick and needy in Christ's name. Idle speculation might be triggered by a priest known to neighborhood residents visiting various apartment houses dressed as a layman."

In many Christian denominations, ministers wear robes during Sunday services. The robe is one part of the liturgical vestments worn by ordained people, and it is called by different names (surplice, cassock, alb). Depending on the denomination, vestments can also include a stole (the narrow strip of fabric draped around a minister's neck), a chasuble (the outermost decorated robe often worn over other layers of robes), and an amice (a piece of fabric that covers the collar of the street clothes worn under all the robes), to list just a few. Putting on the vestments—or vesting—is part of a minister's prayerful preparation for worship. Because sexism is so brutal on and to women's bodies, wearing a clerical robe came as a relief to many of the ministers I interviewed. For the few hours every week—when they were literally undercover—they did not have to worry about what they wore or what their congregations would think about what they wore. They welcomed the chance to cover their bodies, which is understandable to all women living in a culture obsessed with our appearance.

Pamela Sanders,* a UCC minister, works with a senior minister in his late fifties and has never heard a single person in the congregation say anything to him about his appearance. Parishioners say things to her about how she looks quite regularly. "Never do I hear anyone comment on his suit or his hair, or ask him, have you lost weight?" she said. "There is some sense of ownership because I am a woman, almost a sense of owning me, and therefore they're able to make comments that we wouldn't make to the other senior minister."

Sometimes parishioners' comments don't bother Pamela, especially when they are nice and seemingly harmless, even flattering, like telling her that she looks fabulous in her new dress. But other times, the comments have a sexual edge to them that makes Pamela uncomfortable. One man followed Pamela up the stairs to the parish offices one afternoon and said, "Lovely hip-huggers you have on." Pamela thought to herself, "This man is commenting on my ass. I don't think this is appropriate." Another time, during the summer when it was really hot, she wore a sleeveless shirt and a pair of pants to work. "I thought it was very cute," she said. "I mean, I got it from Ann Taylor, for the love of God." She got more comments than she can count about "the associate minister in the halter top in the pulpit." Never mind that it wasn't a halter top.

Constant comments about her appearance make Pamela feel that she is not being taken seriously as a minister. She believes that she has to work twice as hard as the male senior minister to prove that she is an intellectual and ministerial force to be reckoned with, not just a pretty face. "I want to have people noticing my abilities and not my boobs or anything that makes me female," she said. Pamela tries to ignore parishioners' comments. "It is almost like an immunity system, and it has taken me a while, like it does for anybody. It has taken me a couple years in ministry to get that thicker skin and immunity system to the crap they throw at you," she said.

Robes and collars visibly mark women as "ministers." Many women struggle with being taken seriously as ministers, by their senior minister, by their congregations, and, more important, by themselves. Vestments help them affirm the authority that comes with being ordained.

Stacey wears her collar to claim her ordination. Working in a male-centered, rector-centered, wealthy, large church, she feels that it is important for women who are priests to own their roles as priests, visibly. Wearing the collar enables her to do this. When she wears it outside the church—on a subway, in the doctor's office, in the grocery store—people usually do a double take, trying to figure out what a woman is doing wearing a collar. In her historically Catholic town, women in collars are still a strange sight for many, even though local Episcopal churches have had women priests for decades. Stacey's favorite reaction to her collar occurred at six o'clock one morning when she was walking to work. She passed a homeless man sitting on the sidewalk, and when he looked up and saw Stacey wearing her collar, he began to laugh. "He looked at me, and he began to howl with laughter and point at me," Stacey said. "That's it, I thought, right in a nutshell. Even the street guys don't get it."

Although it helps her live into her role as priest, Stacey admits wearing a clerical shirt and collar is a fashion nightmare, especially when you are pregnant. "I was getting these clerical shirts bigger and bigger to fit my growing belly, but my neck wasn't growing anymore. I looked ridiculous," she said.

I met Stacey in her office, a small room with no windows but filled with beautiful art. I had a sense while we talked that maybe it had been a mistake to meet her at her workplace. Throughout our conversation, the answers she gave me seemed measured, as if she thought people might be able to hear what she was saying. Although there are no written rules about the clerical collar where she works, wearing a collar is expected of every ordained person on staff. One day, Stacey, tired of putting on the same black shirt and black pants and white collar every day, didn't wear her collar when she went to visit a parishioner in the hospital. "I got reprimanded," she said. "The other priest working in the office that day said, you know, when you go to see someone in the hospital, when somebody wants a pastoral call, they don't really want to see Stacey, they are waiting to see a priest. You need to show up in your collar."

Stacey's reprimand reminded me of one of my own. One Sunday, my friend Amy came to see me preach. I was giving people wine at the altar during Communion, and Amy knelt in front of me at the rail. Although she grew up Roman Catholic, she had not been to church, much less to Communion, in years. She had never taken Communion at an Episcopal church.

"What do I do?" she whispered.

"Just guide the cup to your lips and take a sip," I whispered back. And then I kissed her on the cheek.

After church, the rector pulled me into her office. "What was that I saw at the Communion rail?" she asked.

I didn't remember anything of note happening that morning.

"You kissed your friend," she said.

"She was nervous," I said. "I was telling her how to take Communion."

"Communion is not about you," she said. "People do not come up to the rail to see you. They come to get Communion. You are just a vessel."

I asked Stacey what she thought about the idea that people in the hospital just want to see a "priest," that they do not want to see "Stacey." "I see God as being relational, so I would push back on that a little bit," she said. "At the same time, when we studied the Eucharist at seminary, one of the things we studied is that no matter if we are flawed and don't celebrate with heart and prayerfully, the bread and the wine still become holy. We don't have the power to make it not holy. God supercedes us in that." Given her belief that God works through her, that her behavior or thoughts cannot get in the way, Stacey understands why her colleague insisted she wear her collar to hospital visits. Wearing the collar also helps her conform to parishioners' expectations of their priests. "It is not that you are less priestly without the collar. It's not that you can't have the same encounter," she said. "It's because that is how people understand priests, that is what priests look like, so you are wearing the physical appearance of a priest."

Stacey wears her collar because people expect to see a collar when they see a priest. Is it a priest's duty to live up to the expectations congregations have for their priests? Or is it part of their holy work to disrupt those expectations, to challenge them, to expand them? Perhaps wearing the collar allows Stacey to do just that.

As a minister, Jamie feels she is called to speak truth to power, and she understands that dressing like a minister gives her the freedom to do that work. "When you out yourself as a person who works for the church, as an agent of God loving the universe, as a minister, people have a different approach to you. When I was standing there wearing a robe and a collar protesting in Washington with a bunch of priests and nuns and imams, they weren't going to grab me by the back of my neck and drop-kick me in front of the media. They might have, but they were much less inclined to do that. If I had been there in my hoodie and in my cargo pants, with black nail polish or whatever, looking surly, even with the same look on my face, holding the same sign, they wouldn't have been so respectful. The people on the bus wouldn't say, hey, why don't you give us a word. You're expected to get up and have a word," she said.

Laurie, the Episcopal priest who works in Alabama, wore a clerical collar every day when she was first ordained. Like Stacey, she understood that as a woman, she needed to be visible as a priest. Now she wears her collar mainly when she celebrates the Eucharist or visits people in the hospital, and she only wears it in the hospital because it is "a shortcut to the doctor." She doesn't really have a problem with the collar. It is the clergy shirts that she has to put on when she wears the collar that drive her mad. "My dream is for Ann Taylor Loft or Calvin Klein to make clergy shirts. Because we are not all fifty years old and 350 pounds, okay?" she said, laughing. "Really, could it be that hard to make a shirt with nice lines?"

Laurie wears pantsuits when she wears her collar, and sometimes she even wears jeans. In seminary, she was taught to create a sense of uniformity with her clothing, that when she is at the altar she should wear her collar, black shoes, and a cassock. She tried to follow these fashion rules for priests, but then she got tired of black shoes. "My first act of rebellion was this really great pair of turquoise suede shoes that I bought," Laurie said. "I wore them, and what was funny was how many people really liked them." The turquoise shoes were just the beginning—then she wore red leather shoes, then pink loafers, and she hopes someday to show up in a really hot pair of Manolo Blahniks.

Laurie is convinced that part of her role as an ordained woman is to be herself at the altar, and that includes looking like herself. If you like to wear lipstick, wear lipstick, she thinks. If you like to wear pretty earrings, wear pretty earrings. If you like pink suede shoes, wear pink suede shoes. If you paint your nails crazy colors, paint your nails crazy colors. "How far are we going to pull back into that '80s power-suit thing, where to be taken seriously we try to become men?" she asked.

Laurie's fondness for wearing lipstick creates liturgical problems for her because when priests put on their vestments, they are supposed to kiss their stoles. Laurie has managed to avoid staining all of her stoles with lipstick by air kissing them, not letting her lips actually touch the stoles. Once, while she was vesting and air kissing her stole, one of the other women priests in the room noticed and laughed, sharing a story about ruining some of her own stoles by accidentally kissing them while wearing lipstick. Another time, a father and his young son were in the room where she was getting ready, and the son asked his father why Mother Laurie didn't kiss her stole but the other priest did. Laurie was a deacon at the time, not yet a priest, so the dad, assuming he knew the answer to his son's question, said, "Mother Laurie does not kiss her stole because she is a deacon. Only priests can kiss stoles."

Laurie corrected him. "No," she said. "It is because Mother Laurie wears lipstick, and it is really a symbolic act anyway."

They all laughed until the bishop, who was also in the room, spoke. "If you were my deacon, you wouldn't wear lipstick," he said.

Laurie insists the bishop was not being a jerk with his comment, that he was simply revealing that in his mind, women priests should look and act like men, and that means they shouldn't wear lipstick or jewelry. Laurie said, "God called me, and that includes me as a woman. God calls us as who we are." For Laurie, being a woman means lipstick and pink suede shoes and a longing for some kick-ass high heels, but she thinks the freedom to look like you choose to look belongs to everyone—lipstick or no lipstick, earrings or no earrings, combat boots or no combat boots, shaved head or no shaved head. Laurie said, "It really is about who God calls to be ordained. You don't have to make yourself into what you are not."

Like Laurie, Jamie experiments with her shoes. She did a sermon series on heaven and hell, and when she preached those sermons, she wore what she refers to as her *en fuego* shoes, a pair of shoes she bought in New Orleans that have flames coming up the sides. "I was like, I can bust them out for hell and Pentecost," Jamie said, laughing. (In addition to her shoes, her favorite part about the series was what she got to put on the signboard in front of the church: "This week: Hell. Next week: Paradise.") Jamie is not required to wear a collar, but she does wear a robe when she preaches. "I wear a robe because I find, for the most part, shoes aside, I try to not be distracting," she said. "I mean, it is frustrating to put a lot of time and thought and prayer into a sermon, and then to have people say, wow, those were some slamming boots. That's not what I want them to come away with." I have been walking with Jamie when she stops traffic. People literally hang out of their cars to watch her walk down the street. "I don't look like people expect me to look," she said. "They don't think I'm an American Baptist pastor." But Jamie finds this liberating rather than burdensome. "I think, as a woman, as a young woman, I have more freedom because already I don't fit in that box. So, they don't try to put me in there at all."

Monica was not required to wear a collar, but she always had to wear black and white suits or dresses. She enjoyed seeing how far she could push the boundaries, and she found creative ways to put black and white together—a black jacket with big white stripes and big gold buttons, a long black skirt with a high slit in the front. "It wasn't just to be ostentatious or audacious," she said. "I have to buy these clothes with my money. I want to look cute. I'm not dead. I'm just called to preach." Although many congregations in her tradition buy their male pastors' suits, they did not buy hers.

Monica's creative use of black and white clothing was one of the ways she responded to the sexism and ageism of the pastor of her sponsoring church, the church where she grew up. In her conference, being young, female, and a Harvard graduate made her an unusual candidate. Monica was not the first woman to come forward in her conference, but she was the first young woman. Most women who preceded her were older and already married, usually to pastors. "There were other women, but they weren't as young as I was," she said. "I felt a lot of discrimination on that level. The most common age for clergy in my conference in Michigan in the AME Church was sixty-five." Monica was twenty. "They didn't quite know what to do with me because there had not been someone like me in a long time," she said. "And the bishop who was the bishop at the time was notorious for how much he hated women."

Trying to discern her call, people in her denomination asked Monica questions she insists they would never ask men. Their first question was whether or not she would marry a Baptist.

"Would marrying a Baptist have been a bad thing for them?" I asked.

"Yes," she said. "I happened to be dating a Baptist minister, and I think that had come out somehow. I was going to keep it a secret because I was just dating him."

Monica told the questioners that she was nowhere near getting married, but that she was sure whoever she married would understand her vocation and her commitment to the AME Church. The committee was not satisfied. They asked, "But where will the kids go to church?"

Throughout the process, Monica continually broke the mold of how her church thought a pastor ought to look. "I don't enjoy breaking the mold," she said. "I think of it as just being me, but I am glad to be able to give another option to people out there. God calls you as who you are, however you are. And if you are a makeup-wearing, straight-hair-having, matching-suit-and-shoe-wearing person, great, but if you're not, there's still room."

After delaying her ordination process as long as he could, the pastor at her home church finally agreed to let her preach her trial sermon. Monica's whole family attended. She preached a month after she graduated from Harvard, and many of her relatives chose to attend her trial sermon as a way to celebrate both her degree and her call. Her cousins came, her godmother came, and so did her parents, her gym teachers from high school, and her Girl Scout troop leader. Her mother had a suit made for Monica for the occasion, a dark burgundy suit with an African print and gold trim. It even had a matching crown (though her pastor wouldn't let her wear it in the pulpit).

One Sunday morning before church, Monica was sitting in the office with a couple of other ministers. Monica described for me what happened. The pastor turned to her and said, "It's about time for the service. Aren't you going to change?"

"No," Monica said.

"But you are wearing pants," he said.

"So are you," Monica replied.

"I thought we had a conversation about what you are supposed to wear."

"We did," Monica said. "You said I should wear a dark suit or dress. This is a suit. A pantsuit."

Then the minister changed tactics. He told Monica she could wear the pants, but she would have to leave her purse in the office.

"Are you leaving your wallet in the office?" Monica asked.

"Oh no," he said. "But you can't walk down the aisle with your purse."

"Why not?" Monica asked. "When you leave your wallet in the office, then I'll leave my purse."

The minister at Monica's home church perceived her as a troublemaker. He thought she did things to annoy him, to push him, to make him mad. "In some ways I did," Monica said. "But it wasn't just because I wanted to annoy the hell out of him. It was because I believe in equity. I wanted to be treated the same way. You know like, y'all put on some panty hose. They are not comfortable. It's August. It's hot. There's no AC. Some things just don't make sense."

The male pastor at Monica's sponsoring church was not the only person concerned about how she dressed. Female parishioners at a church in Nashville where she later worked weren't too fond of her short skirts. They kept giving her lap cloths.

"Do you know what a lap cloth is?" Monica asked me.

"No," I said.

"It is a very big handkerchief with a lot of lace on the edges. You put the lap cloth on your lap when you wear a short skirt so people can't see."

A woman from the congregation would give her a lap cloth, and Monica would put it in her closet and never use it. Then another woman from the congregation would see Monica wear a short skirt and not use a lap cloth. She would assume Monica did not own a lap cloth, so she would make Monica another one. Monica now has a nice collection of never-used lap cloths.

Monica wrote an article called "Why I Wear Short Skirts in the Pulpit." She finds the desire to cover up her body strange given the fact that the sexuality of male pastors is so often celebrated. "Everyone wants to be in love with their pastor, and because our church is predominantly women, women are in a love affair with their pastor," Monica said. "That's why female pastors catch hell, because we can't be in love with them, at least not straight women. They don't like to think of themselves as in love with women." Monica has seen women sitting in the front row open their legs so the male pastor can see they are not wearing any underwear. Funny that Monica is the one who is given lap cloths.

Monica's church—like most religions—had an ambivalent relationship to her sexuality. They denied her sexuality, desperately insisting she dress modestly and cover her body with long skirts, panty hose, and lap cloths, and yet it was their *emphasis* on women's sexuality that led to demands for modesty. They feared her sexuality and were afraid of the power it had to divert people from their real business in church, worship. "We don't want people looking at you and having their minds distracted," they told her.

The desire to hide women's bodies so they won't be a temptation blames women for men's inability to keep their hands to themselves. "People are going to be distracted no matter what I'm wearing," Monica said. "It's that whole kind of Jezebel, Potiphar's wife, that-woman-you-gave-me-made-me-do-it crap. Like, if we can keep the women from looking too hot, then we'll act right." She cannot count the number of times she has been hit on by married male clergy. "You could have a paper bag on," she said. "And if they're going to be lewd, they are going to be lewd."

For many of the women I interviewed, and I imagine for many men, too, part of deciding to be a minister included grappling with the fear that they would have to give up parts of themselves to fit the role. They knew instinctively that being a minister translated into looking like a minister and dressing like a minister, whatever that might mean.

As a high school student and in college, Eve loved using her clothing as a kind of costume. When she moved in with her father in high school, she left the rigid social hierarchy of a junior high in a wealthy suburban town for a public high school in an urban area. "It was a kind of free-for-all, and that was really liberating for me," she said. She shopped at the dollar-a-pound used clothing store. She wore gas station attendant shirts and vintage dresses together, even at the preppy Ivy League college she attended.

When seminary emerged for Eve as a possibility, she realized that although she wanted to be a minister, she did not want to give up the way she dressed. "I didn't want to give up vintage suede miniskirts and boots to my knees and catsuits and nose rings, which I had at that point," Eve said. She asked a friend who had gone to seminary about his experience, wanting to know what it was like. She asked, "What do you do in seminary? What am I going to have to give up?"

He said, "Well, what we did in seminary was we would get drunk and watch the dogs fuck."

Eve said, "Okay, that gives me a lot of leeway."

I laughed hard when she told me that part of the story. "Sign me up!" I said.

"But that was a beautiful way to put it," Eve said. "It sort of says you get to bring your whole humanity to seminary. I figured as long as I'm a student, I have permission. Until I'm somebody's pastor, I have permission. So I wore miniskirts and got my tattoos and was in a band, stuff like that."

When Eve started working as an associate at the church where the parishioners circulated a petition to have her fired, she wanted to establish herself as a person with authority, and she understood that clothes had something to do with that. She asked herself, "Well, now that I am somebody's minister, and I am in the suburbs, what's expected of me?" Eve chose to dress how she thought her congregation expected her to dress, even though they never explicitly told her what they wanted her to wear. She wore what she describes as a "uniform": tailored pants from Ann Taylor, conservative button-down shirts, and little sweaters. "I almost never wore dresses, even though for a long time I had always been like a fun dress, skirt person," she said. Everything in her closet was gray, khaki, navy, or black. Even when she was pregnant, she stuck with this dark color palette, something she recently noticed when, pregnant with her second child, she went through her pregnancy clothes in storage.

Eve worked with the youth group at the church, and she was careful about making sure she set boundaries. Knowing she would probably be an object of crush for some of the teenage boys in the group, she wanted to diminish the sexual side of herself. "I still tend to de-sexualize myself," she said.

Eve was never comfortable in her uniform, but her clothing did what she needed it to do. "It worked," she said. "Basically I wanted the clothes to disappear. I didn't want the clothes to be an issue. I figured I would have more room to have crazy ideas if my dress was not distracting. I wanted to use up all my capital with my words, with my actions."

Eve has always enjoyed painting her toenails crazy colors. "It is just a little thing, but it is also significant," she said. "One of the patriarchs in the church once, sort of good-naturedly but pointedly, chided me on my blue toenail polish." Eve made a crack about it, asking him if he would prefer that she wear green instead of blue, and laughed it off. But she knew at that moment that she had not made up their expectations of her. She knew she had been absolutely right.

Eve realized that if being a minister was her vocation, that if this was work she wanted to do for the next thirty years, she needed to find a way to be herself while being a minister, and that included how she dressed. "I had to find a way that was more me," she said. "I couldn't keep buttoning myself, zipping myself into uncomfortable clothes every day, literally or metaphorically. I just couldn't sustain it. A lot of people can sustain bad marriages. A lot of people can sustain bad clothes. For a long time. I don't know where they get that stamina, because I can't do it."

Eve left the church where she was an associate for a position as a solo pastor where she has been for the last two years. Her time there has been, in part, about reintegrating her identity as a minister with her identity as Eve. She feels free in her new congregation to dress as she pleases. Some of the freedom comes from being in a city, as opposed to the suburbs where her first church was. "In the city, there's a lot more leeway for all kinds of behavior," she said. "The suburbs are still very much about looking the same, acting the same, and not letting your stuff show. In the city, there are tons of homeless people, not just barking on the streets but sitting in the pews. Being here is a lot about tolerance and diversity, so there is just more room."

When I met with Eve in a coffee shop just down the street from her church, she was almost nine months pregnant. She looked so pregnant that I worried she would have her baby in the middle of our conversation. She wore a fabulous, silky, peacock blue jacket over her round belly. I noticed she was wearing a nose ring, and I asked her about it. She told me she had recently decided to wear it again. "I told my congregation I was having my midlife crisis, which is why I put it back in," Eve said. "But I think the real reason was to say I am not just your minister. I am a whole person."

Eve's painted toenails also remain symbolic for her. During her second interview at the church where she now works, she took a risk. She decided to wear a dress with sandals, and she painted her toenails blue. "They took me for dinner around the corner, and then we went for an interview," Eve said. "And they were like, I love your toenail polish!"

And she knew that she had found a church where she could be herself. She was home.

Chapter Eight

SEX

The first time I went to a new yoga studio in Ketchum, Idaho, the town where I lived while I wrote this book, the teacher asked me what I did for a living, and I told her I was a writer.

"What are you writing?" one of the men in the class asked, stretched out on his mat.

"A book about sexism and religion," I said.

"Right on," he said.

Somehow, in that class, my book about sexism and religion became a book about sex. Whenever anyone in the class told a dirty joke or talked about sex or body parts in any way (it was quite a lively yoga class), someone would say, "Put that in your sex book, Sarah."

The transformation of this book about sexism to a "sex book" reminded me of one of my favorite scenes in the movie *This Is Spinal Tap* when a record company executive tells the band that their new album is being banned by American stores because the album cover—an image of a greased, naked woman on all fours with a dog collar around her neck and a man holding on to the leash and pushing a black glove in her face to sniff—is sexist. Nigel, one of the band members, says, "What's wrong with being sexy?"

In a way, my yoga class was right. This is a book about sex. It is a book about the dangerous combination of religion and sex that has generated ideas about sexual behavior that are repressive and do not reflect the myriad ways healthy adults engage in sexual activity. It is a book about the fact that so much of what passes as Christian morality is really fear of human sexuality. And it is a book about how this fear of human sexuality is acted out on women's bodies.

Many of the women I interviewed told me that the easiest way to get rid of an annoying person hitting on you in a bar is to say that you are a minister—that is, if you are a woman. While being a male minister is a turn-on, these women told me, being a female minister has the opposite effect. For Jamie, this sometimes comes in handy. "If you ever want to thwart an untoward advance, say you're in a bad situation and someone's like 'hey, mama' and you want them to back off, all you have to say is, I'm a Baptist minister," she said. "You will never have seen the eject button pushed or the emergency brake pulled so fast." If people find out Jamie is a minister and don't leave immediately, Jamie notices that they start behaving differently toward her. "Either they'll start treating you like their grandmother, or I've gotten some rather bizarre proposals that aren't appropriate for a family magazine. It's kind of an odd mix."

Laurie dreads the moment on a first date when she has to admit that she is an Episcopal priest. When her dates ask her what she does, she usually says something vague and noncommittal like, "I work in the church." She said, "I sometimes hedge my bets that most guys aren't really that interested in what you have to say so they just kind of move on by that." When she actually has to admit that she is a priest, Laurie gets one of two reactions: awe or disgust. Those who are in awe of what she does usually set out to prove what great Christians they are, and those who are disgusted often spend the next few hours telling her everything that they think is wrong with organized religion. "You are kind of like a punching bag in that case," Laurie said.

"Which do you prefer?" I asked.

"Disgust," she said.

The more humorous and annoying dates, in retrospect, have been with men who want to show her how religious they are by proving how much they love Jesus. One talked incessantly about how often he reads the Bible and quoted scripture, or rather misquoted scripture, in almost every sentence. On that date, when the meal arrived, Laurie started to eat. The Bible quoter looked at her and asked, "Aren't we going to pray?"

Almost all of her dates stop swearing when they find out she is a priest. Once Laurie realizes the date has stopped swearing, she makes sure she amps up her own swearing to see what happens. Not swearing is one of the ways these men express the fact that they feel the need to be "good" in front of her. It is an item on a checklist in their minds—ministers don't swear, they don't drink, they don't stay out late dancing. "Good" for Laurie, however, doesn't translate into this kind of checklist. "Good to me is that you look out for people who can't look out for themselves, treat yourself with respect, and live with honesty and integrity," she said. "I didn't know when I got ordained that I was never actually going to have a normal date in my life again."

Her male friends who are priests have not had the same set of dating problems. "If a male priest is unmarried, or even if he is married, women cannot stay away from him," she said. "I don't get it. I have watched what happens to a couple of good friends of mine here who are male priests. I will be out to lunch with them, and I see how people behave, and it is like being a male priest is an aphrodisiac."

Jamie echoed Laurie's observation. She described to me some of the things her male ordained friends have seen women do at the communion rail. "There are certain types of young women who want to grow up and marry a pastor," she said. "I don't think there are young boys who harbor those same dreams in the same way. I mean, someone's not waiting at home with the fried chicken for me," she said, laughing.

The structure of the job itself proves challenging for women trying to date. "Tell me about your dating life," I asked the single women I interviewed.

"My what?" they would say, laughing.

Having to work every Sunday morning means Saturday nights are not ideal for dates. The schedule leads many ministers—male and female—to burn out and exhaustion. "We are never really off duty," Laurie said. "We never get to come home and leave everything at the office, even though everyone says you should do that. You never know when the phone is going to ring and somebody is going to say, oh, my husband is at the hospital with a massive heart attack right when you are planning on going out of town for a vacation." Because female ministers are most likely hired by small churches, in rural communities or small towns, they are often isolated. Single women, with no time to date or hang out with friends outside the church, sometimes working additional jobs to make up for the fact that they were only offered part-time or low-paying work, feel alone and overwhelmed.

While dating as an ordained woman is difficult, being in a relationship is not necessarily any easier when you work in a church. Jocelyn had a serious boyfriend when she was an associate minister, and she said she made the mistake of introducing him to the congregation. When the relationship ended, she then had to tell the congregation. "People would ask where he was, and I had to explain that I broke up with my boyfriend," she said. "And what sounds more junior high than that? It was humiliating. I regret so much ever having had him come to church at all."

The fact that she was not married made Jocelyn feel vulnerable. She has had a few creepy experiences with male parishioners. "There was one guy who wasn't really stalking me, but it felt like that," she said. "It aroused that kind of fear in me. He would go to worship and stare at me the whole time." He then found her home phone number and would call her late at night and try to convince her they should go on a date. At the time, she was a proctor at one of the local universities and lived in the dorms. Since he knew her phone number, it would be possible for him to figure out where she lived. "I would not have been surprised if I had met him in the bushes one night," she said. "It was that kind of a feeling. He would be there on Sunday morning, and I could feel his eyes on me. It was just gross." Jocelyn is not sure this experience would not have happened if she were married, but she knows that being single made more of those kinds of experiences possible. "There is something different about being single and being so public," she said.

My discernment process at the church where I worked ended when I told my committee that Eric and I were moving in together. The minute the words were out of my mouth, I wanted to suck them back in. I felt the atmosphere in the room shift. I inhaled loudly.

"Excuse me?" Marsha, one of the women on the committee, said. "You are going to move in with your boyfriend?" Marsha had three daughters; the oldest was in eighth grade.

"I'm not moving into his apartment. We're going to find a new apartment together," I said, trying to clarify.

"You're going to live with your boyfriend?" she asked again.

"Um, yes," I said.

"I would not want my daughters to know that."

The room seemed to explode. My committee was divided. Half was in full support of my decision. Most of these supporters had sons and daughters living with partners, or they themselves had done so before they got married. The other half thought the fact that I was going to live with my boyfriend made me morally suspect. All of a sudden, they were trying to discern not only whether I was called to ordained ministry but whether they even wanted me around their children. They yelled at me for a while, and then they began to fight with one another.

I sat with my hands in my lap for the next forty minutes while they argued. Several of them actually used the phrase "out of wedlock." This language took me back to one of my first days of divinity school when I found myself sitting in the refectory eating lunch with a group of new women friends. We were talking about dating, and then all of a sudden one of the women started talking about "premarital sex." Everyone else at the table nodded, listening intently. I almost spit out the Dr Pepper I was drinking. "They still call it that?" I asked.

Having young women in the pulpit who are not married—women who are dating (or not) or who are in long-term relationships (or not)—brings to the surface the way congregations think about sex: who should be having it and when and how and with whom. The first thing I thought when my committee started arguing about whether or not it was okay that I lived with my boyfriend was, what if I were a heterosexual man? What if I were a man who dated (and slept with) a new woman every week but did not live with the person with whom I was in a committed relationship? And then I thought, what if I were a gay man? What if I were a lesbian? How would the conversation be different?

Perhaps the conversation would not have been any different if I were a man moving in with my girlfriend. Although it is common for couples to live together before they are married, negative opinions about cohabitation abound, remnants of a time when people married younger and living together before being married was something people whispered about and hid from one another. Living with someone with whom you are in a romantic relationship usually means you are sleeping with that person, and so some of the hysteria in church communities must have something to do with the fact that sex is involved. For many denominations, sanctioning sex outside of marriage would require a change in doctrine. But no matter what official doctrine might say, people have been having sex outside of marriage for years and years and years. In fact, Lawrence Finer, director of domestic research at the Guttmacher Institute, a non-profit organization focused on sexual and reproductive health, discovered that not only had more than nine out of ten people had premarital sex but the rate of premarital sex has been consistent for more than fifty years.

Pamela, the woman in the hip-huggers, lives in the parsonage of the church where she works, and her house is located on one of the town's main drags, a highly traveled street. On Sunday mornings, parishioners ask her about cars they saw in the driveway, saying things like, "So, I saw the red car in the driveway all week. Who was staying at your house?"

"And I'm like, yeah, my freaking mother is here," Pamela said.

Pamela was afraid about what it might be like to be a minister as a single woman. She was up front about this with the search committee when she interviewed for the job. "At the time I was dating somebody, a man who was a person of color, and I had some conversations with them about that. I asked, what do you do in a lily-White congregation when the associate minister's Black boyfriend is sitting in the second row. Is everyone in the congregation concentrating on this man or on what is happening in worship?"

The answer to that question, if you're wondering, would be that everyone is concentrating on the man in the second row.

Whether you live on the main drag in church housing or not, ministers are public figures, on display and highly visible. When I was a teacher, my elementary school students would freak out whenever they saw me outside the classroom—in the grocery store, at the gas station, driving down the street. It was as if they were surprised that I was a real person with a life outside our classroom. Congregations seem similarly surprised to learn that ministers are human beings—fallible, sexual, irritable human beings. People pay a great deal of attention to their ministers' personal lives. Perhaps this increased attention results from the fact that members of the congregation share so much of their own personal information with their ministers that they expect their ministers to do the same. Or maybe the Catholic requirement that priests be celibate has seeped into our subconscious ideas about Protestant ministers. Or perhaps people pay so much attention to their ministers' personal lives because we have unrealistic cultural expectations for our religious leaders. We expect them to be holier, more pure, extra good, better than we are. Whatever the reason, congregations keep a close eye on their ministers, and they seem shocked when they behave like human beings and sit at a bar for a drink, or exercise at the gym, or have sex, or go on a date.

When single women are ministers, people seem to think there is more to keep an eye on. Single women in the pulpit are a relatively new and still fairly rare phenomenon. Many of the first women ordained in denominations were married, and, more recently, a high percentage of women seeking ordination are second-career women, in their forties or fifties, often married or divorced and with grown children. Although many denominations are slowly becoming accustomed to (if not supportive of) older women in positions of ministerial authority, and although they are quite pleased to see young men in these same positions, they are not used to young women.

I remember asking my mother when I was young why Catholic priests were not allowed to get married. She told me it was because not having a wife or children would allow the priest to focus all his time and energy on the congregation. The priest's family is the congregation, she told me. He has to be available to the people in his church. Not only has the expectation about celibacy leaked into the Protestant vision of ministers, the idea that the priest is at the congregation's beck and call has also made its way into Protestant ideas about ministers' availability. The Episcopal survey administered in 2003 revealed that one of the criteria that determined whether or not Episcopalians were willing to hire women priests was whether or not she had young children. Congregations would hire a woman only if she would give her full attention to the church. (They don't seem worried if the priest with young children is a man. He'll have a wife to care for them.)

Even though many religions only officially sanction sexual intercourse in committed heterosexual marriages that leads to pregnancy, not all church communities are prepared to support pregnant ministers, much less ministers who have children. Pregnant ministers' bodies seem to make congregations uneasy. Eve's first congregation circulated the petition to have her fired when she was eight months pregnant. "I think whenever our womanness gets foregrounded, it makes congregations very uncomfortable," she said.

I interviewed several other women who were either pregnant or had just given birth, and they echoed Eve's feeling that having children seemed to threaten their congregations. One woman who had just finished breast-feeding her infant said that now that she has had the experience of breast-feeding, she realizes her congregation has been, symbolically, breast-feeding, claiming her as their sole source of sustenance. She said, "Even before I breast-fed, I have often wanted to say to my congregation, 'My tits aren't big enough for you people.' I've never said that to them, but I feel that. It's like, I cannot nurse all of you."

Some church communities, however, do support women ministers who are pregnant. Stacey's church reveled in her pregnancy. "It was really, really moving, particularly for some of the Roman Catholics in our life who have come into the church, to see a nine-month pregnant woman at the altar celebrating," she said. Stacey is the first ordained woman on staff to be pregnant. "It was so strange, but being pregnant and being at the altar it was as if the two things I feel God is most doing in my life were right there together. That was really powerful for me, and people knew that. I was the happiest pregnant person. I was just on fire with love." When their daughter was born, Stacey and her husband had her baptized at the church, and the community claimed the baby as theirs, loving her, showering her with gifts, and celebrating the new life. When she returned to work after maternity leave, one member of the congregation, a professor, pulled her aside and said, "You are definitely back in a different way. You have claimed something. You have changed. Having that child gave you some gravitas." Stacey said, "I found that very interesting. I thought, fair enough, that is her perception. I didn't come back feeling differently about myself, but for them, I think, something changed. Because I became a mother, I wasn't just a young girl for them."

Although being a minister does offer some flexibility, ministers' schedules can also compound the issues faced by working parents. Stacey married an Episcopalian. Even though they were not yet married when Stacey was going through the ordination process, he was required to meet with the Commission on Ministry and to go to counseling with her. Stacey said, "I don't think he is a doubter. He is faithful in that he believes, but he is doubtful of the institution, and he is very honest about that."

Stacey's fiancé's doubts about the institutional church were not a problem for the Commission. They wanted to meet with him not to force him to prove he was Episcopalian or Christian enough to marry a minister but to make sure he knew what he was getting into by marrying a priest. "I think they are checking on whether your spouse knows that you are about to sell your soul to an institution," Stacey said. "I think they want to be clear: Do you know the way people are going to invade your privacy, or try to? Do you know what it means to raise your family in this fishbowl life? Do you know what it means to have a spouse who works weekends when you work during the week?"

Throughout her journey to the priesthood, her husband has been supportive of her career choice. Since their daughter was born, however, things have gotten more difficult. "Obviously I work Sundays. So Saturday would be our one day to have together, and since I work so many Saturdays, we very rarely have a day together, and he is starting to really pull at that, starting to say that he understands why priests' kids are so messed up." Stacey's husband spends the weekend with their daughter, without Stacey. Mondays are Stacey's day off, and she spends that day with their daughter. "He is doing the lion's share of the load on the weekends," she said. "So, it is tricky."

"I always thought it would be good to have church on Wednesdays," I said.

"Why can't we have church at noon on Wednesdays?" Stacey asked, and laughed. "I mean the thing that people don't understand is that we are asking people to come into our life when they are not at their jobs, so we have to work when other people are not working, and that is always going to be the rub. If I am in a church of 300 or if I am in a church of 3,000, it is what it is." Stacey is beginning to ask herself whether she might need to take a break from ministry while her child is young. She wonders whether staying home for a few years might be a good idea. "I think that I will at some point," she said. "I think that is the only way to have some semblance of family life."

Because ministers' schedules are already different than the schedules of other professionals, churches have an opportunity to take the lead in rethinking what a workweek might look like—flexible hours, day care on site, living wage, job share, health care for all. Churches could reframe the problems faced by working mothers, helping people recognize that they are challenges faced by working *parents* and communities as a whole.

Similarly, churches could take the lead in discussions about human sexuality. The dominant religious voices shouting that birth control, homosexuality, and sex outside of marriage are sinful pretend to be protecting the sanctity of marriage and the holiness of sexual intercourse. Their words, however, do the opposite. By supporting only a narrow sliver of sexual behavior, these voices have perverted our understanding of healthy human sexuality, a perversion that has contributed to the AIDS epidemic and to behaviors that put everyone at risk—as well as to the American sexual culture with all its nonsense.

Irene Monroe's ministry recognizes that the failure to celebrate human sexuality threatens lives. Irene was abandoned in a trash can in New York City when she was six months old. The head nun at the Catholic orphanage who took her in was named Sister Irene, and Sister Irene loved Marilyn Monroe—so she gave the baby the name

Irene Monroe. "Here you have a kid who has, in the conventional sense, no documentation, no sense of being, really," Irene said. For Irene, the Black church was a place where she was somebody. She said, "The Black church certainly operated as the place that really understood the plight of the damned, the disrespected, the dispossessed, and it was a place you could be somebody, meaning, you might just be a maid or a street sweeper in everyday life, but when you come into the Black church you are Deacon Jones or Sister Williams." Irene is passionate about the notion that "we lift as we climb," a central ethos in the Black church and in Black theology. "I could not have made it to where I have made it without the undergirding of the Black church, the generosity of people seen and unseen," she said.

Irene's experience as a child in church—an experience she refers to as her "Romantic Era" in the Black church—shaped her desire to enter the ministry. She understands her vocation as a testimony to the good that can come out of the Black church and to the collective and collaborative effort of the people who nurtured her. She said, "I felt it was important to go back to my community having benefited from the fruits of the civil rights movement and do this kind of work." The church was at its best, Irene thinks, during the abolitionist movement and the civil rights movement, when the social gospel worked to change laws and move the hearts and minds of people throughout the country.

Irene knew that when she turned eighteen, she would be aged out of foster care, no longer a ward of New York. "You have to fend for yourself," Irene said. "And what happens is that a lot of us end up on the street, and we are homeless. How do we make it on the street? Drugs. Prostitution. By any means necessary." When Irene was twelve, she realized that she needed to avoid that situation, and to avoid it, she needed a plan. "I was watching the Macy's Thanksgiving Day Parade on television, and I decided what I was going to do. I decided I was going to work for Macy's department store," Irene said. Her decision was driven by two pragmatic considerations. First, she would get a discount on clothes. Second, all employees of Macy's were allowed to be in the Macy's parade. Irene's visions of marching in the parade and waving at her friends convinced her this was the job for her. She said, "My goal was to work for Macy's, get a discount on clothes, be in the parade, get my little apartment, and life can't be any better. This is as good as it gets."

Irene scored in the 98th percentile on every standardized test she ever took as a public school student in New York City, and she did extremely well on the SATs. Some of her teachers were incredulous. Her teachers' surprise at Irene's ability to do well on standardized tests annoyed her. She didn't see why they thought it was so hard to do well on the tests. "No offense, darling, and to all of my White friends in America," she said when she told me that the tests were easy for her. "But one of the things they do not understand is that if you are trying to navigate through a White world, or as I say to folks, trying to do right in a White world, you always know more about your oppressor than your oppressor knows about you. People of color can mimic White speech, even though we don't speak it among ourselves, or mimic White dance. We can also mimic the way in which White people think about something," she said. "So the exam to me was not to test how Irene really thought about something, because given my social location, my standpoint, it would be very different. It really was about, standing in the feet of White people, how would a White person answer this damn exam? You know, I always say this, and this is from street hustling, you don't enter the game unless you know the rules, and not only do you have to know the rules, you have to master the rules."

Irene was valedictorian of her high school class. She had a guidance counselor who believed in her. He told her he thought she should go to college, not work at Macy's, so Irene applied to many colleges and was accepted to every single one—Wellesley, Vassar, Barnard, Radcliffe, to name just a few. Irene and her social worker visited several of the schools, and she chose Wellesley.

During her senior year at Wellesley, Irene realized she was a lesbian and that the fact that she was a lesbian was going to be a real problem for her, especially in the context of the church in which she grew up. Irene wrestled with her sexual orientation, and, at the same time, she wrestled with the thought that she wanted to be a minister. "At some point, I decided that in spite of all of these challenges I wanted to go to seminary because the Black church at the time was the locus of transformation," she said. "It certainly transformed a bigoted world that had been bigoted for many centuries about civil rights."

She also decided to go to seminary to overcome her own internalized homophobia, to claim, in her words, what a blessing it is to be gay. "I kind of sound like a born-again Christian in the way that I am evangelical in my enthusiasm about being gay," she said, and then she started laughing. "Do you know that I'm gay and I'm Christian. I am gay and I am Christian and I am Black. Certainly God planned it because I felt like my focus was to pastor a Black church." Irene came out of the Bapticostal tradition, a mix between Pentecostal and Baptist traditions. She feels called to make a change in that place, a change for gay people and for women. "So I decided who could better teach me about the Black church than a Black seminary?"

Irene applied to the two Black seminaries in the country at that time, Interdenominational Theological Center (ITC) in Atlanta and Howard. She was rejected by both.

"Why?" I asked.

"Because I'm gay," she said.

"You knew that was why?" I asked.

"Yes," she said. "ITC told me that they didn't have any homosexuals at ITC, and I told the woman who told me that that I was very, very surprised that as a female she was bringing such a message because once upon a time, Black women couldn't enter seminaries, and certainly couldn't enter ITC, because it was considered a male haven."

The woman said, "You have to understand that being in the MDiv program you have to have a field education placement, and our students are placed in local churches throughout the greater Atlanta area." She made it very clear that no church in Atlanta would ever hire Irene.

After being rejected from both seminaries, Irene needed to find somewhere to go to school. She chose to attend Union Theological Seminary in New York City because they had a gay caucus. At the time, Union also housed an incredible group of Black male liberation theologians: Jim Washington, Jim Forbes, James Cone, and Cornel West. Although they have all now changed their positions on GLBTQ people, they were not pro-GLBTQ while Irene was there. "They were just as homophobic as could be. So there really was no support from them," she said. She turned to Beverly Harrison, a professor of feminist ethics, to be her adviser.

Irene was called to her first church, Soundview Presbyterian Church, in the Bronx. "I get to this church not because they want me, I assure you, but simply because there is a paucity of Black Presbyterian ministers," Irene said. "And they had to take me because it was a matter of survival. Had they not taken me, the doors of their church would close."

She arrived at the church in the Bronx at an intense time. Something was happening in that community with gay men—GRID, which later became known as AIDS. Irene said, "The African American community is just dying. Of course, that statistic is not being shown. They are talking about White gay men dying, but we could assure you that Black gay men were dying, and long before the CDC recognized it when trying to track the expansiveness of this virus, we knew Black women were dying and were becoming the newly infected group. Long before data, believe me."

Irene realized this was the ministry for her. It combined GLBTQ issues, women, race, and sexuality. People were dying, and communities were embarrassed, avoiding each other, feeling ashamed, not coming back to church because a member of their family had died of this disease. Some people refused to name it. Irene said, "Black folks were coding this illness as consumption. They would say the child died of anything, anything other than this."

Like most Americans and like most Christians, the people she encountered were not comfortable talking about sex. "We are kind of backwards as a first-world nation when it comes to issues around gender and sexuality. A whole lot of other not-first-world countries are way ahead of us," she said. The refusal to talk about the disease resulted, Irene understands, from a politics of silence and respectability that developed in response to the legacy of slavery. "I realized that I needed to talk about it by coming in through the back door. I needed to talk about it in terms of how we construct Blackness. I wanted to emphasize the interconnections of oppression," she said. Irene conducted workshops with Black ministers during which she framed both the AIDS epidemic and the construction of Blackness as a moral and health imperative. She wanted to create a liberation movement in her community that embraced not only straight Black men but all African American people. "You are not just Black, although clearly when you are profiled it is just about being Black. When we live fully as Black people we are not just Black. We're Black female. We're Black gay males," she said. "We need to address that. You cannot have a liberation movement that three-quarters of your damn population ain't in. I don't know what the hell you are doing other than perpetuating Black patriarchy."

Irene's church, although resistant to her, eventually embraced her. Irene said, "They realize that I have something to say about how you make a way out of no way, how you make it on broken pieces, how you make it with an unwavering faith, believing even in the face of what you don't see. I still have something to tell them about how to make it on nothing that they need to hear." Her message was important for a church community in the middle of an economically depressed enclave of New York that felt ignored by the denomination. "Ward of New York State. On child welfare. Former number runner. I really mirror the life of the people I was ministering to.

Folks got to like me, believe it or not," she said. "They knew very well that I was a warrior about fighting racism within the presbytery." In addition to fighting racism, Irene addressed literacy issues within her community and created a health ministry. "Our bodies are our temples," she said. "I cloaked it in religious language, and I included AIDS under health issues, along with Black folks dealing with obesity, diabetes, high blood pressure, hypertension. It is a health issue, although it is political." She framed the health ministry as part of overcoming the trauma of slavery. The posttraumatic stress of slavery, Irene told her community, not only disconnects people with one another but also from their own bodies.

"Did they go for it?" I asked.

"Some did," Irene said. "Some just say, you know, that child's crazy. That child is a homosexual." Then she said, "The sin of the Black church is that in the face of an epidemic, and in the face of an institution that is born out of struggle, and—I have to say it again, I know I sound like I am preaching, but I am passionate about this— in the face of an institution that has always functioned as a multiple site, not just a place of worship, but a place of politics, a place of health, all of that, it has not addressed the AIDS issue. And that is its sin." Irene has strong words for the damage wrought by her church's failure to act. "It contributes, really, in my estimation, not to the death of African Americans, but much larger than that, to the genocide of its people."

In the United States, someone is sexually assaulted every two and a half minutes. One in six American women and one in thirty-three American men are victims of sexual assault. About 44 percent of rape victims are under age eighteen, and 80 percent are under age thirty. Contrary to the belief that rapists are strangers who hide in bushes or alleys or parking garages, almost two-thirds of all rapes were committed by someone the victim knows. Seventy-three percent of sexual assaults were perpetrated by a nonstranger, 38 percent of perpetrators were a friend or acquaintance of the victim, 28 percent were an intimate, and 7 percent were another relative. Because sexual assault is one of the most underreported crimes, the number of sexual assault victims and survivors is undoubtedly much higher than the recorded statistics.

The refusal of church communities to talk about or honor or recognize human sexuality means that most have been unable to develop healing rituals or organized institutional responses to the survivors that undoubtedly exist in their midst. Because the loudest voices shaming people about sexual behavior are so often religious voices, many survivors of sexual violence feel alone and afraid, shut down and shut out of the religious communities that once sustained them.

During Monica's first year of seminary, in the spring semester, she was raped by her ex-boyfriend, a Baptist minister. At first she did not name it "rape" because she did not want to think about it that way. She kept having anxiety attacks. Monica told the pastor where she was working what had happened. "When I told the pastor that I had been raped, he kept watching a baseball game on the television over my head in his office," she said. "I was going to leave before then, but I was really going to leave at that point. I just wasn't happy at the church." The pastor told her he had heard that things like that happened to women, but no one had ever told him about it before. "I was like, well, I wonder why," Monica said. "That was the last time I ever worked there."

After she left that church, she had to find another where she could work to meet the field education requirements at her seminary. She picked an AME church that had a female pastor. Monica was depressed and posttraumatic. She was going to therapy at a rape crisis center. She shared this with the pastor, who then told Monica that depression was a tool of the enemy and that she should cast it out in the name of Jesus. "I knew not to fight that battle," Monica said.

After a few disagreements, the pastor told Monica that her placement at the church was not working out, and she handed Monica a list of other churches she might like to try. Monica's tenure there lasted two weeks.

One of her friends at seminary took Monica to the interdenominational church he attended. The church had a Saturday service. Monica went to the service, and she remembers thinking that if she could just get to the altar, it would all be okay. After the service, she went to the altar and started to pray. She prayed and screamed and cried for an hour and a half. She had never been to the church before. She knew no one except her friend who brought her. The pastor stayed and kept the church open for her until nine o'clock at night. Several months later, Monica went to a Sunday morning service there. She knew it was the church for her.

When she sat down to meet with the pastor to discuss the possibility of working at that church for her field education placement, she told him her situation—that she was in the ordination process to become an AME minister, that she was recently raped and was posttraumatic, and that she never knew until she woke up whether she was going to have a good day or a bad one. "I can't promise you anything," she said. "I don't know what I can do. I really need someone to minister to me."

"Why don't you just show up," he said. "The ministry will find you." And that's what she did. She showed up. And, soon, the ministry found her.

"It was a very comfortable place for me," Monica said. "A place where it felt like I could have what I call a ministry of the brokenhearted." There were a lot of people at the church who were recovering from drug and alcohol abuse, and it was a very open church. "Although it was not officially declared a GLBT church," she said, "if you were going to go to a Black church and be gay and be open, that was where you went. We would say, alienating to none, inclusive of all." Liberation theology was preached from the pulpit, and the liturgy used only inclusive language. The staff made Monica the designated watch guard for all things sexist. "I was kind of the theological barometer," she said.

Once she felt comfortable, Monica began a ministry in the church around sexual violence. It started out small. "I told the pastor I just wanted to do a little ceremony, a little healing thing with friends," Monica said. The pastor told her he thought it could be bigger than that. And he was right. Monica's ministry—eventually called The Dinah Project—was huge. She created an organized church response to sexual violence that became a community-wide nonprofit and a book, *The Dinah Project.* "I felt called to speak out against sexual violence," she said. "Getting raped was not the plan. And doing this work is not an easy thing to do."

The Dinah Project is a handbook for churches that want to create a response to sexual violence through worship, community education, and counseling. In the book Monica writes that she talked to God throughout the rape and begged for intervention, "pleading that somehow, some way, God would stop this thing from happening to me." She continues, "After the rape, there was no more pleading and no more praying." She felt disconnected from God and did not know how to pray or worship, did not know whether she should be thankful that she survived or angry that the rape happened. Monica then writes, "Honestly, I was absolutely disgusted that the God to whom I prayed and whom I worshipped was the same God to whom my rapist would pray and worship. It was too much for me to handle." Eventually, Monica decided that she wanted to include God in her healing, and The Dinah Project was born.

The story of Dinah (pronounced Dee-nah) is found in Genesis 34. Dinah, Leah and Jacob's daughter, is on her way to visit some women friends. Shechem, prince of the region, sees her, seizes her, and rapes her. After he rapes her, he realizes he loves her and speaks "tenderly" to her. He orders his father to "Get me this girl to be my wife." When Jacob discovers that his daughter has been raped, he and his sons come up with a plan for revenge. When Shechem's father, Hamor, comes to ask for Dinah to marry his son—in fact,

Hamor asks for all of Jacob's daughters—and says he will meet whatever demands Jacob asks for in exchange, Jacob pretends he will agree to the marriage if all the men in Hamor's family will get circumcised. Hamor agrees. Three days after the men are circumcised, when, the story tells us, they are "still in pain," two of Dinah's brothers come to their city with swords and kill every male. We never again read anything about Dinah in the biblical text—not her reaction to the rape, not if she heals, not what she feels or thinks, not whether revenge was something she demanded. She disappears.

Monica points out that "there is a large amount of biblical ambiguity about sexual violence"—the attempted gang rape of Lot's visitors is not condemned, Dinah's rape involves vengeance and no mention of Dinah outside the fact of her rape, Tamar's incestuous rape results in silence, some Levitical rules condemn rape but others don't, Potiphar and Joseph's story leads readers to believe that most women lie about rape, the second chapter of Revelation justifies Jezebel's rape as punishment for false prophecy. Due to this ambiguity, religious communities must speak out clearly against rape and sexual violence of all kinds so survivors will not, like Dinah, disappear.

Although the church where Monica worked accepted her and her ministry, others in the larger community did not. Monica was known as "the girl who got raped." She said, "There were clergy who would say, well, I'm not surprised, you see how Monica dresses." Some people even told men not to date her, telling her boyfriend at the time that Monica would say he raped her.

Despite the fact that Monica created a thriving healing ministry, the pastor at her home church continued to try to stall her ordination. He protested the fact that she worked at an interdenominational church and not an AME church (even though she attended AME services at a church down the street from her interdenominational church every Sunday morning before going to work). During her fourth year in the process, Monica had to take a class with the pastor at her home church during which she had to write several papers. One of the assignments was to write a paper on preaching. Monica, knowing just how to push his buttons, wrote a paper about how "preaching is like sex in a healthy relationship." Monica said, "I argued that preaching is the most glamorous and exciting thing about being a pastor, but it is really only 10 percent of what you do."

Monica insists she did not write the paper to make the pastor upset. "It is what I think," she said.

He called Monica and told her that what she wrote was inappropriate. "Would you agree?" he asked.

"I really think what I wrote is true," she said.

"But preaching is very important," he said.

Monica justified her topic choice by the fact that this was her area of expertise given that she had a degree in religion, gender, and sexuality. He could not argue with that and passed the paper. "I was delighted with myself," she said, laughing.

Monica's experience at the interdenominational church where she developed The Dinah Project restored her faith in Christianity, and her relationship with her mentor there restored her faith in male ministers. "He never once acted inappropriately towards me sexually, which happens a lot, and never once doubted my calling. He continues to be kind of a father figure to me. He let me do what I'm called to do and provided the structure and support for doing it." Even though he never used the word "rape" in the pulpit, he let Monica use it. He funded The Dinah Project, and even paid honorariums for guest speakers. "It was one of the best experiences of my life, to be able to do that and to be in that church," Monica said.

If Monica had not worked in that church, she thinks she would have left the Christian faith. Instead, working there gave her the opportunity to think of herself as a minister who provides the kind of ministry she never had access to. "I was able to give people something I didn't have," she said. "My experiences with churches and clergy have been so negative, and I'm someone who's called to preach. That can't happen to other women. I want survivors to encounter churches that can help them, not hurt them more. I wanted to be able to offer a ministry I hadn't found." Monica understands her ministry as working to make churches safe places—theologically and physically—for survivors of sexual violence. "The world is not a safe place," she said. "But the church should be, and it is our job to make it that way."

Chapter Nine

GAY

In 2003, Gene Robinson became the first openly gay, noncelibate priest to be ordained a bishop. His election by the Episcopal diocese of New Hampshire—and the debates and protests that followed—revealed the intense homophobia of many in the Episcopal Church. Some Episcopal churches and dioceses went so far as to threaten secession, some seceded, and some joined groups like the Anglican Communion Network (or "The Network"), a coalition of churches that have stated they no longer want to be under the authority of bishops in the United States and have demanded to be accountable only to the archbishop of Canterbury. If they leave, they promise to take the church's property with them.

Like most Christians against homosexuality, these people maintain they are following the apostles' teachings, Jesus Christ, and the Bible. I don't know about you, but I've never found a single passage in the Bible in which any of the disciples or Jesus talk about being gay. Whenever someone cites the Bible as an authoritative source for rules about sex, I always want to ask, "Have you actually read the Bible?" Maybe there is a passage or two or three that forbids men having sex with other men, but there are many more passages that show support for sexual behavior that I imagine these literalists do not follow: polygamy, sleeping with slaves, giving a daughter to guests to gang-rape and then butcher. The Bible prohibits activities that are culturally acceptable for many people today (divorce, eating pork), and it encourages activities most would never consider doing anymore (animal sacrifice, death penalty for adultery). Usually the very same people who insist they are simply following the rules of the Bible *don't* follow most of the rules of the Bible. They don't keep kosher or stone their neighbors or bloodlet their ox the way the Bible instructs them to. They probably eat shellfish and don't eat locust. They also don't regularly clothe the naked, feed the hungry, turn the other cheek, or visit prisoners.

One of the texts most often cited by those who profess to take the Bible literally is Leviticus 18, verse 22: "You shall not lie with a male as with a woman; it is an abomination." The book of Leviticus has six parts: laws dealing with sacrifices; the consecration of priests to their office; laws setting forth the distinction between clean and unclean; the ceremony for the annual day of atonement; laws to govern Israel's life as a holy people; and an appendix of religious vows. Chapter 18 is part of the "laws to govern Israel's life as a holy people" section. The passage—clearly addressed to men—is one prohibition in a list of many: You shall not approach anyone near of kin to uncover nakedness; you shall not have sexual relations with your kinsman's wife; you shall not see any woman naked when she is menstruating. Leviticus 19 lists other things God prohibits: You shall not steal; you shall not lie; if a man has sexual relations with a woman who is a slave designated for another man, they shall not be put to death and the priest shall make atonement for them with a ram; if you plant a tree for food you shall not eat the fruit until the fifth year; you shall not eat anything with its blood; you shall not make gashes in your flesh for the dead or tattoo any marks on you; you shall not make your daughter a prostitute; you shall not turn to wizards. Leviticus 20 talks about punishments for disobeying the law: adultery, having sex with a woman who has her period, and a man lying with a man as with a woman all carry the death penalty. (Even if you follow all of these laws, it seems that lesbianism is A-OK. Whew.)

Another biblical text referred to as proof that homosexuality is against the will of God is the story of Sodom and Gomorrah found in the book of Genesis. Right after three men visit Sarah and Abraham to tell them they will have a son, Abraham leads the men to Sodom and Gomorrah. The Lord has heard that the cities have been doing terrible things (we are not told just what these terrible things are), and he sends the three men to see if Sodom and Gomorrah will live up to their reputation. Abraham pleads with God to find out if there might be a few good people to save, asking God not to destroy the righteous with the wicked. God says if fifty righteous people are to be found in Sodom, the whole town will be spared. Abraham bargains God down to ten.

Two angels then go to Sodom, and in Sodom, they visit Lot. Lot begs them to stay at his home as his guest, and they agree. They feast. Before they can sleep, all the men of Sodom, young and old, surround Lot's house. They demand that Lot send out the two visitors so they can "know them." Lot goes outside to calm the crowd down. He suggests that instead of sending out his two guests, he send out his two virgin daughters for the crowd to "do to them as you please." The crowd is not satisfied with this suggestion and begins to push against the door of Lot's house. The guests grab Lot and pull him inside to safety. The two men tell Lot to take his family and flee because God is going to destroy the city. Lot escapes to a nearby city. And then: "the LORD rained on Sodom and Gomorrah sulfur and fire from the LORD out of heaven; and he overthrew those cities, and all the Plain, and all the inhabitants of the cities, and what grew on the ground. But Lot's wife, behind him, looked back, and she became a pillar of salt." And then, Lot's daughters get him drunk and lie with him so they can preserve their offspring through their father. Both girls get pregnant with sons.

There is no indication in this story just what makes Sodom and Gomorrah so sinful. Even if you read generously in favor of the idea that the cities are destroyed as a result of their homosexual behavior (of which there is none in this story, only a request that two male guests be sent out so a mob may "know" them—a request that is denied), then what are you to make of Lot's suggestion that the angry mob gang-rape his daughters instead? Lot, remember, is one of the "righteous" whose family (except for his wife) is spared. Knowing men is not acceptable, but sending out your daughters to placate an angry mob is?

And then there is Paul's "Letter to the Romans." In the first chapter, Paul lists all the wicked things that wicked people are doing. Chief among them are sexual things: women exchanging natural intercourse for unnatural intercourse; men giving up intercourse with women and instead being consumed with passion for one another; men committing shameless acts with other men. But there are other wicked things Paul lists as well: evil, covetousness, malice, envy, murder, strife, deceit, craftiness, gossip, slander, boasting, inventing evil, rebelling against one's parents. Right after this list, in chapter 2—a verse often left out by those clamoring about homosexuality and sin—Paul writes, "Therefore you have no excuse, whoever you are, when you judge others; for in passing judgment on another, you condemn yourself."

Most biblical scholars have demonstrated that Paul was not writing about homosexuality as we know it today. Whether readers of the biblical text think God or humans composed it, the authors definitely were not talking about being "gay." Paul was condemning homosexual acts committed by force—older men abusing boys, owners abusing slaves. As Reverend Fred Small, a Unitarian Universalist, wrote in a sermon, "Paul had no idea—he had no basis for knowing—that people of the same gender could love each other and God, that they could bind themselves each to the other as faithfully, as devoutly, as tenderly as anyone."

The arguments against the ordination of openly gay priests and bishops are nearly identical to the arguments used to support slavery and to protest the ordination of women and integration. Just like the Bible can be used both to prohibit and to support the ordination of women, it can be used to prohibit and to support the ordination of GLBTQ folks. Last year I was having beers with my brother when the conversation turned to the controversy in the Episcopal Church about ordaining gay and lesbian priests. "I don't get it," he said. "Isn't Jesus's message about love? I mean, if you could boil it down to one word, wouldn't it be love?"

If Jesus's message is primarily a message of love and justice, then what is all the hubbub about? Why so much fierce hatred?

Much like women's ordination, homosexuality has become symbolic. Being against homosexuality has turned into a defining feature of certain kinds of Christianity—the kinds that insist they take the Bible literally, that are against feminism and modernity and the decline of "values" they represent. Opposing homosexuality signals to others that you are against liberal ideas of all kinds. It is a way of seeming to draw strict boundaries.

But using homosexuality as a symbol, just like using women's ordination as a symbol, does violence to actual human beings. Gene Robinson, the recipient of so much hatred, checked himself into a rehabilitation center for alcoholism. According to the Centers for Disease Control and Prevention and the Massachusetts Department of Education Youth Risk Behavior Survey, 33 percent of gay youth will attempt suicide, about four times the rate of heterosexual teenagers. We have pumped youth full of misinformation about how wrong homosexuality is—and some of the most vehement providers of this misinformation in the United States are Christians. Homophobia takes its toll on lives and bodies.

Throughout the Gene Robinson saga that brought into relief the deep and violent homophobia of the Episcopal Church, I was mortified. I could barely admit in public that I was an Episcopalian. I was ashamed of the hatred, but I was even more ashamed of the so-called liberals in the church who were supposed to be standing up for justice and love. They were so worried about losing power and property and prestige that they ran around trying to placate all the churches and bishops who were threatening to leave, rather than simply letting them go. William Sloan Coffin once said, "Those who fear disorder more than injustice invariably produce more of both." And he was right.

Trying to find the "middle way" is not new behavior for Episcopalians. In his book *Episcopalians and Race: Civil War to Civil Rights,* Gardiner H. Shattuck documents the Episcopal Church's response (or lack of response) to slavery, integration, and the civil rights crisis of the 1960s. Again and again, Shattuck shows, they used the theological concept of "the unity of humankind" to repress divergent voices within the church. "Unity," while sometimes employed to the benefit of racial justice, more often than not functioned as a repressive myth, Shattuck writes, "akin to the myth of the harmonious, biracial plantation of the Old South, [that] has tended to promote the invisibility (to use Ralph Ellison's famous metaphor) of black people within decision-making areas in the Episcopal Church." Although individual Episcopal priests and parishioners took strong stands against injustice, the church as an institution usually did not—even as recently as 1991.

In 1990, voters in the state of Arizona defeated a referendum that would have created a holiday honoring Martin Luther King Jr. A number of groups protested the outcome of this vote, including the National Football League (NFL), which declared that the 1993 Super Bowl would be moved to another state as a result. The NFL commissioner, Paul Tagliabue, said, "Americans, of all races and backgrounds, perceive the Arizona position as a slap in the face at Dr. King and his message." The Episcopal Church faced a similar situation. The General Convention was scheduled to be held in Phoenix in July 1991. Atlanta, the city where King had lived, offered to host the convention. Episcopalians debated what to do. The presiding bishop at the time, Edmond Browning, opted to keep the convention in Phoenix. Shattuck writes, "In his eyes and in the eyes of many other white Episcopalians...voters in the state of Arizona had done nothing to merit categorical rejection, and whatever mistake they might have made, an understanding 'Christian' approach was preferable to a self-righteous, judgmental one." Black Episcopalians saw things differently. Although many Black and some White Episcopalians protested holding the convention in Phoenix, the leaders of the denomination ignored them. Shattuck writes, "Whites, after all, had always called the shots and simply expected blacks to follow their lead, even in matters that affected blacks more than whites." White Episcopalians cast the Phoenix controversy as a matter of "reconciliation and unity" rather than "race and equality." Concerns about unity trumped concerns about justice.

Bishop Browning used the rhetoric of pastoral care to justify his decision to keep the convention in Phoenix, framing his decision as a relational one. But his was pastoral care for some, not others; the people of Arizona were recipients of his pastoral care, but Black Episcopalians were not. Pastoral care should not be used as a way to avoid holding people accountable for racist behavior. Or homophobic behavior. Or sexist behavior.

Laurie was new to her church in Mobile, Alabama, when Gene Robinson was consecrated as a bishop, and the rector of her church had just gone on sabbatical. Some people in the parish were extremely upset. A small group demanded that Laurie make a public statement against his ordination. They wanted her to declare her opposition to ordaining an openly gay man as bishop. Laurie, however, was not opposed to Robinson's ordination. The group continued to pressure her, demanding that she oppose the ordination, and Laurie continued to refuse. Two people on the vestry told her that her days were numbered. They suggested she start packing her boxes.

Laurie met with the bishop of her diocese. She told him about the conflict in her church, and, almost jokingly, added that she thought soon people would begin to attack her by calling her a lesbian. She told me he said, "Oh, funny that you mention that. I got an e-mail from one of your parishioners that said that I ought to know that there were three lesbian priests in the city of Mobile." The bishop responded to the e-mail by telling its sender that her behavior was completely inappropriate and probably illegal.

When word got out about the e-mail, several people told Laurie that she should publicly deny that she was a lesbian. Again, Laurie refused. "What am I going to do?" she asked. "Bring up every man that I have ever had sex with? How do you deny this?" Furthermore, she thought such a denial would make being a lesbian look like something negative, like being a homicidal maniac. "You can't defend against being called a lesbian," she said. "And to try to diminishes those wonderful people I know who are lesbians."

Soon other people in the church noticed how destructive and hateful the group's behavior was. Even people who agreed with the group's stance against Robinson's ordination started to distance themselves from the group. Southern hospitality won out over homophobia. Laurie watched the group self-destruct.

Laurie felt terribly alone while she defended the ordination of Robinson, even though she now knows there were parish priests all over the country doing the same and feeling just as alone as she did. To make matters worse, when all was said and done, the conflict was blamed on Laurie. People in the congregation suggested she didn't handle the situation well because she is a woman. "I wanted to say, my vagina didn't help me make these decisions," Laurie said. That wasn't the only time a conflict was blamed on Laurie's sex. "Whenever the female priest does something wrong, and I put that 'wrong' in quotations, then it is somehow because she's a woman."

After months of threats and accusations and abuse, Laurie struggles to be in relationship with the people who attacked her. No one in the group ever apologized to her. "I have never abandoned them," Laurie said. "But it is an effort to do that." Laurie used prayer to help her let go of her anger. First, she simply tried to say their names out loud. "I remember when I would say evening prayer, I would just say their names, and I would be really mad and I would feel my blood pressure rise, and then I remember getting to the point where I could say their names and not feel that way." Soon she was able to say their names, even to look at them, and know what they did had nothing to do with her. "I can sit there and honestly wish them the best of God's love," she said. "Forgiveness is not an event, it is a process. But, you know, it comes at a cost."

Samantha Martin* fought to get ordained in the Episcopal Church for more than twenty years. She was raised in the United Methodist Church, and then in high school she became involved with more fundamentalist churches—Baptists, Assembly of God, independent Christian churches. She did not know any women ministers. After college, she got a summer job at an Episcopal camp and retreat center. The summer job turned into a yearlong position, and she ended up staying for almost eight years. "When I first went there," Samantha said, "I didn't even know how to spell Episcopal." But she fell in love with the liturgy and decided to make the Episcopal Church her spiritual home.

One evening, after dinner, Samantha walked through the dining hall and saw a copy of the *New York Times* lying on one of the tables. In the paper was a photograph of a woman priest sitting on the stone front steps of her parish wearing a black short-sleeve clergy shirt and clerical collar with blue jeans and sandals. "I looked at that picture and I saw myself," Samantha said. "I looked around. No one seemed to own the paper. So I grabbed it, tucked it under my arm, went to my little apartment, and literally stared at that picture." She knew she wanted to get ordained.

When Samantha began the ordination process in the mid-1980s, things went fairly smoothly. While attending seminary, however, she realized she was gay. "Finally the penny dropped regarding my sexual orientation," she said. "At that point I was already well into the process. That realization was rather traumatic." With her fundamentalist background, Samantha had plenty of information about how wrong many in the church thought homosexuality was. She knew every passage in the Bible that said it was a sin. Working through her internalized homophobia was "rather tough work." She struggled on an intellectual level and on a spiritual level. She read multiple books on both sides of the issue. She saw a therapist who specialized in sexuality. And she began, slowly, to develop an alternative spirituality that supported her. The spirituality piece was the hardest part. "That was really agonizing," she said. "I went on a weekend retreat at a monastery and really engaged in prayer." She asked God to help her, to sort through her shame and confusion, and then, in prayer, she was overwhelmed by a sense of God's love. "That was the major turning point," Samantha said. "I knew I was loved by God." After years of having the wrongness of homosexuality pounded in her head, she needed this spiritual experience to be comfortable in her own skin.

That experience empowered her to claim her sexual orientation, and she soon realized she was in love with a woman who had been a good friend for years. The woman, however, was a nun. "It wasn't like the relationship could physically go anywhere," Samantha said, laughing. "So in some ways it really gave me this safe space to work out who I was." Because she was not in a romantic relationship with anyone, Samantha did not feel she needed to say anything to anyone official involved in her ordination process. Despite her personal struggles, the ordination process continued to go smoothly.

After she finished seminary, Samantha got a job as an assistant minister in an Episcopal church. In 1987 in the Episcopal Church, you had to have a call from a church to be ordained. This job was her call, so she was ordained as a deacon in February. And then she met Joan Randall.* Joan came to Samantha's church to do a talk about the AIDS epidemic during a Sunday morning adult forum. When Samantha saw Joan, she said, "The gay radar went off."

Samantha called Joan after that Sunday and asked if she would do a presentation on the AIDS epidemic for the youth group. "Nothing like doing an AIDS presentation for a youth group to get the romantic feelings going," I said. We both laughed. Their relationship blossomed.

During the October meeting of her state's Diocesan Convention that year, there was much debate about what the official stance should be toward the ordination of gay and lesbian people to the priesthood. Samantha began to get scared. The rector of the church where she was an associate minister was planning to go on sabbatical the following summer, and Samantha knew she would be left alone as the priest-in-charge. She worried what would happen if people found out she was gay.

In the meantime, her ordination to the priesthood was approaching. She was scheduled to be ordained at the end of November, and she was getting more frightened by the minute. Invitations were printed, the church choir had rehearsed all the songs they would sing, and her parents had made arrangements to come to her ordination. Just three weeks before her ordination, the rector called Samantha into his office.

"He said to me, 'Your ordination is coming up, and you don't seem to be as excited as I would expect about that. You seem to be anxious. Something seems to be troubling you.'" He pointed out how well things were going at the church—that she was a great preacher, that the congregation loved her. "It must be something in your personal life," Samantha recalls he said. "What's happening?"

Samantha felt she had no choice but to tell him the truth, since, she says, "You can read me like a book. Basically, I came out. I told him what was going on."

The rector said, "We need to go to the bishop about this."

The next day, the rector revealed how scared he was. He was afraid there would be a huge conflict in the church about Samantha's sexual orientation, and he had already faced one about the number of times a month they did morning prayer or Holy Communion. He didn't want to have to deal with another conflict. He told Samantha that until "things got worked out" he wanted Joan to stay out of town.

The bishop met with Samantha and her rector. He postponed her ordination. Indefinitely. He told Samantha, however, that the bishops had decided that if she broke off her relationship with Joan, they might reconsider her ordination in six months.

Samantha said no. "I knew that was wrong. They were asking me to take a vow of celibacy—and even then there was no guarantee. That violated me, and it violated this person I was seeing. No, I cannot go there."

After Samantha refused to break off her relationship with Joan, the rector demanded her immediate resignation. Samantha was living in the rectory at the time. She depended on her position as the assistant minister not only for her income and for her ordination but also for a place to live. Suddenly, she was without everything—no job, no home, no ordination.

What the church did to Samantha is typical of how many Episcopalians like to deal with conflict. They didn't spout biblical texts to her. They didn't make a huge production out of her homosexuality and defrock her, stripping her of her ordination as a deacon. Instead, they kept the conflict at an individual level that could easily be contained. "They didn't want to go on a witch hunt, because if they had defrocked me, then it would be like, okay, what about all these other gay priests that the bishops knew about? If you start defrocking, then you've got all this gay clergy that you know are gay, and what are you going to do about it? It would create huge turmoil. They did not want to go in that direction, but they didn't want to make the affirmative move, either. I was in a very strange limbo status."

What's more, Samantha had not yet come out to her parents, but she had to call them to tell them that her ordination was cancelled. She told them the reasons for the cancellation were too complicated to share over the phone. She said she would write them a letter, and then she would follow the letter with a phone call. "That's how I came out to them," Samantha said. It was close to Thanksgiving, so

Samantha returned home to see her family, and they were wonderful, overwhelmingly supportive.

When she returned from visiting her family, Samantha was not sure what to do. She didn't want to disappear like a fugitive in the middle of the night without telling her congregation what had happened. She decided to write another letter, this time to the congregation. The rector agreed to meet with anyone who wanted to know why Samantha left and to read the letter.

The last Sunday that she was at the church, there was a very awkward farewell party, a kind of charade in the church basement: Most people did not know why she was leaving, but everyone pretended there was something to celebrate.

After going from almost being ordained to losing her job, her home, and her call in a matter of weeks, Samantha was stunned. She said, "I was in shock. I left the rectory, and needed a place to live, and so I moved in with Joan. A major jump." Her mind was reeling. At first she thought, "This is all a big mistake, and soon people will realize that, and it will be okay." Friends and colleagues offered to write letters in support of her, but she told them not to. She didn't want to cause a ruckus. She didn't contact newspapers. She just lay low. "I kept thinking if I am good, if I am a good girl, then they will realize I am not trying to cause any trouble, and then they will realize this is a horrible mistake."

Samantha later learned that while she was working hard to show how "good" she was, several rectors of other churches contacted the bishop about hiring her as a deacon. Her bishop refused to let them hire her, and he did not tell Samantha that anyone was trying to recruit her. In effect, she was barred from having any kind of paid position in any church in any diocese.

Samantha's partner, Joan, was also in the ordination process in the Episcopal Church. There are two tracks for ordination—one for becoming a priest and one for becoming a permanent deacon. Priests are ordained as deacons before they are ordained as priests; for priests, being a deacon is a transitional position, not a permanent one. Joan wanted to become a permanent deacon, an ordained position that emphasizes service in the world. Technically, the only things deacons cannot do that priests can are the sacraments.

Six months after Samantha was kicked out of her job and her home, people in the denomination connected Joan with Samantha, and Joan was tossed out of the process immediately. There was no discussion. "It was then that I realized being a good girl wasn't going to work," Samantha said.

After they both got kicked out of the ordination process, Samantha and Joan decided to make a formal commitment to each other. After the Great Vigil of Easter, they quietly knelt down in the church after everyone else had left and privately exchanged rings and vows. They renew their vows after the Great Vigil every year.

When they shared this part of their story, I wondered how many people who have been abused by institutional religions use sacred spaces this way, gathering in corners, after hours, in basements, in the back of churches, claiming what is rightfully theirs but has been denied them. The image of Samantha and Joan kneeling in a dark corner of an empty church making a lifelong commitment to each other has stayed with me. I think of them huddled there in the moments when I feel most hopeless. It reminds me that bigotry cannot keep people from God.

Newspaper articles began to come out about their story. The articles did not name them. Samantha and Joan were just referred to as "two lesbians." Samantha said, "We became Exhibit A and Exhibit B regarding the issue of ordaining gays and lesbians in the church." They soon discovered that there was a fairly sizable gay clergy group in their diocese, and they got connected with the group. At the time, it was made up mostly of men. This was the era of "don't ask, don't tell"—an era in which many churches still remain today.

Samantha began to work in a homeless shelter, and she started attending a church where the priest let her work as an unpaid deacon. She preached once a month and often read the gospel. Two years later, that church had a job opening. The priest informally approached the bishop about hiring Samantha for that position, with the understanding that she would not be ordained as a priest. He was simply asking that she be paid for the work she was already doing. The bishop said no.

Meanwhile, Joan was trying to figure out what to do next. Her first career was in the Department of Corrections, where she worked for twenty-five years. Throughout that time, her sense of call surfaced and resurfaced. Eventually she reached a point where she thought she should do something about the feeling that would not go away. She started a small volunteer chaplaincy at a local short-term detention center. She would visit people, going cell to cell, talking to anyone who was interested, but mostly just listening. "I started by myself," Joan said. "I did it for six years, and by the end of the sixth year, there were five regular people going into the center. We had two services every Sunday. We were inviting clergy from the community to come in and celebrate. We had a pretty comprehensive pastoral care program."

She talked with the Episcopal church that she attended about the possibility of getting ordained as a priest. They steered her instead toward ordination as a deacon. Joan agreed. At the time, in her diocese, there was a program developed for vocational deacons, and Joan was accepted into that program—and was later kicked out of it.

Nevertheless, Joan still felt an incredible pull to ordained ministry. When she retired, she decided to enter a yearlong Clinical Pastoral Education (CPE) residency program at a local hospital, and during that residency she came to the conclusion that she needed to go to seminary. She enrolled the following September. During her first semester she took a course on history, polity, and cannon law in the Episcopal Church. "We were doing a historical piece on the Episcopal Church and slavery, and I said, you know if this church couldn't get its act together on slavery, there's not much hope for me, and that was basically when I said I'm out of here," Joan said. "If this church mucked around this way around an issue like slavery, it's going to be a long time before they start having anything to do with justice for queer people."

The other issue that pushed her toward leaving the Episcopal Church and pursuing other options was her age. She was going to graduate from seminary when she was fifty-two, and she felt that she didn't have time to wait around for the Episcopal Church to change. She and Samantha formed a Women Church community that met in their living room for the rest of the time that she was in seminary. In the spring of 1992 that community ordained her.

While she was in seminary, she continued to work with prisoners. She had an internship at a hospital. Part of the hospital was a maximum-security prison and part of the hospital was a designated AIDS unit. "Those two units were where I did my work, back and forth between those two," she said.

Joan realized that if she wanted to continue to be a chaplain, she would need more institutional endorsement than her Women Church ordination could provide. "The reality was that there were not a whole lot of choices at that point in the mid-'90s," Joan said. "It basically boiled down to Unitarian Universalism and the United Church of Christ, and, since I am Trinitarian, I went back to the church of my youth." She spoke to one of the area ministers where she lived, and he told her she needed to get connected to a UCC church. She joined a small, aging UCC congregation. She told them her story, and they offered her a job.

Joan continued to work at the hospital even though she did not get paid for that work. She was barely getting paid as a part-time associate minister at the UCC church, but that job made it possible for her to enter the ordination process in the UCC, and, after a truncated process, she was ordained ten months later. The contrast between the ordination process in the Episcopal Church and the one in the UCC could not have been more pronounced.

No longer functioning as a deacon, Samantha felt cut off from parish life. She also began to hear traumatic stories from other people in dioceses across the country who were gay. "Watching the body count, I began to question whether I even wanted to continue to be a deacon. I was questioning my call, asking myself if I wanted to stay indefinitely frozen," Samantha said. "I needed to make a move. I needed to move forward or back out."

Samantha and Joan knew the Episcopal bishop of New Hampshire was supportive of gays and lesbians. Joan's parents lived in New Hampshire, and Joan and Samantha were driving to New Hampshire every weekend to take care of them. Samantha approached the bishop, and he told her to find a parish home and see how the diocese felt to her. She had heard about a small church that might be supportive, and she went to the church one Sunday. "As soon as the priest appeared," Samantha said, "the gay radar went off—no question." After the service, Samantha noticed that the priest's partner was floating around at coffee hour, the two of them wearing the same rings. The church was warm and welcoming, so she went back for several Sundays. A few weeks later, Samantha attended church wearing her deacon's collar, and she made an appointment to meet with the priest.

Samantha told the priest what had happened to her, and the priest told Samantha that she was one of the first women ordained in the diocese. She said she had fought to get women ordained and was still in that battle. She had struggled to find a parish that would hire her, struggled to find full-time work, and she was not going to take on any other fights. "She basically told me to go away," Samantha said. Samantha was welcome to be a member at the church, but the priest did not want her to function as a deacon there. "My coming in and being out would raise that issue in the church. People would be talking about me, and then they would connect the dots about their own rector."

Samantha returned to church at a local monastery in the city where Joan was attending seminary and asked the head of the monastery if he might let her serve occasionally as a deacon at their community Eucharist. He said he would be glad to have her but that he needed permission from the bishops in the diocese that had refused to ordain her to the priesthood and from his own bishop. The bishops in her original diocese granted her permission; the bishop in the monastery's diocese refused.

"That was the straw that broke the camel's back," Samantha said.

She asked the bishop in the diocese where she had been ordained as a deacon to release her from her vows. A man on the standing committee of that diocese tried to talk her out of it. He promised the committee would go to bat for her. Samantha said, "Thank you for your support, but no. Cut me loose. Please." The diocese released her from her vows.

Joan finished seminary, and when her parents passed away, Joan and Samantha decided to move to New Hampshire. Samantha started attending a small Episcopal church near their house. She eventually became a member of the vestry, and, once again, the whole ordination issue began to bubble up in her life. Everyone she knew, everyone she met, kept telling her to try again. She met occasionally with the bishop in New Hampshire for a couple of years, trying to discern whether she should go again in this direction.

He told her that to enter the ordination process in New Hampshire, Samantha would have to be restored to the deaconate by the same diocese that had ordained her as a deacon and had later released her. The person who was now the bishop there was a known homophobe. "Basically I had to wait until he retired," Samantha said. And she did. Once he retired, the newly elected bishop happened to be the man who had tried to persuade her not to give up her ordination as a deacon. Samantha asked for his approval. He agreed. This process—the move to New Hampshire, the conversations with the bishop there, and the approval from her original diocese—took several years.

Once the bishop gave her the go-ahead, she had to meet with the standing committee to get their permission. They did not grant her permission until the bishop, after much struggle, persuaded them to do so. Finally, fifteen years after she was originally ordained a deacon, in a quiet service in a chapel, Samantha was restored as a deacon. Later that year she was ordained a priest.

Samantha found a job at a church, although the congregation was, at first, reluctant to hire an out lesbian. Now happy in her church and ordained after almost two decades of struggle, Samantha feels good about how things turned out. "Sometimes you are struggling ahead, hoping you are going where God wants you to be, and once in a while you have these occasions when you look back and can see the footsteps of the Holy Pigeon. That's one of Joan's sayings," she said. "Then, there are those rare occasions when you know the Holy Spirit is at work, and you are almost kicking back and watching it happen."

There was nothing about Samantha's story that suggested to me she kicked back and let anything happen, and really not very much that showed the workings of the Holy Spirit, however you want to interpret that. I saw a long journey during which she got continually beaten down, a road full of bigotry and oppression and secrecy, a perfect example of homophobia that quietly and privately wreaks havoc on people's lives. I said as much to Samantha. She told me that she didn't need the church to validate her. "I had very much claimed the work I was doing as ministry. I wasn't doing parish ministry, but I was working with the homeless, working with the mentally retarded, doing AIDS work, working with prisoners, and then at the hospice helping people cope with death," she said. "I thought, maybe the church won't ordain me as a priest, but you know what, I'm doing ministry. That was very important for me. I found my call in other ways. For me, the journey was traumatic and terrible, but it was also grace-filled. Working with people of color and different classes has radically transformed my life and ministry," she said. "It is a mixed bag. I see some of my peers who are priests and are my age and have been in ministry for twenty years. I see how far they have gone in their parish ministries and what they have done, and then here I am, just starting out. But on the other hand, I think all of this has made me a better priest."

"What made you stay with the Episcopal Church?" I asked. "How did you even keep going to church?"

"This is where I have made my spiritual home," Samantha said. "This is what feeds me spiritually, the liturgy and the service."

Samantha admits she was disappointed with the Episcopal Church. In some ways, she sympathizes more with fundamentalists' homophobia than she does with Episcopalians'. "The fundamentalists take scripture literally, at least they try to," she said. "It then becomes like a house of cards, and if you pull one card out to say, this is what the Bible says, but maybe they got it wrong, then there is the terrifying prospect of the whole deck of cards coming down. So I can understand where they are coming from." The Episcopal Church, however, does not take the Bible literally. Not only scripture, but reason and science inform the church's ethical decisions. "It felt much more political than it did theological. For the fundamentalists, it is theological—it's faulty, but theological. Whereas with the Episcopal Church and the mainstream denominations, you don't interpret scripture literally, you have science helping you understand the nature of sexual orientation, so what is going on? This has more to do with homophobia."

The UCC has an official process churches can go through to decide to be a congregation that welcomes all people regardless of race, gender, nationality, class, or sexual orientation. When Eve became the pastor of her church it had been officially "open and affirming" for two years. "It technically means we are open to and affirming of all persons," Eve said. "But it is really about sexual orientation." Eve pushed her congregation to realize that although they were open and affirming, they were really what she calls "open and affirming to a point." Eve said, "That can mean you are welcome here, and we will treat you like anyone else, but we don't want you to talk about your relationships, and we don't want you to hold hands in church."

Eve thought her church should fly a pride flag, the rainbow flag that has been a symbol of gay pride for decades. They were already in the process of thinking about their building and the signage on and around it. The church is located on a street with several other religious communities, and there is nothing that distinguishes it from any other church on the street. The church has a sign that indicates the church is open and affirming, but most people who are not UCC have no idea what that means. One of the churches down the street from Eve's, a Methodist church, is a "welcoming church," their language for being open and affirming.

Her church resisted. When Eve first raised the issue of a pride flag, the church fell silent. The people who were in support of the flag were respectful of the elders (leaders elected by the congregation), and not knowing what the elders thought of the flag, the supporters stayed quiet. Finally, two elders spoke. They said, "We don't want people to think we're a gay church."

When Eve told me this part of the story she said, "Like there are so many gay and lesbian people out there just waiting to take over churches. That's what they want to do. It's not about equal rights, it's really about being chairperson of the finance committee."

Eve asked her congregation, "What does that mean, we're a gay church? Does that mean everyone at the church is gay? Or does it mean we're happy? What does that mean?" The group talked, uncomfortably, for a few more minutes, and then they agreed to table the issue until the next meeting.

In between, however, the ruling about gay marriage came out in Massachusetts. Eve went to city hall and shook people's hands. She congratulated couples and handed out her business card. The congregation put a sign in front of the church that said, "Congratulations to same-sex couples! We're open for business!" Eight members of the congregation stood by the sign and handed out bubbles and sparkling cider. Many people who walked by the church thanked them, and most of the people who said thank you were straight couples or straight singles. The group brought that experience back to the church council. Eve said, "And people really heard that, so they were then able to say, we feel like this is the direction we need to go."

I was living in Cambridge at the time, and I can still remember the feeling that night at city hall. At midnight, city hall opened its doors to the long line of in-love couples. Eric and I went to the celebration. We brought roses to hand out to people. The street in front of the building was shut down and masses of people filled the street and the lawn. People waved banners and drank champagne. There were balloons and confetti and streamers. It was like nothing I had ever seen before. I am used to going to protests and feeling hopeless. I usually attend big gatherings *against* something—this was *for* something. A huge victory had been won. Civil rights had been won. And the police were there—not to make sure our gathering didn't cause trouble but to protect us. The feeling was electric.

Eve's congregation talked about the fact that most people who do not attend church assume churches are hostile to GLBTQ people unless there is a clear, explicit symbol that the church is not. "I think that was actually the trigger," she said. "Because our church likes to think of itself as welcoming, and there is a lot of feeling among our elders that because we are a friendly church, we're not like those fundamentalists, we're not like those Catholic churches. That sort of goaded them into doing it."

Convinced by their experience following that historic event in Massachusetts and their commitment to being friendly, Eve and her congregation put up a flagpole on the front lawn of the church. They agreed to rotate the pride flag as one of many they would fly. Eve's church flies the pride flag because they recognize that the loudest voice against GLBTQ people is a religious one. "I am so sick of people saying there's room for faithful people on both sides," Eve said. "It's bigotry. The bigotry of good church folks permits the violence of ordinary folks."

Eve's church's pride flag is bringing people to church in droves. "Frankly, it has been our number one way of bringing people in. I mean, it is not my preaching. It is not our fabulous gay, biracial music director whose music is incredible. I mean, all these things help, but the pride flag has brought in so many people. Gay and straight. Single. Coupled. Because they drive by, and they walk by, and they immediately know."

The pride flag isn't the only thing that sends a signal to people who might otherwise never step foot in a church. Eve sends a signal, too. She is a young, vibrant woman committed to doing the work justice demands. "I could get up there and read the telephone book, and there would be some people who would think, this is so different from what I grew up with, I'm signing on," Eve said.

Because the religious voice is often among the loudest homophobic voices, it is not enough for church communities to be neutral when it comes to justice and full inclusion of all GLBTQ people. It is not enough for churches to insist they are not homophobic. Just as they must actively oppose sexism, they much actively oppose homophobia and heterosexism. And this includes rethinking liturgies and rituals, as well as attitudes and teachings about human sexuality. Congregations and ministers must be held accountable for the thinking and theology that allow and support hatred. As Eve said, it is the bigotry of good church folks that permits the violence of ordinary folks. The debates swirling around homosexuality in religious communities offer yet another opportunity to reconceive radically how we understand what a religious community is, how to be congregations that take a stand for justice, how to recover theology that values human bodies, how to articulate views on human sexuality that are life-giving and unafraid.

I am more encouraged about the Episcopal Church now than I have been in some time. The consecration of Katharine Jefferts Schori as presiding bishop is my main reason for hope. Katharine frames homosexuality as a justice issue. "I think it is a piece of the human sinful condition to want to define some group or some kind of people as unacceptable, as other, as enemy, as unsafe, dangerous, and the church has been dealing with this from the very beginning," she said. "The place of Gentiles—are they okay or not? And certainly in our own history in this country—African Americans, slavery, immigrants, women, gay and lesbian Christians, and there will be another group after that. I don't know who it's going to be, but there will be one."

I could tell when I talked with her that Katharine is good at staying in conversation with people she disagrees with and who disagree with her. I am not very good at that, not very good at staying at the table with people I perceive to be acting in ways that are unjust. I asked Katharine how she does it. "I think the opportunity for conversion only comes in relationship, and therefore I am willing to say that people who don't understand these issues or who don't understand why I may see these as issues of justice need to be in the conversation, too, or else there is no hope for change," she said. "I think a lot of the reactivity is about grief. The church has changed. You hear people say that over and over again. The church has changed out from under me and I don't recognize this. And it produces anger and fear and the pastoral response is to accompany such people in the midst of their pain." Then she laughed and added, "Is it easy? No. But I think that's what we're called to do."

Chapter Ten

TRANS

In the book of Genesis, you can find the story of Jacob—the son of Isaac and Rebecca, twin brother of Esau, born holding his brother's heel, stealer of his brother's birthright. One night, as Jacob waits for Esau and the 400 men Jacob believes are coming to attack him, Jacob prays to God. He feels unworthy of the love God has shown to him, and he begs God to keep him safe from his brother. Jacob puts together a gift for Esau—goats, ewes, rams, camels, cows, and donkeys. He sends his family and everything he has across the stream and waits alone. That night, a man wrestles with Jacob on the banks of the stream until daybreak. When the man realizes he has not prevailed against Jacob, he strikes Jacob on the hip and knocks it out of joint. The man says, "Let me go, for the day is breaking."

But Jacob says, "I will not let you go until you bless me."

The man asks, "What is your name?"

"Jacob."

"You shall no longer be called Jacob, but Israel, for you have striven with God and with humans, and have prevailed."

Jacob, now Israel, having claimed the blessing of God, limps for the rest of his life.

What follows are stories about wrestling with humans, wrestling with God, wrestling with shame, wrestling with yourself, and then claiming, demanding, God's blessing. They are stories about knowing you are beloved, calling yourself beloved, even when everyone else refuses to. They are stories about changed minds and changed names and changed bodies.

One of the biggest gifts I was given while writing this book was the opportunity to listen to the stories of transgender priests, men and women who followed their call by literally opening up everything about themselves to its transformative power. Although at times more dramatic than other stories I listened to, their stories were essentially similar to those of most of the women ministers I interviewed. It was as if everything others experienced was suddenly brought into relief, literalized—being forced to conceal who they were, feeling that they could not be their true embodied selves, knowing that their politics or way of dressing or talking or loving would not be welcome in the church. They hid themselves until they could live that way no more, and then they risked everything and endured violence and loss to be the people they knew God meant them to be. Like all women ministers, they transgressed categories, challenging how we understand what it means to be human, what it means to be a man, a woman, even another gender entirely, what we think a body is, who we think deserves to be loved. They blew categories wide open, so wide that if you listen carefully to their stories the boundaries we draw between the sacred and the profane will disappear. You will discover that we are all holy.

The word "transgender" is often employed as an umbrella term to include people who challenge the boundaries of sex and gender. The prefix "trans" comes from the Latin preposition *trans,* meaning "across," "beyond," or "through." In *Transgender Warriors,* Leslie Feinberg writes, "Trans*gender* people traverse, bridge, or blur the boundary of the *gender expression* they were assigned at birth." Feinberg notes that the word "transgender" is increasingly used inclusively, referring both to those who reassign the sex they were labeled at birth and to those whose gender expression is considered "inappropriate" for their sex.

Feinberg asked self-identified transgender activists who they believed were included under the term transgender, and their list included (but was not limited to): transsexuals (people born with the physical characteristics of one sex but who emotionally and psychologically feel they belong to the other sex; people who have undergone surgery or hormonal treatment to acquire the physical characteristics of a different sex than the one they were assigned at birth); transvestites (people who dress in clothing different from the culturally accepted clothing assigned to their biological sex); bigenders; transgenders; drag queens; drag kings; cross-dressers; masculine women; feminine men; intersexuals; androgynes; cross-genders; shape-shifters; passing women; passing men; gender-benders; gender-blenders; bearded women; and women bodybuilders who have crossed the line of what is considered socially acceptable for a female body.

I would add women ministers to this list. In the spring of 2007, a photograph of Presiding Bishop Katharine Jefferts Schori was vandalized while posted on the Boston University Episcopal Chaplaincy bulletin board. Her eyes were gouged out and male genitalia were drawn on her.

Just by being a woman in the pulpit, you transgress gender boundaries. You are a woman in a job that has been traditionally reserved for men, a job that has shut women out—systemically, spiritually, theologically, institutionally—for thousands of years. Crossing vocational gender boundaries—when women fight wars or fly planes or first voted or worked assembly lines, or when men are nurses or primary schoolteachers—reveals and undermines the gendered, sexist ways we have defined work in this country.

When I began this project, I did not understand being transgender. My version of feminism got in my way. Because I understand gender as constructed—that is, because I do not think there is anything *essential* about being a woman—I could not understand when I heard people say they felt that they had been born into the wrong body. Although I recognize there are biological differences among male, female, and intersex bodies, I understand gender as socially constructed. What it means to be a "woman"—to look like, act like, think like, dress like, walk like, speak like—varies from culture to culture, time period to time period, state to state. The notion of "woman" has been defined against "man," and both categories have been shaped by sexism. In this framework, to say "I feel like a man trapped in a woman's body" or "I feel like a woman trapped in a man's body" made no sense to me.

Interviewing trans priests, though, changed me. I, too, stood on the banks of a river and wrestled—with myself, with my feminism, with fear, with terms and labels and ideas I held on to for dear life. And thanks to the honesty and courage of the trans people who shared their stories with me, I came through the night of wrestling a different person, blessed.

I still remember the first same-sex blessing I attended at All Saints, my church in Pasadena. Two men in my small group for people who were new to the church got married. At the reception, they danced the tango as their first dance, surrounded by all the people who loved them. The room was full. I realized then how freeing it must be to follow your heart—to love who you love, to be who you feel called to be, no matter what the consequences. At that time, I was still trying to be who I thought other people wanted me to be so that I could keep their love—and my performance left me feeling hollow. My two friends, the tango dancers, refused to pretend. They risked everything when they claimed being gay, and their courage led them to that place: dancing with the person each of them loved most in the world, surrounded by people who loved them exactly as they are, celebrated by a community of faith.

I got that same feeling when I talked to Gari, an Episcopal priest. Even her e-mails—just one or two lines about sitting by a lake, walking her dog along a beach, writing her Sunday homilies looking out at the water—radiated peace. Listening to her story I remembered what becomes possible when you are willing to say, this is who I am, what becomes possible when you stop hiding from others and from yourself. When we spoke on the phone for the first time, I said, "I have to tell you there is a real sense of peace that comes across in your e-mails."

"I'm more peaceful than I ever have been in my life," Gari said. "We have a good life, a simple life. Our kids are close. Kate and I still love each other, enjoy each other's company, laugh together."

"Are you where you thought you'd be in your life at this point?"

"No. I didn't plan this," Gari said. "When you get through the fire—and it was a fire—there is a peacefulness on the other side. I don't think you can get that unless you toss the cards on the table and say, this is who I am, and if you like it or not, I'm not going to fake it."

"That's a powerful thing to do," I said.

"It was done for me," Gari said. "Outing me was the oddest gift anyone has ever given me. I don't know what would have happened if they hadn't. I think I probably would have continued to live in two worlds until I couldn't anymore."

Gari knew as a child growing up in the 1950s that she was transgender. However, at that time, she had no information and no way to frame the feelings she was having. "There was no one to talk to," Gari said. "I certainly did not talk to my parents. I wasn't going to talk to clergy or a doctor—your family doctor in all likelihood would have no idea what you were talking about."

"That must have been hard to hold," I said.

"It was and it wasn't," she said. "I think it became hard to hold, Sarah, when I began to realize it didn't have to be held."

Gari was ordained as an Episcopal priest in 1986. When Gari decided to be a priest, she was a married man and had two kids. She took her whole family with her to seminary. Her first job was as a priest for two parishes, and she did that work for four and a half years. Then Gari took a job at a church in a suburb in Milwaukee, where she worked for six years. "It was there that things really got difficult," Gari said.

Gari did the best she could. She had no language to talk about her experience. Occasionally an article in the paper would surface about a "transsexual," but there was no forum for talking about it. Gari and her wife started to deal with being transgender when Gari was in her early forties. "Midlife adds fuel to the fire for unresolved issues," Gari said. "My gender conflict had not gone away. In fact as time went by, it seemed to gain strength." Gari discovered a copy of *Tapestry*, a transgender publication, and suddenly realized she was not alone. "I had the revelation that there were many people, far more than I ever would have guessed, struggling with and resolving this issue of gender identity. It was time to begin to deal with this lifelong issue." Gari and her wife committed to trying to deal with it honestly and privately. They chose not to tell the congregation at that time.

But as Gari said, "Nothing in church communities remains private for very long." Around the same time, there was a conflict in the church. "It was about what all church conflicts are about, power," Gari said. "Who has it and who is forced to knuckle under it." During that conflict, some people in the church, upset with Gari, followed her one Saturday night to a support group meeting. The next morning, a Sunday, they approached Gari and said, "We know where you went last night. If you don't tell the bishop, we will."

Gari resigned immediately and spoke with the bishop. "When I was outed, the kids knew, thank God, but it didn't happen to just me. Our older daughter was a senior in college, and the other one was a senior in high school," Gari said. "It splashed all over everybody." Gari lost her job at the parish she was serving at the time. "When housing is supplied by the parish, the loss of the job also meant the loss of our home."

Gari's bishop suggested she would never work in the church again. "My bishop told me that my prospects for employment in the church were somewhere between slim and none. Unfortunately, an MDiv does not carry much weight in the job market. It was a tough time," she said. "He wasn't angry at me, but he wasn't very helpful, either. I got the feeling that he would be happy if I were to disappear."

Gari tried to separate herself from the church, but she soon realized she couldn't do anything else. "I was called to be a priest," she said. "And I needed to figure out some way that could make sense." She eventually got a job at a small parish, what Gari describes as a "disaffected, cranky little parish that felt neglected by the diocese."

They had been without a priest for seven years. Gari started there as a supply priest, a temporary arrangement, and then, after six months, she became their full-time priest. The church had already heard all the rumors about her, but they offered her the job anyway. "That's what I mean when I say they took me in spite of everything."

Gari was the first transgender person I interviewed, and as I talked to her, I slowly began to realize that none of the categories I held in my head worked anymore. "Are you out?" I asked.

"Am I out? That's kind of a difficult question to answer categorically," Gari said. "I pretty much live my own life, but I have never really taken up a billboard and said, hey, guess what!"

I kept trying to put her in a box that made sense to me. "So you're now in a lesbian relationship."

"More or less," Gari said.

"So that's not an issue for your congregation? That would be a big issue in a lot of places."

Gari was quiet for a while, and then she spoke. "I mean, we've been together for more than thirty years. In practical terms now, yes, it's a lesbian relationship, but it is just that we've never not been together, so people don't...how can I explain this...I'm not really sure that they perceive everything, if you know what I mean. It's kind of right there in front of them, but we're a same-gender marriage, and that's not supposed to be able to happen. But because we were married before, that break that exists in some cases just doesn't exist for us."

Listening to the recording of my conversation with Gari, listening to the kinds of questions I asked, I began to realize that none of the labels we use to sort people hold. "All the categories are up for grabs," Gari said. "Honestly, if somebody were to ask me today, are you gay or straight, I would say, well, I'm not straight, but those categories don't have any meaning for me."

When Gari's bishop came to visit her for the first time, Gari didn't know how much he knew. Gari said, "Well, you know, I'm transgender."

The bishop said, "I had heard." And then he asked, "So you live part of your life as a female?"

"I just kind of try to live as myself," Gari said. "I'm not trying to be a smart-ass. If I feel like letting my hair down one day, it will be down one day. If I want to pull it back, it will be back. Some people think I'm female, and some people think I'm male, and other people don't know. I don't think it's my business to make sure they have it all figured out."

Much like they want to do with Gari, people want to manage God. Gari is more comfortable with mystery, with change, with what cannot be known for sure. She seems to embody in her theology and her ministry—and her body—what philosopher Richard Rorty meant when he wrote about "the priority of the need to create new ways of being human, and a new heaven and a new earth for these new humans to inhabit, over the desire for stability, security and order." Gari said, "For me, God is the unseen presence wherever we are. Nongendered, nonhuman, nonmaterial, personal in a sense and yet in other ways not as personal as we have traditionally assumed, always present if we care to look, if you think about looking."

Gari confessed to having an ambivalent relationship with the institutional church. "I don't consider myself a religious person," she said, and when I laughed, she said, "People always laugh about that. By definition, religion is a structure. It's doctrinal, in our understanding. It's hierarchical, it's patriarchal, and I'm not interested in that. I'm not any of those things. God doesn't disapprove of us or approve of us based on what we believe or don't believe." And then she added, "But I'm a priest, and I'd be a priest whether it was my job or not."

For Gari, being a priest means walking with people on their journey, being willing to admit you don't have all the answers, and trying to be in touch with God, however you may understand what that means. It means being open to questions, being honest, trying to live with integrity. "I try to give people permission to think for themselves," Gari said.

"That is a beautiful gift," I said.

"It's a dangerous gift," she said, laughing. "Because if you give people the permission to think for themselves, then you have to value their opinions."

On Sunday mornings, Gari does not preach. She offers what she calls a reflection. Every Sunday, the reflection is followed by an open mike, during which she asks her congregation, "So how do you see it?" They love it. Gari said, "If the place is truly going to be open for everyone, you have to find a way to listen."

Michelle Hansen was ordained a priest in 1971, before women were allowed to be priests in the Episcopal Church. "I had very long hair at the time, and so I wasn't your typical guy even then," she said. "I got ordained before I got married, and at the time I think no one knew that I was transsexual. I wouldn't even accept it myself." Once ordained, Michelle worked as a youth minister and then "got a rather standard job as an assistant in one of the big churches in West Hartford, Connecticut." While working as an assistant, Michelle got married. "I thought maybe that would cure me of this desire to be a woman, this need to be a woman. Of course that doesn't work, but

I continued the illusion for quite a while." After working in Hartford, Michelle became a chaplain at the University of Kansas and began, in secret, to take female hormones and to cross-dress. Then she worked as a director at an Episcopal camp and was a part-time priest in a parish. She worked both jobs—"Each was supposed to be half-time, but it turned out they were really two full-time jobs"—for five years, until the schedule became untenable. Michelle asked the bishop if she could do one of the jobs full-time instead of trying to do both, and he refused. "He said, well, I guess you are going to do neither job full-time." Out of a job, Michelle began working in computers, doing the "clergy thing" part-time.

Michelle cross-dressed and took hormones she wrote false prescriptions for until her wife found pictures of Michelle in a bra and panties and a secret stash of women's clothes. Confronted by her wife, Michelle promised to stop, and she did for the next thirteen years. Michelle did not begin to transition until she was fifty-eight years old.

"What happened when you turned fifty-eight?" I asked.

"Believe it or not, I encountered a bar of soap," she said.

Michelle had fallen and scraped her leg, a wound that became infected. The doctor told Michelle to use a moisturizing soap to avoid drying out the skin around the wound. "And so, I got in the shower, and the feelings of the moisturizer soap awakened something in me that was very sensual," she said. "And my problem of trying to deal with the feminine thing inside me just came right back."

After taking a few part-time positions at different churches, Michelle worked for a cluster of five parishes and at a computer company. Michelle was part of a staff of two full-time clergy (both women) and three part-time clergy (all men)—that is, until Michelle transitioned. "As soon as I said the word 'transsexual' to the computer company, they laid me off. The church actually was far better." The bishop of her diocese was supportive. "Of course, he was an old friend, but still, it is a pretty unusual thing for someone to say I have lived all these years as a man, and now I am going to live as a woman and go the whole way and do everything, surgery and everything, but he was very supportive." The bishop told Michelle's story to the other bishops in Connecticut, and they, too, were supportive. Together they worked out a plan for Michelle to transition while continuing to work in the church. "They gave me six months to visit the churches that I had been working in, and the diocese would pay my salary. I wouldn't do any real work; I would just visit and get people used to me."

When Michelle announced her plan to the other clergy working in the cluster, all were compassionate and encouraging. Together they announced their plan to a group of leaders from the five churches. "There didn't seem to be any sort of opposition, which surprised us," Michelle said. "But then, the proverbial shit hit the fan." Part of the plan was to let each church on its own decide whether or not they were comfortable letting Michelle work as a priest. "One of the churches, actually the biggest one, had this huge controversy and they started attacking everybody in sight, practically." They directed much of their outrage at the two full-time female clergy, but they also disinvited Michelle from working there. "Pretty immediately following that, another church in the cluster invited me, wholeheartedly, to the altar, and then another one followed." A third church in the cluster invited her back, as long as she would only stay two weeks at a time. "There were some people there who were hemming and hawing and saying well, if she's there, we won't be there." The final church in the cluster didn't make a decision one way or the other. "That church kept on sitting on their hands and refusing to decide," she said. "In the middle of all this I was diagnosed with cancer. It sounds like a real disaster, doesn't it?"

Michelle was diagnosed with stage-three colon cancer and had to undergo surgery and then chemotherapy (during which she developed kidney stones and discovered that she had an aneurysm). "I went through that as a woman with male parts still," she said. "Not a very comfortable thing, but it is what I did." There was a period of time when Michelle could not work because of her cancer. When she was finally well enough, she underwent genital reassignment surgery. "In many ways, I think we all thought that things might get a little better once that was done. I was no longer a woman with man parts," she said. "But we were wrong, because things got more and more difficult in the church from there. Not only were people in the one church that I wasn't invited to attacking me, but in the church that had sat on its hands, a minority of people there got very vocal, and the other people catered to them. I got a clear picture that I wasn't going to be able to go there and work because of their attitude." Not only did things get bad for Michelle, they also got bad for the two women who were clergy in the cluster. They risked their jobs to support Michelle. "I owe them so much," she said. "They held my hand, strategized, and fended off the wolves for a year and a half." Michelle knew she would have to resign, so she did right after the Christmas season.

After she resigned, she tried to get the diocesan convention to approve a statement against discrimination on the basis of sexual orientation or gender identity. "That resolution failed by about seven votes," she said. "And, since then, I have done maybe a handful of services, but have pretty much been out of things, licking my wounds."

"Do you think you would ever want to return to parish ministry?" I asked.

"I don't know, to be honest with you. So much grief that I am still..." She trailed off, and then she said, "I don't know if I want to fight the battle. Maybe I'll change my mind at some point, but right now I am not sure how much more I want to get into the fray. It was tough because I was so accepted as a guy, and then I turned into a female, and you know, people were saying, well, it's fine, we accept her, but she can't be a priest. She can't have the authority for us. And I thought, what difference does it make?"

Michelle thinks part of the resistance she encountered resulted from the fact that she was working in rural areas of Connecticut. "They were kind of refugees looking to get away from the problems of cities in Connecticut, and of course, my problem was seen as a city problem. I think that was part of it," she said. "That and, you know, God made you this way and that's the way you should stay."

Michelle also lost her marriage. Her wife did not want to be married to a woman. The two remain friends, and Michelle is in "fairly good graces" with her three sons. She also has one granddaughter.

I asked Michelle how it feels to be a woman, whether or not it is radically different from being a man. "Men open doors for me," she said, laughing. "The guys at the auto repair place treat me like I am an idiot."

"Welcome," I said.

Michelle's transition and the violent reaction of some of the people in the church communities where she worked helped her more fully claim the fact that God loves everybody. "I just cannot imagine that someone like me doesn't have a place in God's kingdom," she said. "And not only me, but others who are unusual or different. It brought that home." Michelle lived fifty-eight years of her life as a straight, White male. "You know, with all the privileges and no real discrimination in my background, so being discriminated against is a new experience for me. I can say it is not pleasant, but it is also very enlightening, understanding the position of people who have been discriminated against, and theologically, feeling that God doesn't do that discrimination. It is just people who do it."

Throughout the interview, Michelle's voice brimmed with sadness. "I have seen some of the worst of humanity in this whole thing," she said. "You know, it could be worse. I could have had violence done against me." And yet, even given everything she has lost, Michelle experiences her transition as an incredible relief. "I don't have to be something that I wasn't anymore," she said. "You just cannot imagine, my whole life trying to be something I wasn't, feeling ashamed of a certain part of myself, something I couldn't control. And you will find that all transsexuals feel like this."

Michelle's earliest memories have to do with feeling female, even before she had any idea what "genitals were about." She said, "I was sensitive. I felt more affinity to being like my mother. I got picked on by the boys." Michelle's father was in the air force, so her family moved around a lot, allowing Michelle to reinvent herself every time they landed in a new place. "I finally figured out how not to get picked on, but people who stay in one place, they live with that," she said.

Although Michelle was driven from the church by a group of people who made her life and the lives of her female colleagues miserable, Michelle knows that this group was in the minority. "I think more people in those churches accepted me than didn't, except for that one church. But I tell you, the ones who didn't made life just miserable. They were very vocal and very nasty. It is kind of sad. I have a bad taste in my mouth, but I have to say there were so many fine and accepting and truly Christian people." That seems to be the case in most forms of discrimination. The people who discriminate shout the loudest, and those who don't discriminate rarely raise their voices at all. If the people who are supportive of justice for all human beings cannot learn to be as loud and as forceful as those who support bigotry, then the bigots will continue to prevail.

I never imagined that meeting a priest who is a transman would make me feel hopeful about and welcomed in the Episcopal Church. Eli* was born female and is now living life as a man. I interviewed Eli in the home he shares with his partner, Anne. Eli picked me up at the train station and drove me back to his house. Before we went inside, we walked around their yard and he showed me his garden. He had recently planted flowers along the chain-link fence that marks the boundary of their yard. His garden, like his life, makes borders beautiful. Eli's apartment is filled with photographs—wedding photographs, family photographs—three cats, and the sound of a neighbor's dog that howls all day long.

Eli transitioned from female to male while he was in the ordination process to be an Episcopal priest. Eli began the process as an out lesbian with a partner, Anne, and was eventually ordained as a transman.

A cradle Episcopalian, Eli grew up in Washington and attended a conservative Episcopal church in the middle of a liberal town. The church's rector refused to use the 1979 prayer book and was against the ordination of women. The liturgy was high church—"high and dry," Eli said. Eli hated Sunday school, so she spent most Sundays in church with her mother, kind of bored, but also fascinated. Eli loved listening to prayers said in unison. She thought the sound was beautiful, like a wave of water rushing over her.

When it was time for her to be confirmed, she was in a class led by the assistant minister who was rumored to be gay. He toured the class around the church and pointed out all the symbols, explaining what they meant. "I felt I was in the midst of this symbolic universe, and the rabbit hole goes a lot deeper than this, and I want to dive in."

At first, how deeply Eli could dive was limited by the fact that girls at Eli's church were not allowed to be acolytes. Soon things changed. Eli was not in the first group of girls who were trained as acolytes, but she was in the second group. "I took a lot of pride in getting compliments on how well I acolyted," Eli said, laughing. "I was really into it."

Eli spent summers at conservative, evangelical Christian camps. The personal relationship with Jesus that the camps introduced her to filled a place in her that had been left open. Eli said, "I was in such hell as a fairly transgressively gendered teen whose dad had left and whose mom was sick with a neuromuscular disease, and I was absolutely miserable. Going to camp and having someone address Christianity to the misery of my life was really amazing, and helped get me clear that that could be part of the larger picture for me. I brought that back to my church within myself."

The summer before tenth grade Eli had a camp counselor she aspired to be like. Eli had never met someone, fairly butch like herself, who was in a position of pastoral leadership. Over the week the counselor became an icon of possibility to Eli. "I suddenly could see myself," Eli reflected. Yet, in later correspondence Eli felt awkward as her counselor warned her about the dangers of women's colleges and lesbians. Where was this coming from? Eli had never before considered queerness as something about which Christians had opinions one way or another. This was her introduction to a now all-too-familiar controversy.

Eli was fourteen when she returned home with a sense that being a minister was something she might like to do. "It was just kind of bubbling," Eli said. "But I thought it was nuts. Nuts." Eli attended a progressive private school, and being Christian was not all that cool. "Plus I was a queer kid," Eli said.

"Did you understand yourself that way?" I asked.

"No," Eli said. "I understood myself as a tomboy, and I was a big athlete, and that was how I channeled that part of myself. I did sports. Every season I was doing a sport. So, a big part of my identity in high school was as an athlete."

Although she found refuge playing sports, she struggled in the homophobic culture of high school athletics. "It is horribly homophobic. Sort of endemically," Eli said. "I understand why that happens. There is an association of female masculinity with gayness, so if you are a serious female athlete, you have to automatically combat that stereotype. It creates a homophobia at its very foundation. I always had to fight that."

Eli remembers one day in high school when gay and bisexual speakers were brought in to talk to a group of students in the library. After the talk, Eli went to basketball practice, where the rest of the team was already talking about how disgusting the speakers were. "I remember being really disgusted with them for saying that," Eli said. "Had you asked me, I would have denied being gay, but there was an undercurrent of identity that was there. I was desperately trying to keep myself Christian and not queer." As if the two could never coexist.

One major high school problem for Eli was how to wear her hair. Eli told me his "haircut history." Eli said, "I had short hair in kindergarten, and then I grew it out. In fifth grade, I was totally into Billie Jean King. I thought she was the bee's knees. I have a little essay I wrote about her. I cut my hair in fifth grade, and it was short. And from then on I was always trying to ride the line between how short I could cut it without looking like a boy. I really did want to look like a boy, but I couldn't. So in fifth grade it was short, short, short." In ninth grade, due to the enforced girliness of her basketball experience, she started growing her hair out. In Eli's tenth-grade basketball picture, her hair is still too short to pull back into a ponytail, but by the end of that year, Eli was able to wear a ponytail, and from that point on Eli always had long hair, although she never wore it down. When she got to college, Eli wore her hair in a bun.

Every night beginning in elementary school, Eli's mother would tuck Eli into bed and would pray with her. One night during their evening ritual, Eli's mother said that she could see Eli being a priest. She asked Eli if she had ever thought about it, and then she said, "I think you would be a really great priest."

Eli felt that if she were to tell anyone that she wanted to be a priest they would think she was, in Eli's words, a "total freak." Claiming that identity felt a lot like claiming being gay, and Eli was not ready to do either. She turned away from those parts of herself and turned toward academic work, focusing intently on art history, in particular on early Christian art. Eli said, "I thought, I want to study art history and get a doctorate and be an art historian. I can't be a priest, so I'll do that."

In her last semester of high school, Eli took a women's literature class. "I actually didn't want to touch it because I thought people would think I was a feminist, and I had this antifeminist thing going on," Eli said. "But the same teacher who taught Russian literature was teaching feminist literature, and I thought she was a great teacher." Eli signed up for the class, but three weeks into it, the teacher had a dispute with the administration of the high school over her contract and left the school. A teacher who had recently graduated from college as a women's studies major replaced her. She turned the class into a feminist theory class. "It rocked my world," Eli said. "It opened my eyes." The image that comes to mind when Eli thinks about his experience in that class is the scene in the movie *The Matrix* when the main character, Neo, is first plugged into the system's software, and all the experiences and information he needs to learn kung fu are downloaded into his brain. "That is what it felt like. I want more. Give me more. Show me," Eli said, imitating Keanu Reeves's voice as Neo. Suddenly, the experiences Eli had been having in high school began to make sense, especially her experiences in athletics, how masculinity and femininity got worked out on the field and the court, how fans called her a "she-man" from the stands. "I became a feminist, and suddenly all this rage came out. I could see stuff that I had seen before but could not make sense of. Suddenly I could see, and I was furious."

Eli had not seen any women priests in the Episcopal Church. Her conservative parish had hired one woman as a priest, but they would not let her celebrate the Eucharist. "The parish was in an uproar over it, and she ended up leaving," Eli said. As she struggled, secretly, in high school with the possibility of being a priest, Eli visited other parishes. One Sunday, Eli attended a small parish in the Sierras, and the interim priest—a woman—delivered the sermon. Eli was in tears.

When Eli's conservative church hired a new rector, Eli confided in him that she wanted to be a priest. The rector was supportive and thought Eli might be just the person to bring the church around on the issue of ordaining women. He suggested Eli talk to his assistant priest, a man named Mike. Eli did, and Mike took Eli under his wing.

The summer before she went to college, Eli worked as a counselor at a sports camp. Eli had just been introduced to the music of the Indigo Girls, and she knew they were gay, could hear it in the lyrics of their early songs. One afternoon, Eli was listening to their music, lying on the grass in the sunshine, and she realized she was gay. It just washed over her.

Despite her counselor's warnings—or maybe because of them—Eli went to a women's college, and she loved it. During the first semester, while procrastinating to avoid writing a paper, Eli was fooling around on the computer in the library and discovered a book called *Womanpriest* by Alla Bozarth-Campbell. Although she had grown up as an Episcopalian, Eli had never heard about the Philadelphia Eleven until she found this book. When she read their story, she knew she was going to be a priest. Eli said, "I read this book, and I was like, there is no doubt in my mind that I will do this. I don't know how. Maybe it won't happen, but if it's up to me I will do this." Soon after, Eli had a spiritual experience in prayer that confirmed her sense of vocation. "I'm not usually one to say the 'voice of God' came through or whatever," Eli said, laughing. "But this was one of those communicative synergistic moments where I was very clear that I somehow needed to try to do that."

Meanwhile, Eli fell in love with Anne. The experience of falling in love with a woman was both exhilarating and traumatic for Eli. "The very first thing I thought about was the priesthood, the very first thing," Eli said. "Because I knew being a priest was something I wanted to do, and it was so important to me, and I thought, I'm losing it. I'm losing it right here, right now." Being gay would make an already difficult process more difficult, if not impossible.

Eli came out to her parents. Then she immediately cut her hair. Eli said, "I thought, forget this. I don't have to try to not be gay anymore."

Mike called Eli and invited her to go with him to a reunion at his seminary, which was known at that time as evangelical and conservative. Eli took the train to meet Mike, and they went directly from the train station to visit one of Mike's mentors. Eli said, "I had done the haircut thing, and a certain butchness is more obvious." The three of them sat down to talk, and Mike's mentor immediately launched into an antigay tirade, seemingly out of the blue. "There are some people in this place who want to allow our married student housing to be open to gay couples," he said. "And it'll be over my dead body." Eli felt her stomach fall to the floor.

It was raining when Mike took Eli back to the train station. Eli remembers looking out the windshield, watching the wipers go back and forth and realizing she needed to tell Mike that she was gay.

Mike said, "I didn't know, but I figured it was a possibility. I guess this wouldn't be the seminary for you."

Eli returned to school and found an Episcopal church through a friend at a neighboring college. The church had an incredible woman priest who wore men's suits and was in her seventies. Eli adored her. Although it was quite an ordeal to get to the church from school, Eli took the bus there every Sunday. Anne was raised Roman Catholic and was wary of organized religion, but she was intrigued enough by Eli's stories about the priest that she decided to attend. On the first Sunday that Anne went to church with Eli, the liturgy was Eucharistic Prayer C. "The one with the planets and the sun," Eli said. "And Anne burst into tears. She felt like she had come home."

Mike told Eli that she needed to talk to the rector at her home church in Washington and tell him she was gay. He advised that Eli not let it be a secret. "It's one thing for you to be a woman who is presumably straight to be ordained out of that church," he said. "But if you are gay in addition, that's another thing, so you'll have to see what he says." When Eli went home that summer, she met with the rector and told him she was gay. He pointed out that it was already a huge stretch for the congregation that she was a woman who wanted to be a priest. If Eli was gay, it would be too much. The issue would split the parish, so Eli should seek support from another congregation. And when she came out to a future sponsoring parish, he added, she should emphasize that she wanted to be a priest—a priest who happened to be a woman and gay, not a "gay priest" or a "woman priest."

That was not the last time Eli heard the "priest who happens to be a woman" or "priest who happens to be gay" kind of reasoning. Whenever he hears this argument, Eli wants to ask, "What does that mean?"

The rhetoric, Eli insists, is about containment, and it reveals the fear that is behind the resistance to ordaining gay people to the priesthood. "If you let gay people be priests, then what else is going to happen? If you let trans people be priests, then what? If you let gay people get married, then what?" Eli said. "Well, the answer is, we don't know. You don't know. People want to say, oh no, that doesn't mean that a whole bunch of other things are going to happen that might scare you. You know, it could. Norms change. And we have to sit with that. There is a lot of ambiguity. As much as we like our Anglican middle way as a political strategy to appear to be moderate, it is really a call to get better at sitting with ambiguity. That doesn't mean that we automatically are good at it, because we very much are not. We're working on it. I think we're on the right path. There is hope."

Eli was a religion major in college. Much like her feminist awakening in high school, Eli had a theological awakening when she encountered feminist theology. She fell in love with the process of looking at theological systems and imagining how they might be better. And yet, she found herself dissatisfied with feminist theology. The politics were not progressive enough, and their theology was not, in Eli's words, "thick enough." Eli said, "They weren't doing the classical stuff, like incarnation. They focused on the social justice-oriented Jesus, which I like. I'm totally down with that, but it wasn't satisfying for me. It didn't feel like..." Eli paused, looking for the right words. Then he started again. "If I were going to articulate a theological system, I wouldn't have that be my center."

Because of her conversation with the priest at her home church, Eli knew she could not apply to the ordination process in Washington. Knowing that she would be required to get a master's of divinity as part of the ordination process, and wanting to discern her call more deeply, Eli decided to apply to graduate school before she applied to the ordination process. She and Anne applied to graduate schools together, Eli to master's programs and Anne to doctoral programs in physics, and they chose to attend schools in the same city.

During the first semester in graduate school, Eli reread the Definition of Chalcedon, a doctrinal formula written in 451 C.E. A compromise between two factions within Christianity that understood

Jesus's divinity differently, Chalcedon emphasizes Jesus's "two natures" in "one person": Christ is "recognized in two natures [one human, the other divine], without confusion, without change, without division, without separation; the distinction of natures being in no way annulled by the union, but rather the characteristics of each nature being preserved and coming together to form one person and subsistence, not as parted into two persons, but one and the same Son and Only-begotten God the Word, Lord Jesus Christ." As Eli pondered that definition, something about it struck her as queer—the paradox of Christ's identity, two and yet one, distinct and yet inseparable. She read it and thought, "That's the Christology that's in my bones."

While at divinity school, Eli tried to find a church to attend so she could enter the ordination process in that diocese. She first went to a large and very wealthy church because her mentor, Mike, was now working there. Mike told her she would have to wear a skirt, that her discernment committee would need to see a professional, feminine person when they looked at her. Anne and Eli attended the church and happened to show up during stewardship season. Even though several homeless people were part of the congregation, the person who stood in the pulpit asking for money seemed to assume everyone in the congregation had as much money as she did.

Although the church was vibrant and ran great programs, Eli could not call that church home. "Class dynamics are really wrapped up with gender norms," Eli said. "The more upper class you get, the more rigid the gender norms can get, as far as dressing up is concerned. Working classness can allow you to be more casual, and when you are more casual, you can be more gender transgressive, and it isn't perceived as transgressive to the same extent." Eli explained to me how difficult it is for people who are gender transgressive—whether they identify as trans, or gay, or straight—to get jobs in professional work environments. In most professional settings, the expectations for how people will dress are highly gender bifurcated: Women wear one kind of clothing, and men wear another.

After that church, Anne and Eli visited a local church that had an out lesbian rector. "There were plenty of queer folks in the pews, and plenty of nonqueer folks," Eli said. "And we have a lot of developmentally delayed people there. It is a neighborhood parish. It is a very real place, and people can just be who they are." Signed up for an internship at this church, Eli entered the ordination process as an out lesbian.

And then, new "gender stuff" started to surface for Eli, and Eli didn't know what to do with it. Eli had been exposed to the umbrella notion of transgender, a way of thinking about being gender transgressive in general, and Eli thought maybe that term could include her. Leslie Feinberg's book *Transgender Warriors* had just been published, and Eli rode her bike to a local feminist bookstore and bought it. Eli said, "I was terrified to put the book on the counter. I was like, how can I enter the ordination process when this is unresolved? I don't know what to do. They could never deal with this. I don't even know where it is going."

And then the senior warden of Eli's church died. He was in his fifties, and he had cancer. Eli said, "That process of going through his death and wake and funeral totally wrenched my attention away from the gender stuff, and I was grateful for that. I was like, death. I can think about death. Let's do death." The parish held an all-night vigil. The coffin was at the back of the church, open, and people gathered all night to pray around it. The following morning, watching the rector lead the congregation through that ritual, through their grief, confirmed that Eli was ready to move forward in the ordination process. "I was like, okay, I'm ready to put my bread on the water and see what happens," Eli said.

Eli confided in the rector about struggling with what it might mean to be transgender. She was the only person other than Anne that Eli talked to about it. The rector was very supportive, and suggested that Eli needed to take the gender issues to a therapist and work them through, but Eli could not deal with that yet. "I just couldn't," Eli said. "I wouldn't dare do it."

Instead Eli entered a Clinical Pastoral Education program at a local hospital. She was the chaplain, by choice, on the unit in the hospital that had the highest death rate. "I immersed myself in death," Eli said. Although Eli had intended to write her master's thesis on Chalcedon, she could not face it anymore because it was too connected to what she was afraid was going on in her own body. Instead, she chose to write about death, focusing on the crucifixion.

Eli knew that in addition to becoming a priest, she wanted to get a doctorate. Although Eli was advised not to tell anyone about wanting to apply to doctoral programs because the process favored parish ministers and not academics, Eli decided to be honest. "I was just like, forget it. I'm not going to lie. I know this is part of my vocation. I don't know what's going to happen with it, but I have to put it out there, that I'm going to do this." Eli was also open about being a lesbian with a partner.

As soon as Eli was no longer in school, Eli could not stop thinking about gender. And, like a good academic, Eli decided to read more about it and bought as many books as she could about transgender issues. Anne started getting nervous. Anne was a lesbian, in relationship with a woman. What would it mean if Eli transitioned to become a man?

Eli began to wonder when she would need to tell her bishop what she was thinking about. At first, Eli justified the choice not to say anything because Eli had no plans to do anything physical about the things she was feeling, no plans to alter her body in any way. But then, increasingly, what the diocese thought about Eli did not match what Eli was beginning to feel about herself.

Eli discovered a group advertised on a queer women's e-mail list, called FTX, which stood for "Female to ?" Part of Eli's fear about transitioning was being plopped into a box, that to choose not to be female anymore would necessarily mean that she was a man. The ambiguity of the "X" appealed to Eli. Like it had for me, Eli's version of feminism at that time made it seem to her that becoming a man would mean abandoning her feminism. "I didn't have a naive idea that I'd be joining the enemy or anything, but it was more like I was participating in gender bifurcation by transitioning, that's the way I saw it. There was no way to understand transition as anything other than assimilation," Eli said. Eli started attending the FTX group. "I came to realize that there is no way you can stop other people from assimilating you to the norms that they have," Eli said. "But you can also tweak them, even as you are being placed in the boxes you don't want to be placed in."

Eli attended divinity school, and her diocese required that Eli complete what is called an Anglican year, one year of study at an Episcopal seminary. The powers that be steered Eli away from a known liberal seminary—Eli was feminist enough, they reasoned—and toward one on the East Coast. Her relationship with Anne became a long-distance one. Before Eli left, they talked and talked and talked about what was happening. They decided together that Eli would make the year away about gender discernment.

Eli arrived at seminary and found a spiritual director. Although the spiritual director had never known anyone who was trans before, she walked with Eli through discernment, helping Eli think about embodiment.

Eli began to think about the possibility of chest surgery. "I really didn't want to have scars," Eli said. During graduate school, Eli had encountered theologians who meditated on what the wounds in Jesus's side might mean, the wounds that are part of Jesus's resurrected body. Some called the wounds a kind of womb. Eli said, "It is like Jesus's body has this opening out of which the church is born, and we are always being born, that process of being given birth to is continuous." In a high school art history course, Eli had been fascinated by one particular image of Thomas who, doubting that the visitor was really Jesus, reached out to touch Jesus's side. "Jesus has his hand up above his head, and Thomas is climbing up his side, getting ready to explore the wound. I remember reading the description and underlining it and starring it in the textbook." As Eli struggled with thinking about the scars on her body that chest surgery would leave, Eli remembered this image. "The scars in that scene show that the resurrected body is a body that has died. It is not a body that just survived. It is a body that died, and the scar is the sign of that, and you are invited into that death, into that process of death that leads to resurrection."

Once Eli realized chest surgery was in her future, Eli wondered if it was now necessary to tell the bishop what was going on. Eli thought, "If I just have chest surgery, do I tell my bishop that? Well, no, I don't need to tell him that. Why would he need to know that? Well, maybe he would. I would go round and round and round." Eli was applying to doctoral programs and having panic attacks. "I could not stop throwing up," Eli said. Anne applied for postdocs, and she decided to go to California. Now, instead of being several hours apart, they were thousands of miles apart.

When Eli started a doctoral program on the East Coast, "It was, as my friend Joel puts it, just like the gender rock hit me smack on the head, and there was nothing I could do about it. I had been dealing with it, but living in the not-yetness of it was too much. I couldn't deal with that anymore. At some point that fall I realized my name wasn't right."

Eli was not named Eli at birth. Eli chose the name Eli, looked it up on epregnancy.com and gave birth to himself. And then he realized he would have to tell Anne. "When your own partner has to start calling you by a different name, that's hard," Eli said. "It was very hard for her as it would be for anybody, and she handled it incredibly well, and she did eventually start calling me that, within a couple of weeks." Then Eli called his mom to tell her, and she was very upset. Eli's mother said, "Do you understand? You're going to be a priest! Has anybody done this?"

Eli said, "I don't know, Mom. I don't know, I don't know, I don't know."

"You're going to end up being a poster child!" she shouted.

After Eli's conversation with his mother, all he could do was crawl into bed. Eli was miserable and terrified and exhilarated all at the same time. The process had a sense of rightness to it, and yet Eli was afraid of everything that might be lost—friends, Anne, family, and the priesthood. The next morning, he felt like he had been run over by a truck. Eli went to church anyway, and outside the church, on the yard of the neighborhood day-care center, was a sign: "Now opening: Bright Futures." Eli interpreted the sign as a message that everything would be okay. Eli walked into church, and the priest asked if he would be willing to be one of the readers for the day. Eli said yes. He took the Bible and sat down to look at the readings, and the first reading was from Genesis—the story of Jacob wrestling with the angel. Wrestling with God changes his body. He will always limp. He is given a new name. Eli realized he, too, had been wrestling with God all night and had emerged physically changed and with a new name.

Eli's anxiety and the throwing up continued. He was in therapy. "I wanted to work with someone who was a gender therapist, so that if and when I was ready to deal with this, she could help me," Eli said. "That, in fact, was true, and she was really great and really open. She didn't walk me down any particular primrose path toward transition. It was totally up to me to figure out how I wanted to embody my gender. I really was grateful for that because I felt very empowered to do things at my own pace and in my own time."

Once Eli changed his name, things progressed quickly. "This happens to a lot of people when they are transitioning. It is sort of like they have been holding it back and then suddenly—whoosh—everything happens really quickly, and everyone in their lives is like, slow down! Have you lost it? You've gone off the deep end! But the people who are going through it are like, this is not fast enough because it suddenly becomes clear." What became clear was that Eli wanted to identify as "genderqueer"—gendered in a way that is neither male nor female—*and* as a man. "I went through a tortured journey to try to avoid reifying the gender binary, and then I realized I was called to live out my gender as a man who is genderqueer, to define my own identity as a transman."

Eli realized that his voice—still stereotypically female—kept causing people to plunk him into a box that didn't feel right. His voice became unbearable to him. Anne guessed what was happening before Eli told her. The day Eli realized that he would have to change his voice, Anne called from California. "I had a dream last night that you were transitioning," Anne said. "And I woke up, and I was really upset. I just knew. You are going to transition hormonally. The voice is the next thing to go." They both cried.

Once Eli decided he would change his name, pursue chest surgery, and take testosterone, Eli knew that he had to tell his bishop. He made an appointment. Coincidentally, the week before the meeting, the Episcopal news service sent out a story about a deacon in Oklahoma who had transitioned from male to female. In the story the bishop in Oklahoma sounded supportive of her, but, in the end, her parish protested, and she left the church. Eli brought the article with him. "The bishop was actually quite amazing," Eli said. "He is a good pastor. He freely admitted that he had never thought much about trans stuff before, and he had never known anyone who was trans, but he hoped that I would be willing to help him learn."

During spring break, Eli flew to California for chest surgery. It was scheduled during Holy Week, a time in the church year filled with imagery about Jesus's side wounds. As he began healing, the anxiety began to dissipate. He still threw up occasionally, but he also felt a tremendous sense of peace. About a month after surgery, Eli began taking testosterone. To give himself more space to heal, to let the hormones take effect, and to be with Anne in California, Eli decided to take a year off from both his doctoral program and the ordination process.

Eli has always loved to sing, and one of his fears about testosterone was that he would lose his singing voice, something that happens to some people who transition. But Eli got to keep a singing voice. With his new voice, Eli joined a choir. He sang bass and tenor. "It was weird to adjust the clef that I would look at," he said. "It would especially affect me when I turned pages because my eye would go to the wrong place."

Eli's grandfather also lived in California. He was ninety-two. His nickname for Eli had long been Champ. "Champ," he would say. "What's going on with your voice? You got a little cold?" His grandfather did not really understand what was happening to Eli's body and voice, but he loved Eli, and he made that clear. Eli and his grandfather spent a lot of time together. That year, when Eli transitioned, was the last year of his grandfather's life.

When Eli returned from California, he and the bishop decided he needed to tell the other people in the ordination process with him. Two years before there had been a retreat, and during the weekend, they did an activity called the circle of oppression. Everyone stands in a circle, and the person leading the activity names a particular marginalized group, and if you are part of it, you step into the circle for a moment, and then you step back out again. The activity happened during what Eli calls the oh-my-God-what-do-I-do-about-this-thing time. Eli stood at the edge of the circle praying. "I was like, please don't let this leader separate out transgender from anything else because if she does I'll die because I'll have to step in the circle, and then I will be out." The leader didn't. Instead she said, "If you're gay, bi, trans, or lesbian, step in the circle." Eli did, with lots of other people.

And then the leader said, "If you're a woman, step in the circle."

"And I was like, oh no! What do I do?" Eli didn't step into the circle. He just wiggled his toe a little bit and hoped no one noticed. But someone did notice. She made a beeline for Eli at the end of the activity. "I saw what you did in the circle," she said. "And I don't know how you identify, but my partner identifies as trans."

This time, two years later, with his relationship with Anne intact, Eli returned to the group post–chest surgery and with a deep voice. Eli arrived at the retreat holding copies of a letter he had written telling the other people in the process what was happening. He had to put a name tag on, and he wrote his new name—Eli—even though he had not yet told most people there he had changed his name. The housing for the retreat was divided by gender—men in one wing, women in the other. The organizers of the retreat who knew Eli was transitioning didn't know where to house him. One of the organizers approached him and said, "We put you in no-man's-land. There are some nuns and the bishop in the same house that you're in."

That first night of the retreat Eli had a dream. In the dream he is back in the house where he grew up. The doorbell rings, and he re-alizes he is at a birthday party, his own birthday party. He runs down-stairs and opens the door to let all his friends in, and he looks down and realizes he is wearing a white dress, tied with a yellow ribbon around the middle. "I look at myself in horror," he said, laughing. "And—this is the best part—I think the ribbon should be in the back! The ribbon is in the wrong place! And then I am like, wait a minute, I'm wearing a dress! What is this?" In the dream, Eli runs back upstairs and rummages through his closet trying to find some-thing to wear. And then he woke up. It was time to tell the gathered group that he was transitioning.

After the morning Eucharist, the bishop brought everyone to-gether and said, "I want to tell you something about Eli. Eli is tran-sitioning from being a woman to being a man." He described Eli as courageous. Eli told the group that if anyone had any questions, he would be happy to talk with them. Only one person talked to him. "Everybody else was like, right on," Eli said. That retreat happened during March 2003. That summer the General Convention of the Episcopal Church confirmed the election of Gene Robinson as a bishop.

Part Three

CREATION

MINISTRY

*Finally she called the women to her. "Cry," she told them.
"For the living and the dead. Just cry." And without
covering their eyes the women let loose.*

*It started that way: laughing children, dancing men, crying
women and then it got mixed up. Women stopped crying and
danced; men sat down and cried; children danced, women
laughed, children cried until, exhausted and riven, all and
each lay about the Clearing damp and gasping for breath.
In the silence that followed, Baby Suggs, holy, offered up to
them her great big heart.*

*She did not tell them to clean up their lives or to go and
sin no more. She did not tell them they were the blessed of
the earth, its inheriting meek or its glorybound pure.*

*She told them that the only grace they could have was the
grace they could imagine. That if they could not see it, they
would not have it.*

—TONI MORRISON, *Beloved*

When people discover I was almost a priest, still study theology, and now do not attend church, they often ask, confused, "Are you still a Christian?"

Am I?

The Religious Right has laid claim to some of the most powerful words in the English language: God, life, Christian, morality, patriot, American, family, faith. When I am asked that question, part of me wants to say no, I am not a Christian. I do not want to be associated with what seems to pass in some circles as Christianity in this country—prowar, antigay, antichoice, antiother, antiequality, anti-immigrant. But the other part of me wants to insist that I am a Christian. If I can say I am a Christian, then that stretches boundaries, expands what it means to be a minister, what it means to be a person of faith.

Words like God and life and morality and family belong to everyone. No one group owns these fundamental categories. Elisabeth Schüssler Fiorenza argues that feminists must continue to interpret biblical texts critically not to keep women in biblical religions, "but because biblical texts affect all women in Western society." The same is true for the religious language we use. These words affect all of us. They shape—or misshape—our public policy, our laws, and our foreign policy, determine what happens in our doctors' offices, kitchens, and workplaces. Feminist philosopher Mary Daly writes that for centuries "women have had the power of *naming* stolen from us" and "have not been free to use our own power to name ourselves, the world, or God." Recognizing the damage wrought by religious language not of our own making, Daly engages in renaming, reclaiming, revising, and re-creating. "It is the creative potential itself in human beings that is the image of God," she writes.

The terms, doctrines, and beliefs of Christianity have been hotly contested since the very beginning. Although many Christians seem to forget this, Jesus was Jewish, and so were his earliest followers. Jesus did not think he was founding a new religion. He understood himself as laying claim to Judaism itself. He was a critic, a prophet, a dissident. Christianity was the result of an argument about how to live a faithful life. Its history is marked by change and revolution, schism and dissolution, splintering and breaks.

Christianity—it might be better to write Christianit*ies*—has always been in flux. History reveals that human beings continuously debate what it means to be Christian, to be a person of faith, to follow Jesus. Almost every "new" idea we think we have has been thought before. Ideas considered heretical today were orthodox to someone else in another time. What we understand as Christianity has been changed by institutions, edicts, individuals, and communities, and then changed again by other institutions, edicts, individuals, and communities.

I took a class at Harvard Divinity School on orthodoxy and heresy with Karen King, one of the best teachers I have ever had. During her class, we read *The Gospel of Mary.* Written in the second century, *The Gospel of Mary* disappeared for more than 1,500 years, until a single, fragmentary copy came to light in the late nineteenth century and provided a glimpse into a kind of Christianity that had been lost. The brief narrative presents a radical interpretation of Jesus's teachings. In her book on the text King writes, "It rejects his suffering and death as the path to eternal life; it exposes the erroneous view that Mary of Magdala was a prostitute for what it is—a piece of theological fiction; it presents the most straightforward and convincing argument in any early Christian writing for the legitimacy of women's leadership; it offers a sharp critique of illegitimate power and a utopian vision of spiritual perfection; it challenges our rather romantic views about the harmony and unanimity of the first Christians; and it asks us to rethink the basis for church authority. All written in the name of a woman."

The first six pages of the text are missing, so the version we have begins in the middle of a scene, a discussion between the Savior and the disciples after the resurrection. They are talking about the nature of the material world and of sin. The Savior warns against those who would delude them into following a heroic leader or a set of rules and laws. King writes, "Instead they are to seek the true Humanity within themselves and gain inward peace. After commissioning them to go forth and preach the gospel, the Savior departs." Then controversy erupts. The only disciple in the room who seems to understand Jesus's teachings is Mary. The rest of the disciples are afraid to go out and preach the gospel. If they do, they think they will share his violent fate. Mary comforts them and shares a teaching she received from the Savior in a vision. When she finishes, two of the disciples, Andrew and Peter, challenge her. Peter calls her a liar and insists Jesus never would have shared this with a woman. Mary cries. Levi comes to her defense, telling the people gathered in that room that they should stop arguing among themselves and go out and preach the gospel as the Savior told them to do. The story ends there.

We also read other texts that, like the *Gospel of Mary,* had been excluded from the New Testament, *The Thunder: Perfect Mind, The Gospel of Truth,* and *The Gospel of Thomas,* books that were, for some early Christian communities, sacred and revelatory. They are part of the *Nag Hammadi Library,* a collection of papyrus fragments found by two brothers in 1945 in a jar buried in the desert but not published until the 1970s. When the brothers broke open the jar, they discovered thirteen leather-bound codices (papyrus books) containing more than fifty tractates. Historians believe the books were buried in 400 C.E. and are among some of the earliest texts written by Jesus's followers. Written in Coptic, an ancient Egyptian language, they are believed to be translations of works originally written in Greek.

The Thunder: Perfect Mind is a revelation discourse by a female figure. Imagine if this text had been included as one of the gospels:

> For I am knowledge and ignorance.
> I am shame and boldness.
> I am shameless; I am ashamed.
> I am strength and I am fear.
> I am war and peace.
> Give heed to me.
> I am the one who is disgraced and the great one.

Or this:

> I am the union and the dissolution.
> I am the abiding and I am the dissolution.
> I am the one below,
> and they come up to me.
> I am the judgment and the acquittal.
> I, I am sinless,
> and the root of sin derives from me.
> I am lust in (outward) appearance,
> and interior self-control exists within me.
> I am the hearing which is attainable to everyone
> and the speech which cannot be grasped.
> I am a mute who does not speak,
> and great is my multitude of words.

Or this:

> For what is inside of you is what is outside of you,
> and the one who fashions you on the outside
> is the one who shaped the inside of you.
> And what you see outside of you,
> you see inside of you;
> it is visible and it is your garment.

And those are passages from just one of the forty-seven texts included in the *Nag Hammadi Library.*

When I first began reading these books, I was furious. I felt betrayed, angry that so much information about my own faith, my own religion, had been kept from me. And when some of that anger passed, I felt strangely hopeful. When people lament the state of religion today—how different it is than "the early church," how modernity has perverted "real" Christianity, how things used to be simpler and more clear—they seem to believe there is a pure version of Christianity that we could get back to. Today's multiple denominations, organizations, and interpretations stem from one early church, they think, and if we could return to that one church, then modernity and all its confusion would disappear. In this version of history, the farther back in time you go the less diversity there is. But, in fact, there was no such thing as "the early church." Tracing Christianity back to its origins, you will not arrive at one, unified community. The first Christians had no New Testament, no Nicene Creed or Apostles Creed, no church buildings, no organized and official hierarchy, and no single understanding of the significance of Jesus. The farther back you go, the more versions of Christianity you will find. Early Christians were wildly diverse groups of people with multiple, conflicting, and contradictory opinions about who Jesus was, what meaning they ought to make out of his life and death, and what was required of people who wanted to follow him. When I discovered this in Karen King's class, there seemed to be a new kind of room for me in Christianity.

Courses like Karen's made me fall in love with theology. Theology—words (*logos*) about God (*theos*)—is the study of words human beings have used to talk about and understand God. It is also the study of the effects our words about God have in the world. How we talk about God matters. For me there is radical hope embedded deep within the theological enterprise: Language about God can change the way the world works. My theological mentor at Harvard,

Gordon Kaufman, once told me that asking whether or not there is a God is not the right question. What interests Gordon is not whether God exists but rather what difference human words about God might make. In his book, *In Face of Mystery,* he writes, "The central question for theology...is a *practical* question: How are we to live? To what should we devote ourselves? To what causes give ourselves?" Christian theology that does not contribute significantly to struggles against inhumanity and injustice has lost sight of its point of being. For Gordon—and for me—theological work is imaginative work. Because he takes God's mystery seriously and believes we must always acknowledge our "*unknowing* with respect to God," he understands theology as human construction. The words we use to talk about God are *human* words, infected with our limitations, interests, and biases. We must engage, therefore, in relentless criticism of our faith and its symbols, always knowing we might be wrong.

The word "religion" comes from the Latin verb *ligo,* which means to bind or to tie. When I remember this root meaning, I ask myself what I have chosen to bind myself to. Each of us—religious or not—orients our life toward something. For some, it is success. For others, money. For still others, justice or peace or family or country or love. What we call sacred tells us our most important values. Changing what we value changes what we call sacred; changing what we call sacred changes what we value.

Ministry is theology in action. Like theology, it reveals what we hold sacred, what we value, what gives our lives meaning. The church can fight as hard as it wants against women or gays and lesbians or people of color or trans people, but, meanwhile, ministers like the ones I interviewed are doing the work of justice—loving those who most need it, combating poverty and racism and sexism, including and celebrating everyone. What we bring to the altar alters us.

Many of the women I listened to felt, in one way or another, excluded by religious institutions. Either they were ordained ministers and someone told them they did not belong or they could not find a home in any of the organized religions with which they were familiar. Across the board, when faced with a sense of not belonging—whether being actively excluded or just feeling like they didn't fit anywhere—these women made something new: They invented rituals, women's groups, and new religions; they wrote books, plays, and liturgies; they created life-giving, world-changing spaces where everyone was welcome. They saw what was missing in the structures we call religion, and they fashioned what they needed so that it could be offered to others. They imagined what might be possible, and they brought it into being. Because they knew what it felt like to be raped and have the church remain silent, knew what it felt like to be abused by a minister, knew what it felt like never to hear "she" uttered Sunday after Sunday after Sunday, knew what it felt like to be hated for loving who you love, knew what it felt like to be shut out and shut down and told to shut up, they worked hard to make sure what happened to them would not happen to anyone else.

In an article published in *The Psychological Bulletin* called "The Need to Belong," Roy F. Baumeister and Mark R. Leary argue that "belongingness"—regular and meaningful connection with a person or group of people by whom you feel included—is nearly as essential for human health and well-being as food. The loss of belongingness often has negative effects: maladjustment, stress, behavioral or psychological pathology, and health problems. Being rejected or ignored leads to anxiety, depression, grief, jealousy, and loneliness. People who lose belongingness will attempt to re-create it even under adverse conditions. For example, women in prison, cut off from the communities to which they belong outside the prison (families, religious communities, friendships, neighborhoods), often create surrogate families, assigning each other roles as spouses, children, cousins, grandmothers, and aunts. Youth, when they are not able to connect meaningfully with their families or with teachers or peers in school, sometimes turn to gangs. As Greg Brown sings, "If you don't get it at home, you're going to go looking."

Cut off from the religious community that provided me with a sense of belonging, suffering from anxiety and depression, I started my own community, WomenChurch, at Harvard Divinity School. I created a feminist space where women gathered and used their imaginations to enact rituals that provided healing and fought injustice, a democratic space shaped by whoever attended. We explored what rituals might look like that took our bodies seriously. All emotions were welcome—anger, rage, grief, joy, celebration, frustration. The monthly services were held in the school's chapel, a location that felt wonderfully subversive to me. We danced. We practiced alternative communion rituals. We made body maps, life-sized outlines of our bodies that we then collaged with images, marking our scars and strengths. We celebrated Eve's hunger for knowledge and willful breaking of taboos by eating apples. During one service, we built our own version of the Wailing Wall. Adah Reed brought the scarf her abusive mentor knit for her. She sat on the steps of the chapel and shared her story with us. As she talked about what her mentor did to her, she cut a section of the scarf into pieces. She laid the pieces at the foot of the wall.

Clinging to a community, to a sense of belonging, can come at great cost. I struggled to figure out if I should stay in the ordination process, and then I struggled to figure out if I should stay in the church at all. Leaving the ordination process and the church not only meant leaving a community, part of my identity, and a profession, it also seemed to mean leaving God. If not in the Episcopal Church, then where did I fit? How could I practice my faith? Even more, how could I change the church if I no longer belonged to one? After watching me suffer with migraines and cry through many a dinner, Eric framed the situation differently: If your relationship with the church were a relationship with an abusive boyfriend, you would have left long ago.

How much of a price—emotional, physical, spiritual—do you have to pay to stay in the struggle? What does it mean to belong? Who gets to draw community boundaries? How do you decide whether to stay or to go? Is change best made from within an institution or from without? Who gets to speak for God? The women I interviewed answered these questions differently. Some remained within their institutions, and others left. Some created pockets of transformation on the margins of their churches, and others created entirely new religious communities. Some were ordained, others ordained themselves, and still others did the work of ministry without ordination ever crossing their minds.

Throughout my time in graduate school I was in a women's group with three other women. After my ordination process and my faith dissolved, the women in my group ordained me. "You are called to let your light shine in the world; to be your best, biggest self; and to remember that you are always beloved," they told me. I took vows, promising to work for peace and justice, to care for the world and for myself. They anointed me, laid hands on me, blessed me. They claimed me as a minister when I could not claim myself.

What makes a minister *real*? The emphasis on ordination—a religiously sanctioned and institutionally monitored rite that marks some as ministers and others as not ministers—has resulted both in a narrow understanding of what it means to be a minister and in a failure to claim much of the radical work being done in the world as ministry. At the same time, ministry is a skilled profession that requires, even demands, training, oversight, and institutional accountability. What might empowering people to live their ministries in daily life look like? How would it change the church? How would it change ordination? What might be lost? What gained?

In my interviews, the women to whom I was most drawn were those who took themselves and their ministries seriously, who were comfortable in their own skin, who radiated power and peace and confidence. Sometimes they were ordained within mainline Protestant denominations, but other times they were not. They helped me glimpse what Katharine Jefferts Schori calls "baptismal ministry, total ministry." She said, "Baptism begins a person's vocation to ministry. I think every Christian is called to ministry somewhere, and most of it is in the world, in daily living. I think the vital churches in our denomination are the ones that are equipping people to live their ministries in daily life. Our mission as Christians is to reconcile the world, and yes, a little piece of that happens inside the church walls, but most of it happens out there in the world, and when we are doing our job as an institution, we are equipping people to be reconcilers in myriad ways—on the playground, in work situations, in politics, in restoring creation, in feeding the poor."

The women I interviewed were engaged in total ministry, and in this work they moved in and through structures that have been shaped and defined primarily by men. Part of their ministries involved redefining and reclaiming spaces, terms, and roles from which they had been excluded. Sometimes they had to stake out their territory, to insist that they, too, had a right to a word or a belief or a building. And in so doing, they made room for the rest of us.

Chapter Eleven

CATHOLIC
WOMENPRIESTS

I started writing this book with a definite anti-Catholic-women bias. Why do they stay in the Catholic Church? I thought to myself smugly, as if my own tradition was oh-so-much-less sexist than theirs. The first Catholic woman I interviewed, Nicole Sotelo, set me straight. Not only did I begin to understand why some women remain Catholic, I also discovered (as I mentioned in the introduction) how much more articulate they are about sexism than many of the Protestant women I interviewed, who, no matter what denomination, seem to have internalized sexism. Rather than rage, many Protestant women feel shame. Much in the same way that some Protestant versions of Christianity have been individualized—it is all about the individual's direct and unmediated relationship with God—Protestant sexism has been individualized. Women ministers who endure misogyny, sexism, and oppression in Protestant communities think that what is happening to them is their fault, even when they have an intellectual understanding that what they are experiencing is sexism. What do they have to complain about? they ask themselves. Their denominations ordain women.

The Catholic women I interviewed, on the other hand, understand their experiences of misogyny, sexism, and oppression as institutional and systemic, not simply individual. They also recognize that ordaining women is not the endpoint, but simply the beginning. Those fighting for the ordination of women in the Catholic Church claim the church's radical social justice tradition and expand that tradition to include the rights of women as part of it. There is a huge grassroots movement in the Catholic Church made up of people fighting against poverty, war, and injustice both within and beyond the church. They understand that people of faith make the church what it is, not the hierarchy. As a result, there is a vast difference between the "official" pronouncements of the Vatican and the real, on-the-ground practices of actual church communities. Although the Vatican publishes statement after misogynist statement against the ordination of women and outlining the acceptable role of women in the church, not all Catholics agree with this position. And, in fact, due to a shortage of priests, many Catholic churches are actually led by women.

Nicole was invited to deliver a speech at the 2006 event "Conversation and Celebration of Women Called," held in Santa Barbara, California, and hosted by the Women's Ordination Conference, a group fighting for the right of women to be ordained as priests and deacons in the Catholic Church. In her speech titled, "Woman, why are you weeping?" Nicole placed the fight for women's ordination in the context of the fight against injustice of all kinds. She opened with the story of Mary Magdalene, who arrives at the tomb of her friend Jesus to find it empty. Mary turns from the empty tomb in grief and anger and sees a gardener. The gardener—who turns out to be Jesus—asks, "Woman, why are you weeping?" Nicole transformed this question that Jesus asks the first person to witness his resurrection—a woman—into a question that must be asked of all women:

"Woman, why are *you* weeping?" Nicole asked.

"I am weeping because the nights are cold here in Pakistan where the earthquake shook my home to the ground and buried my husband and children."

"Woman, why are *you* weeping?"

"I am weeping because my child died without medicines in a country where U.S.-imposed sanctions led to the deaths of half a million Iraqis."

"Woman, why are *you* weeping?"

"I am weeping because my church had a Eucharistic synod recently where church leaders were more concerned about continuing the practices of patriarchy than the practices of breaking bread with the hungry and marginalized."

As I sat across from Nicole at my kitchen table, I could see that the oppression of women within the Roman Catholic Church visibly pains her. She carries it in her body, in her eyes. "I see so much potential in the church if we could just get our act together," she said. "My vision is that the church would live out its own teachings on social justice, that it would live out and embody its teachings on God coming into human form, that it would live out Jesus's example of reaching out to those who are marginalized and welcoming them into the fold." For Nicole, the fact that the Catholic Church is organized, with members all over the world, makes it an amazing place for change. "If the church lived out Jesus's message of justice, we could transform the world, and really use our church as a social justice movement," she said. "I think we, as a church, are committing a huge collective sin by not mobilizing ourselves as Jesus hoped we would to transform the world."

As I mentioned earlier, one of the ways the Roman Catholic Church justifies its refusal to ordain women is through a sacramental argument. In the Roman Catholic Church (and in the Episcopal Church, the Eastern Orthodox Church, and some forms of Lutheranism), the communion ritual is not (officially) thought of as a *symbolic* reenactment of Jesus's last meal with his disciples. Instead, the ritual is believed to transform bread and wine into the *literal* blood and body of Christ. The ritual's ability to effect this change depends on the priest's resemblance to Jesus, specifically the priest's biological resemblance. In other words, for the bread and wine to be turned into the body and blood of Christ, the priest must look like Christ, and to look like Christ, the priest must be a biological male: Jesus was male, so the priest must be male. Otherwise, the magic words and hand motions won't work. Bread and wine will remain bread and wine. There is no reason, however—as Mark Chavez points out in *Ordaining Women* and as many Catholic theologians have argued—that this "resemblance" has to rest on biological sex. Jesus was not just male. Jesus was Jewish. He probably had a beard and dark skin. Chavez writes, "Insisting that gender is the primary dimension of literal resemblance between the priest and Christ seems an arbitrary addition to the requirements of the sacrament rather than a straightforward outcome of them."

Well versed in the multiple arguments used to keep women from being ordained in the Roman Catholic Church, Nicole can counter every one of them, as she did in her speech at the conference in Santa Barbara. In the gospels, she reminded her audience, you will not find the sacrament of ordination: Jesus is not ordained, no disciple is ordained, no ceremony of ordination is held or created. The Vatican points to scripture as a reason that women cannot be ordained, but, as Nicole reveals, although Jesus may not have ordained any women, he also didn't ordain any men, either. In fact, Jesus didn't create any formal church structures at all. He didn't divide people into priest and laity. He doesn't ever use the word "priest" in reference to himself or to anyone else. People who used their gifts in various forms of ministry were called by many names, most often prophet, teacher, and apostle. Although when people think about apostles today most imagine the twelve apostles, Elisabeth Schüssler Fiorenza reminded the first audience of the Women's Ordination Conference that all Christians who were eyewitnesses to the resurrection or who were commissioned to do missionary work were considered apostles, and all four gospels reveal that women fulfilled these criteria of apostleship. Quoting Kenan Osborne's book *Priesthood: A History of the Ordained Ministry in the Roman Catholic Church*, Nicole relayed that there isn't any historical evidence of an ordination ritual until the second century. A second-century document, "The Apostolic Tradition," refers to an ordination ritual for *episkopos,* presbyters, and deacons—and when outlining the requirements for episkopos, the document dictates that the person holding this office is required to be at least fifty years old and, as a general rule, the husband of only one wife. So much for a celibate priesthood!

Nicole remembers one day in high school when her religion teacher told the class that the Trinity—the idea that God is simultaneously one and three: Father, Son, and Holy Spirit—was constructed by early male church leaders. "I remember thinking, what?" she said, laughing. "Why had I been going to church for seventeen years and no one had ever told me this? Did they think that people in church could not handle that? I was just stunned. Why had this information been kept from me and my family? Does the church dare to think that people who are not part of the clergy are incapable of handling this information?" This moment of glimpsing the man—or men—behind the curtain and the theological information and history that had been hidden from her infuriated Nicole and opened up new ways of thinking about God. She wondered what ideas about God she might have if she were to dream about possibilities beyond the doctrine that had been handed to her. "I think that opened the stage for me to begin thinking about God the mother. If the Trinity was constructed, then maybe God the father was, too. These are all just symbols for us," she said. "And how beautiful, too, that God is more than just a threesome. God can break through that and be all sorts of great and wondrous things."

During her sophomore year in college at Wellesley, Nicole was invited to a Call to Action regional conference. Call to Action, a movement working for equality and justice in the Roman Catholic Church and society with a membership of approximately 25,000 people, understands the Spirit of God to be at work in the whole church, not just in its appointed leaders. In its mission statement, Call to Action declares that it works to produce a vision of the Catholic Church as it can and should be, promoting a progressive, engaged Catholicism. Nicole and a friend piled into a small car with four other women who had been fighting for church reform since Vatican II and drove to Worcester, Massachusetts, for the conference. Realizing how many other people were engaged in trying to reform the church was a turning point for Nicole. She heard Bishop Thomas Gumbleton give a talk about Iraq and the devastation U.S. sanctions had effected in that country. Nicole and her friend attended a workshop about embodied prayer. "It was an amazing experience," she said. "So embodied and life-giving, like church rarely was, and I remember coming back from that conference and thinking, this is an organization I need to be in touch with. They are truly a living, breathing body of Christ." The Call to Action conference was her first encounter with groups struggling for change in the church. She realized that if there were other people feeling the same things she was feeling, then it would be possible to build a movement.

Nicole is active in Call to Action's Next Generation group, young adults ages forty and under interested in changing the church. Next Generation recognizes that many people who want to change the church end up leaving the church. "We are trying to make a place where they can find community in one another's homes like the early Christians, a place to have a community that will support them as a liminal space until the church does change and rebuild," Nicole said. "You can be part of parish life again." Nicole's group meets once a month. The host decides the format for the evening. "There's usually some sort of fellowship, meal or dessert, meditation, Bible study, even just conversation about a particular issue in the church or spiritual development."

The people Nicole encounters in Next Generation and Call to Action recognize the power and importance of their Catholic traditions. "They don't want to cede that power in their own identity to those who are oppressing women in the church, and so they're staying Catholic and meeting with these alternative communities to support one another in our struggle for change until the church is more open to people," Nicole said. "And not just to women, but to people who are gay, lesbian, bisexual, transgender, and people who disagree with the church about reproductive concerns, and people who believe that the church has moved into a mode that is too ethereal and not as grounded as it should be in addressing issues of poverty."

I asked Nicole what she thought was behind excluding women and GLBTQ people from ordination. "I think the church is scared about unleashing the divine that is within each of us because that is what is most powerful, and that is what our faith is based on," she said. "It is about Christ, who was a human who helped us understand that the divine is also part of being human, and that it was a struggle, and it wasn't anything of perfection." To illustrate her point, Nicole told me the gospel story when Jesus tries to restore sight to a blind man—and, in Nicole's words, "messes up." She said, "He puts some spittle in the man's eye and says, can you see? And the man says, no, I see people but they look like walking trees." Jesus, realizing his first attempt at healing did not work, tries again, laying his hands on the man's eyes, restoring his vision. Then she told me about another time when Jesus made a mistake, the story of Jesus and the Syrophoenician woman (which happens right before Jesus heals the blind man in Mark's gospel). A woman whose daughter has an "unclean spirit" bows down at Jesus's feet and asks him to heal her daughter. Jesus says, "Let the children be fed first, for it is not fair to take the children's food and feed it to the dogs."

The woman answers him saying, "Sir, even the dogs under the table eat the children's crumbs."

Jesus then says, "For saying that, you may go—the demon has left your daughter."

The story has been interpreted as revealing that Jesus had the mistaken idea that his ministry was reserved for certain people and not others. The woman corrects him and expands his vision. Nicole said, "Here a woman says, no, your ministry is for all people, and Jesus says, whoops, you're right. Thanks for telling me." She stopped for a minute, and then she added, "Even though he wasn't able to admit it."

"He called her a dog," I pointed out, and we both laughed.

"He's such a beautifully human symbol for us to see," Nicole said. "We are human, things are messy, but we do have a spark of the divine within us. And I think the church worries—maybe not consciously—that if they were to allow laypeople to develop fully as spiritual beings and to invite all people's ministries and gifts into the church, it would release an amazing divine energy like we've never seen before. I think the church is afraid of that because they have been the ones who have tried to hold on to the power of the divine for so long. They would have to admit that they've been wrong, and that is something that power does not like to do."

Part of the reason Nicole stays in the church is because she understands justice work as spiritual work. "I think the only way transformation is going to happen is through spirituality—not just transforming material structures but really transforming people as well," she said. "Because, as we see with so many of the movements even in the U.S., laws are changed, but people's hearts are not. If we don't have a simultaneous spiritual and heart transformation, it does not matter what the law says. Racism will still occur, discrimination will still occur, sexism will still occur." Even more, at the heart of her decision to continue to work for change within the church is that she holds herself accountable to other women in the church, in particular to the generation of women that will come after her. "I know the pain of being in the church, and I don't want to leave it so yet another generation of women in the church can be hurt by it," she said.

Much of Nicole's academic work in divinity school focused on atonement theology and suffering. Nicole said, "The church, through its atonement theories, valorizes Christ's suffering and uses this against women who are in abusive situations. Women then feel that suffering is okay, and that God wants them to suffer like Christ, and so we have a third to half of women experiencing abuse—sexual, physical, emotional—and many probably because of the church." Nicole insists that ordaining women who would speak out against domestic violence, offer new ways of thinking about God, and articulate theology that is liberating would reduce incidents of domestic violence. "Women who are being abused have to go to another man of power in their church when they need help. He might not understand the situation, and tell them to go back to their abuser. This can be deadly to women," she said. "Having more women ministers in the church would save women's lives." Attending church, listening to exclusively male language for God and for human beings, hearing no women's voices from the pulpit, and seeing no women representing Christ at the altar have real effects. "Every single Sunday women are being subtly told that they cannot be near the divine, that they cannot speak for the divine, that the divine does not speak through them, and I think the psychological effects of that on women the world over are devastating," she said. "And it can be seen in a myriad of ways—women having self-esteem problems, body issues, women trying to get rid of the body so that we can access the divine."

I interviewed Nicole after the Vatican smokestacks revealed that a decision had been made about who would be the next pope: Joseph Cardinal Ratzinger, who was the head of the Catholic Church's Congregation for the Doctrine of the Faith, the group that used to be called "The Roman Inquisition." He was the author of many an anti-woman document, part of his charged task to protect Catholic faith and morals and to discipline any and all who offend them. I asked Nicole how she felt when Ratzinger—now Pope Benedict—was named pope. She told me she was asked the same question on a radio show. The man interviewing her told her that women had been calling the Women's Ordination Conference office crying. He asked Nicole if she had cried. "And I said, no, I haven't cried because I believe in the spirit, and I believe there is always a resurrection, meaning change, so I am hopeful that the spirit will infuse Benedict to recognize that the spirit is not just in him but in all people, and that he will be open to change." There was a long pause as Nicole looked at me, and then she said, "But it is devastating," and dissolved into laughter.

Nicole feels called to use the life she has been given to make a difference in the world. "Particularly, I hope that I'm able to make sure that women are not hurt as deeply as they have been because I feel like I've known some pretty painful things in life, and if I can help change the situation so women don't have to experience my pain or other women's pain, what a joyful thing that will be." Part of this work is making sure that human-made church structures do not "squelch the divine that is within us." Nicole recognizes that simply ordaining women will not create justice in church structures. "Women are not perfect, either. Ordaining women into the current church will not fix things. They will have to be ordained into a re-newed church, into a new priesthood, because otherwise women will just become part of the structures whether they want to or not, and change will not happen," she said. For Nicole, ordination and ministry that are not shaped as a response to a community's suffering are neither ordination nor ministry. If the fight for women's ordination is not situated in a larger fight against injustice, then it misunder-stands ordination itself.

Victoria Rue, the oldest of eight children raised in a Roman Catholic family, is an ordained Roman Catholic womanpriest. She is one of roughly one hundred women who have been ordained as priests or deacons through Roman Catholic Womenpriests, an international initiative within the Roman Catholic Church. Roman Catholic Womenpriests prepares, ordains, and supports women and men to minister and is committed to an inclusive model of church. Like Nicole, Victoria recognizes that including women in the patriarchal, hierarchical priesthood is not enough. "You can't just add women and stir," she said. Feeling called to enter the convent in the late 1960s, she did so a year after she finished college. While she was at the convent, her grandmother died, and Victoria was not allowed to go to the funeral because, according to the rules, her grandmother was not a close enough relative to merit allowing Victoria to leave.

"This was an opportunity for me, according to the mistress of postulants, to understand the vow of obedience," Victoria said. "I did not go to the funeral, but three to four months after that, I decided this was not my calling, so I left. The changes that were coming from Vatican II were coming too slowly for me." When Victoria left the convent, she left the church. The theater became her church, theater audiences her congregation. She also became active in the women's movement in New York City and Los Angeles. And in 1974, she came out as a lesbian. "My relationship with my family was a difficult one, especially with my father, but years later, this, too, would heal."

In the early 1980s, Victoria went on a trip to Nicaragua with a group of other theater artists, and there, she visited a *comunidad de base,* a base community. "I began to see the extraordinary connection between social justice and spirituality," Victoria said. "For the first time, I saw the church involved in social justice issues, how a community of Catholic people was addressing social justice issues. What this meant was making clean drinking water could be an act of prayer. Creating streetlights in a village community was an act of prayer." Liberation theology brought her back to the church. At that time, she met a woman who was attending Union Theological Seminary in New York City. Victoria visited the school and knew immediately that she wanted to study liberation theology there. "But of course I then discovered that there was something called feminist theology," she said, laughing. "And I was amazed that theology, like history, philosophy, and literature, was being created by women."

Victoria began her studies at Union in 1985 and during her time there she met her life partner, Kathryn, who was also a student. Victoria and Kathryn have been together for more than fifteen years. "She's Presbyterian, and I am Roman Catholic, and our differences just feed the richness of our relationship."

In 1988, her last year at Union, Victoria was asked to concelebrate a series of Masses on the sidewalk across from St. Patrick's Cathedral. The Masses were held in response to a letter written by

Ratzinger, the famous "Halloween Letter" that came out in October 1987. In that letter, Ratzinger wrote that homosexuality is an intrinsic moral disorder. "We as gay and lesbian people and those that supported us met on the sidewalk across from St. Patrick's, and I stood next to and concelebrated a Mass with an out gay priest," Victoria said. "That was the first time I was ordained. I was ordained by that community, called out by that community, into the understanding that we are church. Each Mass brought together spirituality and social justice. LGBTQ folks and our supporters did both ecclesial and civil disobedience with our actions. After every sidewalk Mass, we would lie down in the middle of Fifth Avenue and be arrested by the cops. We did this to bring attention to the plight of LGBTQ folks, both in the church and in civil society." Victoria graduated from Union with an MDiv and went on to get her Ph.D. at the Graduate Theological Union in Berkeley, California.

While finishing her doctorate, she started another group with Sister Monica Kaufer called A Critical Mass: Women Celebrating the Eucharist. There was a core of twelve women. "Our goal was to open the door of the priesthood to women. Secondly, to enlarge the very definition of what priesthood means. We created a feminist Mass that utilized the arts, gesture, movement—embodied prayer." For seven years, they celebrated the Mass on the first Sunday of every month in an inner-city park, which happened to be the site of the former Oakland Cathedral that had been destroyed during the 1989 earthquake. "It was a very difficult space. The cops called it 'the snake pit,' because it was a site where homeless people not only lived but also did a lot of drug deals." The members of A Critical Mass would arrive well before the Mass started to clean up the park. "When I say clean up, I mean clean up feces, because no toilets, of course, were provided for homeless people there. So we would clean up the feces, sweep up the park, disinfect it," Victoria said. Eventually, a community of Third Order Franciscans approached them and asked if they might start a feeding program that would accompany A Critical Mass. Approximately 150 to 200 people were fed prior to each Critical Mass, and the park began to transform. One Sunday while they were feeding people and holding A Critical Mass, police cars pulled up near them. "We looked at each other and said, oh no, now what?" Victoria said. The officers approached Victoria and Sister Monica and said, "We just want you to know that your presence here has changed this park, and that if you ever need our help, here are our cards."

After seven years of A Critical Mass, Victoria and Kathryn moved to take teaching positions at St. Lawrence University. "While we were there, the Danube Seven ordinations occurred." On June 29, 2002, a group of women from Germany, Austria, and the United States, the Danube Seven—Christine Mayr-Lumetzberger, Adeline Theresia Roitinger, Gisela Forster, Iris Muller, Ida Raming, Pia Brunner, and Angela White—were ordained on a boat on the Danube by a Roman Catholic bishop named Rómulo Antonio Braschi, whose orders are recognized as "valid but illicit" by the Roman Catholic Church. The Danube Seven had been preparing for their ordinations for several years before that moment on the river.

The Roman Catholic Church subscribes to the doctrine of apostolic succession, that is, it is believed that a line can be traced from every bishop and priest now ordained back to St. Peter. It is both a symbolic line—the present-day church is the same church as the church founded by Jesus and the twelve apostles—and a literal one—Peter laid hands on his successor, who laid hands on his successor, who laid hands on his successor. Ordination, which is a sacrament in the Roman Catholic Church, changes the ordained person's being, his (and now her) ontology. It cannot be undone. While apostolic succession and ontological change are key arguments used to oppose women's ordination, once women were ordained by Roman Catholic bishops, these same arguments worked to the women's advantage. Now these seven women had been touched by hands that had been touched by hands that had been touched by hands that had been touched by St. Peter. They, too, had been ontologically changed. It could not be undone.

But they could be excommunicated. And they were. Immediately.

Not one of the priests convicted of pedophilia has been excommunicated.

Following the Danube Seven's excommunication, several other bishops came forward and said they would be willing to ordain any or all of them as bishops, which would grant the women the power to ordain other women to the priesthood. The bishops, in very good standing with the Vatican, asked that they remain anonymous. Two of the Danube Seven stepped forward to be ordained as bishops, Christine and Gisela. "They were ordained bishops in secret, duly notarized, and promises were made not to reveal the identity of the male bishops who had performed the ordinations," Victoria said.

After Christine and Gisela were ordained as bishops, a preparation program for womenpriests was put in place. "A Web page was created, and word started to go out that there were now women bishops, and ordination in the traditional way was going to be available to qualified Catholic women," Victoria said. Women who enter this preparation program are required to have a master's degree in theology. In conjunction with this educational component, women take ten additional units through the preparation program, a distance learning program. Each woman is also partnered with a mentor, some of whom have been members of Corpus, the national organization of married Catholic priests that promotes an expanded and renewed priesthood of married and single men and women in the Catholic Church.

In the summer of 2002, sitting at her computer, Victoria learned that Christine and Gisela had been ordained as bishops. "By chance, I had met Christine in 2002 in Rochester." Victoria e-mailed Christine and asked if she would ordain her. Christine e-mailed Victoria back, writing, "I would be most happy to do that." Victoria said, "We talked, and she knew I had not only a master of divinity, but a Ph.D. in theology, and frankly that is more education than most priests have. However, I did want to go through the preparation program that she had created."

Victoria was mentored by a member of Corpus, a former Jesuit, Don Cordero. Their relationship has changed them both. Victoria learned liturgical practice from Don, and Don learned from Victoria that womenpriests are not simply becoming priests but are changing what it means to be a priest. "He realized that we don't want to just put on cassocks," Victoria said. "I can learn from him the rubrics of the Eucharist that he was taught some years ago, and he can learn from me that I am already revisioning that Eucharist. It is a mutual learning, a mutual transformation."

Victoria completed the preparation program, and in the summer of 2004, she went to Europe to be ordained as a deacon by Christine and Gisela along with five other women in a boat on the Danube. Ordinations are held on rivers for symbolic reasons—"Jesus taught from boats, and the church itself is often spoken of as a kind of boat"—and for practical reasons: Boats on rivers are outside the jurisdiction of dioceses, and, as Victoria pointed out, "you can control who gets on a boat." She said, "It was a joyous occasion, and a beautiful one. The idea of women lying down on the floor of a boat in prostration was such a different idea than on marble floors. The water was moving under the boat, and this was the flow of change, the spirit moving and creating new things." The Danube has a series of locks that control water flow. "Just as the boat was released from the last lock, we received our deacon stoles," she said. "My dear parents were there, and they are both eighty years old. It was an extraordinary moment for all of us on that boat."

Ordained a deacon, Victoria returned to California and started a house church that has since grown into the Sophia Catholic Community. It has thirty members. Victoria also began a new position teaching Women's Studies and Comparative Religious Studies at San Jose State University. During the summer of 2005, Victoria was ordained a womanpriest with three other women on the St. Lawrence Seaway. "After ordination, with no models to observe, I asked myself, what does being a womanpriest mean? How will this change my ministry? Does it change my ministry?"

Roman Catholic women are not all in agreement about how to answer these questions. Some do not think ordaining women is the way to transform the church. For these women, the distinction between lay and cleric is inherently problematic. Elisabeth Schüssler Fiorenza argues that instead of a church in which some are ordained and others are not, we should work to create a priesthood of all believers. In a keynote address delivered at a Women's Ordination Worldwide conference she said that "to be able to call ourselves Reverend, to wear the clerical collar, to don clerical vestments...to receive the 'indelible' mark of ordained hierarchical priesthood" will not transform the church into "a discipleship of equals." She called on those present to end their fixation with ordination and to focus on and acknowledge the varieties of ministries women are already performing. At one point in her speech, she invited feminists to stand and be blessed by the community, claiming the work they already do—teaching, preaching, dancing, healing, caring for the earth—as ministry. She then quoted Rose Wu: "To renew the Church and exorcise it from all forms of oppression, we must tackle the root causes of all these problems. To me, it is a choice between whether we want a community that shares power or whether we want power to be held by only a few."

Others insist that women ought to wait for the Vatican to allow women's ordination. Victoria said, "There are women who are opposed to what we are doing, who feel we should wait until the Vatican opens its door, until it is official, and we shouldn't be stepping out and going forward ourselves." Some of this resistance is pragmatic. The Roman Catholic Church funds programs all over the world that are essential to survival for some communities—feeding programs, schools, health clinics, the list goes on and on. To support the few women seeking ordination would mean putting these programs—putting human lives—at risk.

Victoria asked herself whether she should wait, or whether she should move forward. "I have been waiting a very long time in my life. I think women have been waiting for 2,000 years," she said. "In December, I will be sixty, and in my lifetime, I am not going to wait, and so I stepped forward. I don't think Jesus would be asking us to wait."

Although Victoria, like Elisabeth, firmly believes that we are all priests by our baptism, she also recognizes the importance of ordination for women's leadership in the church. "I feel very strongly that women should be ordained as priests because we need women as leaders in the church, liturgical leaders as well as sacramental leaders." And yet, she emphasized over and over again that hers is only one kind of ordination. Other kinds of ordinations are happening in grassroots Catholic communities all the time. Communities are calling people forward—gay, straight, and married men and women—as leaders and are ordaining them in rituals of their own design. "In my mind, there is no difference between their ordinations and my ordination. I think what is really important as we begin to create a renewed priestly ministry is that each of us, however it is that we are ordained, comes forth from communities."

Women being ordained as womenpriests are walking a fine line between tradition and revolution. By becoming priests, they are forced to take on the baggage that comes with that term and position, and yet, by being womenpriests, they are transforming the term and creating something new. "I am very aware that we as women must not re-create the oppressive, hierarchical structures that we have been in for 2,000 years," she said. "And what a struggle that is. Women who have been kept out of power and kept out of authority for 2,000 years have to be incredibly vigilant. How can we create democratic, accountable, transparent structures? What does it mean to be a bishop? And, of course, then you ask, well, what does it mean to be a priest?"

"So what does it mean to be a priest?" I asked.

"A priest is, I think, ordained to call forth the gifts of the community. I think a priest can also be ordained to liturgical leadership, which is not to say that there cannot be other people in liturgical leadership," Victoria said. A priest invites people into sacraments, what Victoria understands as "doorways of grace." She insists that sacraments, like the priesthood, must be reimagined. "The sacraments need to be looked at anew. Of course, the language needs to be changed, which then begins to change the theology. And we need to also reimagine the authority inside the sacraments. Is it just one person who does anything?" As an example, she pointed to the sacrament of marriage and the fact that the traditional church now understands that the priest is a witness to two people who are marrying themselves. "That's what I think the sacraments in general should be about. The priest is simply a facilitator to what people are doing. Also, perhaps there are more than seven sacraments. Perhaps giving birth is a sacrament."

In some ways, Victoria understands her ordination not as something that flies in the face of tradition but as something that returns the church to its tradition. "Bishops in the early church were members of the community. They were married. They were leaders. Their responsibility was toward the spiritual life of the community," Victoria said. "They weren't CEOs of vast landholdings. They weren't CEOs of big bank accounts, which is what they are now, with no accountability to people, which is why we are in this terrible mess with pedophilia. Cardinals and bishops think of themselves as above the law. This is medieval. This is wrong."

Listening to Victoria, I could tell that she struggles with how to live out her ordination in a way that is new, radical, liberative. And yet, just the fact of her ordination, just the fact that she is an out lesbian, university professor, theater-loving, female Roman Catholic priest means she is already reshaping what it means to be a priest.

The day before I interviewed her, Victoria helped to start a new faith community. With her mentor from Corpus and two women in various stages of the ordination process to become womenpriests, they are creating a new Catholic community that will meet every Sunday in the nondenominational chapel at San Jose State University. Thirty-five people attended their first gathering, including students from San Jose State and from neighboring colleges and universities. "Yesterday we had students there from Santa Clara University, which is a Jesuit University," Victoria said. "The Jesuits probably would invite a womanpriest if they could to come and celebrate at Santa Clara, but the Vatican, of course, would deeply frown on this—probably more than frown, probably take away their charter. At any rate, we are appealing to students at Santa Clara University who would like not only to experience a Eucharist that is embodied but also build a community that is welcoming."

During the Eucharist, the entire congregation consecrates the bread and the wine, not just the priests. "After we tell the story again, we turn to one another, and we take hold of a person's hands or their shoulders, and we look at each other and we say, 'This is my body. This is my blood.' We do this as the mystical body of Christ. It isn't just about the bread and wine. It is the people gathered who are the body of Christ."

One of the people who attended the first service was a seven-year-old Vietnamese American girl named Vee. After the service, Victoria was standing talking to another member of the group, and Vee came and stood next to her. She stands as high as Victoria's hip. "She grabbed hold of my waist, and she said, 'This is my body!' With a big exclamation point behind it," Victoria said. "She knew exactly what that meant. And that is what fuels me."

"I have one technical question: Were you excommunicated?" I asked.

"No, I have not been, and none of us in the USA have been," she said. "If they did excommunicate us, Sarah, it wouldn't matter at all, and that is because we come from communities, and it wouldn't matter to the communities."

Chapter Twelve

MINISTER (N.)
VS. MINISTER (V.)

Minister (n.): clergyman, cleric, ecclesiastic, pastor, shepherd, parson, dominie, man of the cloth, servant of God, reverend, father, padre, priest, liturgist.

Minister (v.): serve, care for, attend to, wait on, accommodate, oblige, befriend, favor, help, aid, assist, abet, succor, relieve, comfort, console, give solace; nurse, heal, cure, remedy.

For the first year that I worked at the Episcopal Church as the director of children's and youth ministries, my office was down the hall from the rector's office. Halfway through my tenure there, the church hired another person who was ordained. The rector told me that I would need to move upstairs so the new priest could have my old office. She wanted all the ordained people to be on the same floor.

That move was one of the most outright ways I was told I was not a real minister, that because I was not ordained, I was somehow less than those who were. The relocation occurred soon after my discernment committee fell apart and I withdrew from the ordination process. I moved from the second floor to the third, and then out of the building—out of the sanctuary—altogether.

The rector probably didn't mean for the move to be so symbolic. I imagine it was a pragmatic decision, not a personal one. But I took it personally. I already struggled to take myself seriously as a minister, to see my work as legitimate. My whole life I have looked outside myself for approval—to parents and teachers, to mentors and supervisors. This need for approval is the underside of my desire to be ordained. This is sanction that is visible—worn as robes and collars. What better source of approval could there be than the church, than God?

The dissolution of my ordination process forced me to stop looking for outside approval. I didn't need the rector to take me seriously as a minister—maybe she did—I needed to take myself seriously as a minister. As Claudia Highbaugh reminded me, "You have to figure out how to know that your call and your work are satisfactory to the cosmos as opposed to the institution because a lot of times the institution doesn't want you to succeed."

Tristy Taylor and Callie Janoff, cofounders of the Church of Craft, unapologetically ordained themselves, and I was drawn to them immediately.

Growing up with a revolutionary UU minister as a father, Tristy spent a lot of time in churches. Her mother had a regular nine-to-five job, so her father, with a more flexible work schedule, was her primary caretaker. "I went to every kind of service imaginable. I spent a lot of time in church," she said. "But I didn't really feel a deep connection to any of those organized religions."

Callie's parents were "various degrees of agnostic." Her father came from a Jewish background but was never religious, and her mother came from a secular Protestant background. "Neither of them practiced when I was a kid, and they were kind of hippies who were really interested in their kids finding their own way," she said, laughing. Although she did not feel like she belonged in any specific religious tradition, Callie still understood herself as spiritual. "I didn't think of myself as a secular person. I thought of myself as a vaguely spiritual person without a religious home, which served me fine for the better part of my young adulthood."

A few years after college, Callie's friends started getting married. "It turned out that all of my friends were having a difficult time finding the right person to perform their ceremonies," she said. "And it didn't seem like a big deal at the time, but one of them asked me if I would perform their ceremony, which sounded really fun." After that first wedding, Callie performed three weddings in one month. She said, "It ended up being more intense than I was prepared for. In a lot of ways it was a spiritual awakening—to be in front of these people and realize there was this totally mystical thing happening that was created by and centered on love and was divine, which begged the question, so, you're spiritual for real, what does that mean? What do you believe? How does God manifest in your life? What does God mean? All kinds of questions like that came up, and I didn't have a lot of answers, and I didn't really know where to go looking for them because my experiences with organized religion had left me cold."

While wrestling with these questions, Callie realized her spiritual practice was tied to her experience of being creative—making artwork, making objects, and making creative decisions in life. "That is when I feel most connected to the divine, or to the God within, however you want to call it," she said. "Which was interesting, and certainly not without precedent. It is a really old idea that creativity is a way to connect with God."

The more excited Callie got about her idea that being creative was a spiritual practice, that making art connected her to the God within, the more people she talked to about it. "And it really captured a lot of people's imaginations, like, oh yeah? Me, too! That is exactly how I think about God, or what I wish religion was, or how I see that happening in my life. The more I talked about it, the more it got around and eventually trickled over to this acquaintance of mine from college named Tristy."

Although they did not know each other well at the time, Callie and Tristy went to college together at the University of California, Santa Cruz. After college, Callie moved to New York City, and so did many of Tristy's friends. Tristy would make an annual pilgrimage to the city. Tristy's friends were friends with Callie, and so they hung out a few times. During one of Tristy's visits, Callie shared with Tristy that she was feeling a call to ministry, and that to marry several of her friends, she had gotten ordained online as a minister in the Universal Life Church. She was in the process of looking for a seminary she might be able to attend, but she could not find a fit. "She kept talking about art and this idea of the church of craft," Tristy said.

Tristy was elated to hear Callie talk about making as a spiritual practice. In San Francisco, where Tristy lived, she had been holding monthly gatherings she called "craft-ons"—"Like, getting your craft on," she said—because she was surrounded by creative, art-making people. "I was noticing my friends saying stuff like, I made this, and I make a lot of stuff, but I am alone when I do it, and I wish I could just go out and make stuff with other people, so I thought, why don't we do that?" She started Sunday afternoon craft-ons, and she realized that they felt like church to her.

When Tristy and Callie talked with each other, each felt like she had discovered the other half of the equation. They were electrified by the idea that they could create a religion from scratch. Callie took Tristy downstairs and ordained her as a minister of the Universal Life Church on the Internet, and Church of Craft was born in 2000 in New York City.

The Church of Craft became a sensation almost overnight. "We accidentally found ourselves on that craft resurgence train that started happening right about that time," Tristy said. "The train is still rolling pretty hard." They were interviewed by the *New York Times,* the *Village Voice,* and National Public Radio (NPR). They are also the subject of a documentary directed and produced by Samantha G. Wiesler. In the spotlight, with all sorts of people paying attention to them, Callie and Tristy had to construct their statement to the world. "We had to get our structure built very quickly," Tristy said. "People were really examining us and poking at our structure and saying, what the hell are you guys doing? What is this? How dare you call yourselves a church! We just got thrown into this pit, really like a lion's den, and we held our own."

Tristy and Callie's choice of the word "church" in Church of Craft was intentional, although they have taken a lot of heat for it. "The word 'church' can be a little prickly," Tristy said. "It is not actually owned by Christians. The true dictionary definition is 'an association of people who share a particular belief system.' It originated from the pre-Christian Germanic term *kirka*."

When Tristy and Callie were on radio talk shows, people would call in to yell at them for using the word "church" and not being Christian. "I think that was part of it," Tristy said. "But thinking about it now, I think there was anger about my being a woman, and about two women starting their own church."

Initially, the people who attended Church of Craft—in San Francisco and in New York City—were their friends. "I sent out an e-mail to everyone I thought would be interested, and a lot of them came, and it totally snowballed from there. People would bring their friends or forward the e-mail on to other people they thought would be interested. Month by month we were collecting more new, interesting, different people," Callie said. "And before we knew it, I had an e-mail list of about 250 people who wanted to be kept abreast of things." Tristy had the same experience on the West Coast. They asked a friend to set up a Listserv and a Web site for the Church of Craft (http://www.churchofcraft.org/), and once the Web site was up and running, people started to find them. "We really haven't done anything in terms of marketing or recruitment or missionary work per se, although that would be my fondest desire," Callie said.

"Missionary work?" I asked.

"Totally," she said. "Missionary work for the Church of Craft. I imagine a cross-country tour in a yellow school bus."

All kinds of people show up at the Church of Craft's monthly gatherings, which are now held in cities all over the world. "Very religious people, seminary students, proclaimed atheists," Tristy said. Most Church of Craft communities meet once a month. Meetings are free form, with people wandering in and out, pulling out their craft of choice, and getting to work. In one short film made by Gotham TV about the group Callie leads in New York City, you can see people making kites, sweaters, lights, photo journals, hemp bracelets, vests, kinetic paper sculptures, cookies, and a skirt.

Tristy's Church of Craft community in Oakland meets in an art gallery. "We settled into a great place called the Rock Paper Scissors Collective, a funky gallery that is funded by the city of Oakland, a place for people to craft."

In addition to being a Universal Life Church minister, Callie is an ordained Church of Craft minister. Because Church of Craft in New York is incorporated as a religious corporation, the organization has the legal right to ordain its own ministers. Callie was ordained during a tea party at the house of a friend who is a trustee of the Church of Craft. Tristy is an interfaith chaplain. She attended the Chaplaincy Institute for Arts and Interfaith Ministries, an interfaith seminary in Berkeley. The ordination program consists of eleven one-week modules, each focusing on a different religious tradition. "Five days each month, from 9 A.M. to 9 P.M., intensive," she said. "They call them intensive for a reason. Every month is a different faith tradition, as well as a different aspect of ministry—weddings, hospitals, prisons." The program requires that those in training engage in personal, self-searching work. "The idea is that we cannot ask other people to do that unless we have done it ourselves," she said.

When they started Church of Craft, Tristy and Callie had no idea their organization would last the seven years that it has. It is still going strong, even growing. "We weren't thinking about how it would become an international organization and we would be on NPR talking about it. It grew on its own. And when that happens, I have to trust God that it's right," Tristy said.

"Do you do it full-time?" I asked.

Tristy laughed hysterically, and when she caught her breath she said, "Don't I wish! There is currently no cash flow whatsoever involved in the Church of Craft, which I kind of like." She is a spiritual director and a Web designer, she sees clients for dream work, and she works in a bookstore on the weekends. "I look at my friends—friends who are getting ordained, an Episcopalian friend, a UU friend just ordained—I see them going through the process, getting placed in a church, getting their community, even though I know it is not a bed of roses, and they are struggling in that process, I still look at that and think, they have structure, they have a community, they have a church, they don't have to build it from scratch, they have a building they can go to," Tristy said. "There is definitely part of me that wishes there were more structure around creative, revolutionary ministry, a way to provide for all of us. It is exhausting to be hustling all the time for money, especially in the Bay Area, where our rent is astronomical, our food is astronomical, gas is astronomical. It is paralyzing sometimes. It is hard to do the work. I have to be the administrator, the bill payer, find the best jobs for me, wrangle my schedule. It is exhausting trying to find a path."

On her side of the country, Callie does not do Church of Craft work full-time either. She does freelance business management for artists, helping artists realize they are independent contractors. She said, "To be a successful artist you have to be a successful business-person, and so a lot of what I do is run the business of their art business for them. I make sure that all the businessy stuff is taken care of so they can be creative." As for her own art, Callie considers the Church of Craft her primary art project at the moment.

When I interviewed Tristy she had just heard an NPR story about the birth of Pentecostalism, that it started with an itinerant preacher who could not find a home anywhere and set up a tent in the middle of nowhere and started preaching. People started showing up. "I talk about that with my husband," Tristy said. "But I think I struggle with the ego part of that. I don't know what people need—only they know what they need."

Callie and Tristy help people believe that they have everything they need to live fulfilling lives, that they can create lives that have meaning and make the world a better place. It is nearly impossible to create a powerful institution based on the idea that each of us has everything we need to be the best person we can be, that God is inside me and inside you and inside of everyone else. You cannot institutionalize that. You cannot maintain power that way, because it is the opposite of maintaining power. It is about empowering everyone.

After I interviewed Tristy and Callie, I went online to determine just how one goes about starting her own religion in the United States. I thought I would be able to find a "start your own religion" link on a government agency Web site, like, for example, the IRS Web site. The process is a little more undercover and a lot more complicated than that, but very doable.

I e-mailed Callie and Tristy to ask if I could talk to them again about the nuts and bolts for starting your own religion, and I ended up talking with Callie on the phone while she was in a Laundromat in New York City felting some old sweaters.

When we talked, Callie reminded me that you don't need governmental permission to get a group of people together. "You just start," she said. "You don't need any kind of sanction from the government to meet and have a nonfinancial relationship with your religious practice. There is no reason you cannot just proclaim it a religion and make that happen." The question of governmental involvement only comes up if it is important to you to be able to perform rites and rituals that the government oversees, marriages, for example, or if you would like people to be able to donate money to your organization.

In the beginning, Tristy and Callie held Church of Craft meetings and did not feel any need to be a religious organization sanctioned by the government. Two years into it, Callie—running the Church of Craft on the East Coast—thought it would be wonderful if her community could rent their own space. There was a lot of enthusiasm for the Church of Craft and people were willing to donate money to purchase a permanent space. Callie knew that if people donated money, they would want their donations to be tax deductible. She began to research what she would need to do to make that possible. She discovered that the Church of Craft could become a religious corporation, and she used a Nolo legal guide for starting a not-for-profit to figure out how to do that. The requirements for becoming a religious corporation vary from state to state, even from county to county.

She researched New York state law online—"which was insane!" she said—and learned what she would need to do for the Church of Craft to become a religious corporation. She arrived at the government office with, she thought, all the necessary paperwork. The woman at the desk looked at what she presented and said, "No, no, no. It has to say this, and this, and this." Callie left the office, made the necessary changes, and returned to try to file her paperwork. Again, she was told what she had done wrong. She went home and tried again. The third visit to the office was the charm. The woman helping Callie reached underneath her desk and pulled out a piece of paper—"a crappy Xerox copy that they had under the desk"—that listed the guidelines for becoming a religious corporation. Callie followed the directions, and the woman looked over what she had done. "Then she stamped it and sent me on my way." Callie paid the required fee ("around $115") and the Church of Craft was officially a religious corporation.

I asked Callie if she would say she started a religion, even if they had not become a religious corporation.

"What makes something real or true?" Callie asked. "It is not like it is all figured out and hard and fast. You make those decisions as you go. What makes something real or true is if you believe in it. You don't need anyone to anoint you."

Even though I know being an Episcopal priest is no longer the right path for me, I still harbor secret fantasies that someday a bishop from an Episcopal diocese will call me on the phone and beg me to be ordained. Parish ministry is not the work I am called to do in this world—it is not the place where my deepest joy and the world's deepest need meet—but, nevertheless, I sometimes want someone to ask me to do it. I want the church to recognize me, claim me as a minister. Secretly, I long for someone to ask me to come back to church.

My fantasy was a reality for Paula Smith. When Paula was fifteen, she left the Catholic Church of her childhood. "Now remember," she said. "I am African American—I consider myself Black. I am a Black American—so my struggle has been mostly around race, gender, and being gay, and also the struggle to love myself and feel equal and realize that I deserve to exist." Paula knew the official position the Catholic Church took on homosexuality. "It didn't reflect who I was. There was nothing wrong with my attraction toward women. Therefore, I left the church." At age twenty, she left her home in Louisiana and joined the navy. During her time in the navy she struggled with addiction until she found her way to a recovery program. "Recovery began my journey toward a relationship with God," she said. "During that process, I was introduced to liberation theology, and feminist, womanist, and Black theology, which gave me a new understanding of the divine. I began to define my own conception of God. God isn't defined through any particular doctrine or any intermediaries. I believe that those theologies allowed me to expand my thinking about God. That was liberating for me."

The path of recovery also freed Paula from the "good-girl syndrome," which she now understands as "smothering a lot of women."

She said, "There is a deep loss of authentic selfhood. I realized that I was paining myself and betraying myself by trying to be good." She began to see herself not as a person trying to be good but as a person trying to be whole. "The church misses that," she said. "I think the goal is to get good by colonizing our minds. The body becomes men's property. They shut down everything from the neck down." She grew to believe her lesbianism was a gift from God. "That was pretty radical for a Catholic girl, but it was liberating. Oh, you know, God created man and woman who will procreate," she said, laughing. "That is true for man and woman, but it wasn't true for Paula. I believe that my sexuality is a gift from God, from my God, who loves me in the dark and in the light. I certainly don't see my sexuality as any darkness. It is probably one of the most beautiful things about me. But I had to learn, I had to embrace that, which meant I had to unlearn or resist, rather, what other people were projecting onto me."

After the navy, Paula began working in prisons as a counselor. "I was working in the prison system and saw women, women like myself, who were addicted, who were sexually abused, who were victims of domestic violence, who were Catholic, who were struggling with sexuality and identity, who were repeatedly incarcerated due to drugs and alcohol, and I became a mentor there, and a group facilitator, and began to teach them about self-esteem and about reentering society."

One of the most surprising things about interviewing women for this book was how many of them worked in prisons at some point or another—Paula, Jackie, Samantha, Joan, Jocelyn, to list a few. "That's where we go. They don't know what to do with us in society, those who don't conform," Paula said. "It is a population that is vulnerable and needs help and is easily accessible, I think. You don't have to follow a particular creed. There is a mix of religious or spiritual backgrounds there. They are open, and they need help. That's what I found there." And then she added, "Women want to tell their stories. This is a place to hear women's stories."

Working in the prison with women, Paula began to feel called to "do something more," and suddenly it seemed that everyone she met was either a priest or had gone to Harvard Divinity School. Although Paula did not have a college degree at the time, she talked with everyone she knew about the possibility of going to seminary, including Janet Cooper Nelson, a UCC minister. "Her church was having a dialogue about how to become open and affirming to gays and lesbians," Paula said. "Now this was a little church in Rhode Island where it is probably 95 percent White and very affluent, and they were having a dialogue about how to become open and inclusive. It appealed to me, and I remember I thought, oh, wow, something is changing in the institutional church."

To go to seminary, Paula knew she needed to get her bachelor's degree, so she began to attend Antioch University in Los Angeles. While in Los Angeles, she went to Unity Fellowship Church. "In its message, Unity felt like the Black invisible church that existed during slavery." The church was founded in the early 1980s; Bishop Carl Bean started the church to minister to people with HIV who were marginalized by society. "Bishop Carl Bean saw the need," Paula said. "He was driving in Los Angeles, on La Brea Avenue, and saw men walking around in their hospital gowns and IVs. When they died, these big churches refused to bury them because they were homosexual and had AIDS. The men had been baking cookies, members of the churches, doing stuff for fifty years, and the churches wouldn't bury them. That's how this church came about." At that church, she began to study liberation theology. "I learned to understand the Bible from a liberative perspective, affirming the life of gays and lesbians, rather than having people use the Bible at me as an oppressive tool." Paula was ordained as a minister by Unity Fellowship Church.

While she was completing her undergraduate degree she was accepted at Harvard Divinity School. An Episcopal priest from the diocese of Los Angeles heard her speak at her graduation from Antioch and mentioned her to the bishop, John Bruno. "The summer before I started going to seminary, I was introduced to the bishop of

Los Angeles. I remember him speaking about taking the church into the twenty-first century. He is all about diversity. He wants the church and church leaders to not look like they have been looking for a thousand years, meaning, he was open to gay priests," she said. Paula was invited to Bishop Bruno's home in Pasadena. He tried to convince her to be ordained in the Episcopal Church. She wasn't an Episcopalian, but that wasn't a problem for him. "He confirmed me right in his living room. Right there! I swear to God!" she said. "And I thought, okay, I am in the ordination process. The bishop wants me! You know, why not?"

With a warning from the bishop not to let Harvard Divinity School turn her too far toward academics and away from the margins, Paula set off for the East Coast. At divinity school, she learned Hebrew, and it empowered her to read and understand the Bible differently. "Studying Hebrew was very important, seeing and understanding how marginalization happened in terms of how the Bible was constructed." She focused her study on the power of women's voices. "I could see myself in the lives of the women in the ancient days, in the ancient Israelite women." She also studied liturgics and Anglican history at the nearby Episcopal Divinity School, and she started going to chapel there.

Despite being handpicked by the bishop, Paula soon discovered the Episcopal Church was not for her. "I didn't feel it, Sarah. I didn't feel it. I'm sorry." The Episcopal services she attended in school— even the nontraditional, creative services she went to at Episcopal Divinity School—rarely moved her. "Fredrica Thompsett, a professor there, tried to help me understand how communion could be a reconnecting with my higher power. I remember feeling that for one second, but I think I felt it more because she had tears in her eyes as she was talking about it. It wasn't really my experience," she said. "The Eucharist is the center of the Episcopal Church, and the fact that I couldn't connect with that was very telling. If one can't connect with the Eucharist, then one shouldn't be a priest. I couldn't feel the liberative God in church that I had experienced. I felt everybody else's, but I couldn't feel mine. I remember going to the services and looking at everybody and wondering if I looked like that. There was such an engagement. I would go to church, and I would feel like I was dying inside. I wanted to know what was moving people, the force moving inside of them. I wanted to know how God was moving in their lives, in church. For me, it felt too smothering, too stifling." Being surrounded by people going through the ordination process in the Massachusetts diocese didn't help. "It began to feel like this corporate, competitive environment. Everybody seemed to be on the ordination track. I was hearing stories about people trying to get internships at fancy elitist downtown churches because it would look good to their commission on ministry. I said, well, shit, I could work for a Fortune 500 company and have it feel this cutthroat and competitive," Paula said. "And I stopped going. I jumped off the ordination-track train."

Paula graduated from Harvard in 2005 with an MDiv, no official denomination, and without any plans for ordination in a mainline Protestant church. "And of course I knew I was going to be on my own, and I knew it was going to be difficult out there with an MDiv and not attached to some institution." She eventually secured a job as a community organizer and went to work in Louisiana helping to rebuild communities after Hurricane Katrina. Paula worked with a minister who had been in the Baptist Church for thirty-six years. "Now, the first thing she told me, and I was very surprised about this, she said, don't come down here talking about the ordination of women. Don't have that as part of your conversations. You are going to be working with a lot of male pastors. Don't let them know that you are educated, because you may intimidate them," Paula said. "I was appalled. And I was even more appalled because I conformed. I think the whole trauma of Katrina just devastated me, anyway, and I wasn't really thinking clearly, but I did conform on some level, and I was very hesitant to share myself totally."

Paula resigned after working there for five months. She found another job at the Baton Rouge Crisis Intervention Center, and she also has her own private counseling practice. "I think it is what I am really called to do. I thought I would do it as a priest, as a UCC minister, and then I thought I would do it as an Episcopal priest, and now I think I am just going to do it as a Harvard Divinity School graduate," she said, laughing. "I call myself an interfaith chaplain. That is how I see myself, not as embracing any one particular denomination but extending my understanding of all faith practices beyond tolerance and into honor, honoring all walks of life and spiritual paths. For me, it is about everybody's voices being at the table. Bring your beliefs, and bring who you are to the discussion." Although Paula has claimed herself as an interfaith chaplain, other people she encounters do not seem to know how to label her. "People don't know what to do with me as a clergyperson. They cannot fathom me as (a) educated at Harvard because that is just too out of their frame of reference, and then as (b) a Black gay clergy person. It is just too foreign for them," she said.

I interviewed Paula on a Sunday morning, and when we were finished, a woman who was trying to quit drinking was on her way to Paula's home office. Paula planned to sit with her for four hours that afternoon, accompanying her on her journey toward sobriety and self-discovery. "It is not happening in the church because it doesn't happen there. The church doesn't allow it to happen. So I can't be there," she said. "I can do it in my home." Churches are too busy trying to be *good* to help the women Paula ministers to. "I believe we are getting away from the real message of Jesus," she said. "I don't think Jesus was good. He frightened many with his radical message. He was a political leader who believed in liberation. He was certainly human."

"He was a troublemaker," I said.

"And the churches don't make trouble," she said. "That is their message. Be good, watch out for the devil—they think you can catch it like the flu—take no responsibility for your actions, and we don't have to be accountable for our actions because we're the church."

———

Sarah Peck grew up in what she describes as a "secular household" with parents who were both "spiritually inclined." Because they did not belong to any particular faith tradition, they created their own rituals—words said before meals, intentional ways of marking important moments. When she was in high school, Sarah wanted to sing, so she joined a church choir that was part of a conservative Presbyterian church. With the church's youth group, she went on four mission trips to Tijuana, Mexico, to build houses. "I was really seduced," she said. "We had contemporary Christian music and praise and worship that I felt really attached to. I was in that phase of life where I really wanted to fall in love, and somehow all that energy was directed toward this idea of Jesus. The praise songs were love songs."

Although her family accepted her enthusiasm for Jesus and for the group, they did not attend the church, which meant they did not pledge any money to the church. This absence of financial support made the group suspicious of Sarah and, as a result, she often felt like an interloper. "I was always sort of an iffy candidate on the mission trips because if I wasn't a member of the church, why would anyone want to sponsor me on this mission trip?" Even more, Sarah was raised to treat the biblical text as a relic of a community, written at a specific time for a specific time. This orientation led her to ask critical questions during youth group when the leaders would read passages from the Bible. "That created a profile for myself that I was resistant to the Bible somehow, although I didn't notice it at the time." When Sarah graduated from high school, the leader of her youth group did not attend her graduation party, even though he attended parties for almost every other member of the group.

At home, Sarah tried to convert her parents to her newfound version of Christianity. "I was very emotionally connected to it, and for a short period of time felt incredibly concerned for my family, and came home and would try to read the Bible to my family," she said, laughing. "I went through a phase where I thought it was important to convert them." During Sarah's senior year, her mother offered to go on the mission trip with her, a gesture that meant the world to Sarah.

When she went to college, Sarah looked for a similar group so she could continue to sing praise music. She joined a praise band, Selah, and was their lead singer. They performed every Sunday night for hundreds of students. She soon discovered, however, that the Christian groups on her campus participated in what she called "Christian gossip." Praying for each other generated a highly efficient rumor mill—holding so-and-so in your prayers because you have heard that she is having sex with her boyfriend was a way to make sure everyone in the community knew that so-and-so was having sex with her boyfriend.

She majored in music in college until her senior year, when she decided to switch to a different major. The requirements of the women's studies major were easy to fulfill because there were only two women's studies classes offered at the entire school. She took the first class during the fall semester of her senior year and the second class the final semester. "Then you had to petition that you had taken a gendered lens in eight other classes. That meant if you had written a paper about women, for example, or if you had taken a class that had any gendered word in the title of it," she said, laughing. Despite the easy requirements, the women's studies classes she took transformed her. Suddenly, Sarah could see how sexism shaped every aspect of women's lives—standardized tests, medical research, medical treatment, and religion. That semester, she was also taking a course on eastern religion. During the seventh week of the semester, with her suspicions raised about religion in general, Sarah reached a breaking point. "One of my professors said that in some really conservative Buddhist monasteries, monks will not allow women to touch them. Even just bumping into a woman is powerful and sinful. It was a weird little side comment in the middle of a lecture that wasn't even about women," she said. "It came at the right moment. I had been building up all of this information about gender treatment, and I jumped out of the class, and I was hysterical. I ran to my adviser, who was a feminist theologian at my college." Sarah went to his office and said, "I can't believe this! Tell me more about this! Are all religions like this?"

Sarah had taken his feminist theologies class her sophomore year and, at that time, thought it was all "bullshit." She said, "I thought, what are all these people worried about? How we call God Father? Who cares?" The combination of a women's studies class and a religious studies class made everything click. "All of a sudden, I felt like I lost my faith."

At that time, Sarah was applying to graduate school programs at divinity schools. She had been working at St. Jude Children's Research Hospital while she was an undergraduate, where she was a chaplain to children who were dying from cancer and to their families. Because of that experience, she was interested in the intersection of God and crisis. She noticed that many patients and their families had expectations about how the world worked based on their religious faith and shaped by biblical passages about the good being rewarded. "I saw people losing their faith all over the place because they realized that's not how the world works, and they were asking, where was God," she said. Writing her statement of purpose for graduate school applications, Sarah realized that she, too, was in crisis. "I realized how patriarchal and male-dominated my religion is, which is Christianity. I felt a hatred for Christianity and a hatred for Jesus for not correcting gender imbalances." She wrote about that crisis in her statement of purpose and mailed the applications. She was accepted.

Sarah chose to attend Harvard Divinity School, intending to be ordained as a hospital chaplain. Because she did not grow up in any institutional religion and because she no longer felt comfortable in the Christianity of her youth group, Sarah was not officially affiliated with any denomination. Almost immediately, students in the master's of divinity program are asked to tell their story, which includes crafting a narrative called a "spiritual autobiography." For those seeking ordination, claiming a tradition—wrestling with that tradition—is an essential part of their identities as ministers-to-be. Sarah decided to tell people she was "shopping" for a denomination. She went to three churches every single Sunday: a Unitarian Church, a UCC church, and Harvard Memorial Church, presided over by Peter Gomes. She also attended WomenChurch, the monthly service I started at Harvard.

"I couldn't help feeling like I was an outsider always," she said. None of the readings assigned for classes about ministry at divinity school spoke to her, either. "All of the readings were about the most conventional types of preachers, over and over again, and there weren't any struggles with faith in any of the readings." The only book she felt she could relate to was Simone Weil's *Waiting for God.* "She has this line in her book where she says she will always stand on the porch of the church because she just can't ever go in and leave those who won't go in behind."

Her second year at divinity school, Sarah worked as a hospital chaplain intern for her field education placement. Chaplains are asked to identify their faith traditions and denominational affiliations so patients can be assigned appropriately. She said, "I decided to say I was unaffiliated and see how that worked." Then she added, "And I decided to only see women patients."

As a chaplain in the hospital, Sarah felt much like she did as a member of the youth group in high school—like somehow she did not belong. Although she felt confident when she was *ministering to* patients in the hospital, other chaplains continued to give her a hard time, continually reminding her that she was not one of them, not a *minister.* "It was such a problem, over and over again, in the communal areas, mainly among chaplains. We shared an office, and I would go in and people would say things like, so, you're unaffiliated, huh? That must be pretty tough being a chaplain around here."

When she was talking to patients, the fact that she was "unaffiliated" was rarely a problem. "I felt like it was almost a relief to patients sometimes," she said. "I didn't go up and say, hi, I'm a Baptist, how are you? I said, I'm Sarah, from the chaplain's department. I started eliminating some vocabulary from the way I would do an introduction."

"Like what things?" I asked.

"Like religion," she said. "I started using words like, we are here to listen, and we talk about anything that is in the realm of your spiritual needs or your emotional needs, instead of saying we provide religious support for patients." Listening to her patients, Sarah realized that most of the women she encountered in the hospital had been, at some point during their care, misdiagnosed. Because of this, she began to ask, "How has your care been here? Have you been satisfied?" And women began to tell her stories about being misdiagnosed, about feeling that no one listened to them.

One woman told Sarah about finding a lump in her breast. She went to the doctor. The doctor could not feel the lump and sent her home. She still felt the lump, and so she went back to the doctor and demanded a mammogram. The results showed nothing. She still felt the lump. It grew more painful. She kept returning to the doctor's office and demanding mammograms. Although she could feel that the lump was growing, she continued to receive mammogram results in the mail with a note in her doctor's handwriting saying "all clear" and stamped with a smiley face. Her breasts grew increasingly painful. She was feeling more and more lumps. And then parts of her breasts started blackening like bruises. She told Sarah that she ran to the clinic. She found her doctor, and when he saw her, he said, "Why are you here? How many times do I have to tell you that you are fine? Go home. You are paranoid." She looked in his face and yelled, "There is blood coming out of my nipple. I am not fine!" Seven surgeries later, her body is covered in scars. Both breasts are gone. She is dying.

Sarah started a weekly chapel service for women at the hospital, loosely based on WomenChurch. They sit in the hospital's chapel in a circle and share readings and prayers. Sarah said, "Recently I have liked poems by women, or I will bring a reading that alludes to what I think are subtle reminders that there are gender differences going on in our world." Six people came to one of the first gatherings Sarah held in the chapel, and she was afraid the service was not going well. She decided to veer away from her planned format and invite women to come forward, drop a marble into a bowl of water she had placed on the altar, and share a prayer with the community. "And this space opened up. Women started naming their mothers, saying the names of their mothers, sharing memories and stories about the way they resembled their mothers. Many of them had just lost a mother in the last year, and then they started naming their friends and their sisters, and praying for all these women in their lives," she said. "It lasted twice as long as the service was supposed to last."

Not having a strict faith tradition to which she felt allegiance gave Sarah the freedom to use whatever religious language her patients used, to reflect back to them the version of God with which they felt most comfortable. She respected the language her patients used to talk about God, even when she thought about God differently than they did. "I was worried that I was being too much of a chameleon, that by not having my own distinctive tradition I was allowing all sorts of assumptions to be made, and not really correcting them," she said. But that fear was trumped by her understanding of what being a good listener requires. For Sarah, the most important part of ministering to women in the hospital was to create the sense that she was "unshockable"—that nothing they could say to her would be met with judgment or offense, only love and acceptance. "I like to think of it like midwifery in a way," she said. "They have something in there. They are being treated for cancer, and they are thinking all sorts of things, but it is not on the outside. You have to just wait for it, and wait for it, and twist for it, and let it come out."

At the end of her first year, when she had to write a paper for Introduction to Theological Education for Ministry—a required class of the MDiv program at that time at Harvard Divinity School—Sarah decided to tackle her discomfort with the word "minister." "I looked up minister, and I saw words like 'man of the cloth,' 'father of the church,' blah blah blah, and I was like, *uuuck,* not a minister! But then, right underneath it, it says 'minister to,' and it has all of these words that reminded me of why I was interested in the MDiv in the first place—to serve, to guide, to teach, to comfort, to be present with, all of these words after 'minister to' that I felt were relevant." Reading the definitions revealed to Sarah that even if she never claims herself as *a minister,* she is already *ministering to.* (She is, however, now considering being ordained in the Disciples of Christ tradition.)

Sarah understands part of ministering to people as stretching what they consider sacred. When she was a student at Harvard Divinity School, she put on a production of Eve Ensler's *The Vagina Monologues* in the school's chapel. "We brought our performance to the altar," she said. Based on interviews with more than two hundred women about their memories and experiences of sexuality, the play celebrates female sexualities and bodies through monologues ranging from funny to heartbreaking. Groups all over the world perform *The Vagina Monologues* as part of V-Day, a global movement to stop violence against women and girls. Each production of *The Vagina Monologues* on V-Day—usually February 14—raises both community awareness and money for local organizations engaged in work to stop violence against women. Not knowing there were official guidelines for how to put on a V-Day performance, Sarah thought she would be able to bring divinity school women together to craft additional monologues. She imagined what other monologues ought to be included given the fact that the performance would take place in a chapel. Sarah wanted to write a monologue about Mary's body. Although Christianity focuses on the bodily sacrifice of Jesus, the first body that is sacrificed, Sarah reminded me, is Mary's. "The first bodily sacrifice is the torn body of Mary, in so many ways, stretched and torn and damaged. That's how Jesus came into the world," she said.

The performances at Harvard Divinity School were a success and raised more than $4,000 for a local domestic violence shelter. The twenty-one performers included students, staff, and faculty, and all three nights were sold out. They sold chocolate vagina pops and

T-shirts with GOD LOVES VAGINAS printed on the back. Sarah's eighty-year-old Catholic grandparents attended. Sarah's monologue was the one titled, "Reclaiming Cunt," and at the end she asked the entire audience to chant the word "cunt" with her. "My grandfather stood up and started pounding his cane to the word cunt. I feel like people just stretched their courage," she said. "*The Vagina Monologues* was one of the most honest things I have ever done in a chapel. It felt holy, and it felt directly connected to my core and everything I find to be divine. It reminded me of what has always been missing for me in the structures that we call religion."

Chapter Thirteen

A CHURCH OF
HER OWN

During the period of time when I was questioning my faith but was still going to church, if you happened to sit in a pew near me and could hear me reciting the words of the Episcopal liturgy, you would have thought you were listening to a cell phone call that was breaking up. If a prayer or hymn contained words I didn't think I could say with integrity anymore, I skipped them. Each Sunday my version of the Nicene Creed shrunk. For those of you who don't recite it every single Sunday, the official version goes like this:

We believe in one God,
the Father, the Almighty,
maker of heaven and earth,
of all that is, seen and unseen.
We believe in one Lord, Jesus Christ,
the only Son of God,
eternally begotten of the Father,
God from God, Light from Light,
true God from true God,
begotten, not made,
of one Being with the Father.
Through him all things were made.

For us and for our salvation
he came down from heaven:
by the power of the Holy Spirit
he became incarnate from the Virgin Mary,
and was made man.
For our sake he was crucified under Pontius Pilate;
he suffered death and was buried.
On the third day he rose again
in accordance with the Scriptures;
he ascended into heaven
and is seated at the right hand of the Father.
He will come again in glory to judge the living and the dead,
and his kingdom will have no end.

At first I dropped only a few words, like "Father" and "man" and "for our sake." But as time went on, more and more words became unutterable for me. Eventually, out of the 154 words in the creed, I was left with eleven: We believe in one God…seen and unseen… light…and…death.

It was time to go.

But where?

I wish I had lived in the same town as Diana Holbert, an ordained Methodist minister—the woman who was a parsonette before she could hear that the call to ordained ministry belonged to her. Diana created ArtSpirit Mission for people who have been "burned" by the church. Because it was a community for those who had been hurt by churches, Diana was careful, watching what she said, how she said it, how often she talked about Jesus, the way she prayed and talked about her faith. "It was like, you don't want to jump on a trampoline with somebody who's got bandages for burns. It's just not going to work."

Diana noticed what she calls a "brain drain" in the United Methodist Church and that her own children, aged twenty-nine and thirty-two and both artists, were leaving the church. "They were bored," she said. She started talking with some of her artist friends to find out what was happening for them, and they, too, were bored with church. She said, "They would read the newspaper, and they would think that Christians were idiots, like the Baptists coming out and saying, women, you should be submissive to your husbands. I mean, most pastors don't even believe that, but the hierarchy said that's what they are supposed to believe, and, so they just felt like, I don't want any part of that." One person Diana talked with said, "It began with the Crusades and it is still going on. I can't stand Christianity. It is harmful."

"And I just thought, well, maybe I can retrieve 2,000 years of Christianity for these people," Diana said. "Maybe we can do this in a way that is not boring, but really enlivening in the same way that Ms. Irene, my Sunday school teacher, was enlivening to me, and Ernestine Hayes, my Sunday school teacher in high school, who helped us develop critical thinking. You could be a Christian and you could doubt. In fact, you were asked to doubt and to ask questions. A lot of these people in ArtSpirit were ones who were told, no, that's a sin, that's heresy."

Before she started ArtSpirit, Diana worked as an ordained minister in a suburban church, the first female minister hired by that congregation. Diana felt inadequate in every aspect of her job—except for her faith. "I am an introvert in an extrovert's profession. I am a woman in a male-dominated profession. I have been the first woman of every church I've served. And breaking those barriers is just so hard," she said. "But on the other side, I love pushing the envelope. I love trying a new thing. I love questioning the status quo and moving out of it. I know that is prophetic."

Even though some members of the congregation resisted having a female minister, Diana took risks. "I danced my first sermon after a month preaching, and heard later that one of the men in the congregation said, what is this? The sacrifice of the vestal virgin? It was just ripping stuff. They were trying to rip me out of there."

The man was one of six men who hated having Diana as their minister. She called them her "six detractors in the sanctuary." (Someone once heard her talking about them and thought she had sixty *tractors* in the sanctuary.) Two of the six would attend the adult education program every Sunday, and then they would stand in the hallway with their arms crossed as everyone else walked past them on their way to the worship service. Other members of the congregation who passed them would ask, "Don't you want to come down and join us?"

And they would answer, again and again, "No, we don't like the leadership. We don't like what's going on here."

"It was hard. It was just plain hard. I remember looking out at the parking lot and crying and thinking, men have an easier job at this than women do. They tell their sports stories and everybody just loves them," she said, laughing. "And I'm not like that."

Despite continual abuse from her six detractors, Diana led the church into a new and financially stable era. "Those six people either changed or left, and the rest of them galvanized around this woman pastor," Diana said. "They loved what was happening. They saw God at work. We had more Bible studies than they'd ever, ever, ever had, and mission trips, and it was beautiful." They started a building program and launched a capital funds campaign. After four and a half years, Diana knew it was time to leave. She said, "I know that's what I'm called to do, healing, and they're healed and they are ready to move." The next minister appointed to take Diana's place was a woman. "They were ecstatic to have her, sight unseen, because she was my friend and because she was a woman."

When she decided it was time to leave, God, in her words, "presented me with this fantastic idea and opportunity to start this mission," that is, ArtSpirit. The United Methodist Church supported her idea. The district superintendent believed in her. She said, "He was a mover and a shaker, and he was able to find me funding from our missionary board in New York for three years." The ArtSpirit congregation later raised enough to keep paying Diana's salary.

"Truly, it was a no-brainer for them because it was mostly women who were in that ministry," she said. "Yes, they wanted a woman minister, yes indeed."

Diana had always felt that an hour on Sunday mornings was too short for a worship service. "I mean, how could you even pray?" she asked. In ArtSpirit, they sat in a circle. Diana shared a five-minute sermon. After she talked, there would be an open dialogue when people shared with the group or with partners or in small groups. And then they would do a hands-on art experience, which was always led by one or several members of the group. Diana shared one example with me.

A psychotherapist and an ex-Catholic, Lila and Karen planned an activity based on the sacrament of confession. Karen and Lila divided the group into partners, and each pair was given a large piece of butcher paper. They sat on the floor, with the butcher paper between them, and were given watercolors, markers, crayons, or whatever other medium they wanted to use. One of the partners would then begin to confess, and while the person was confessing, the listener—the confessor—would respond, not with words, but with images. "It had to be in silence, and it had to be using one of these media," Diana said. When one partner was finished confessing, the other partner had a chance to do the same thing.

Diana told me about her experience in confession. "I started remembering things I needed to confess, and the pain that came with that," she said. "And I remember bright colors, red for blood I think, and real sharp, angular shapes were being formed on my paper, and about halfway through, my partner began to do very soft lines around what I had done, not on what I had done, but around it, almost like an embrace. And I'll tell you what, Sarah, I have done a lot of confessing in my life, either privately with God or with a therapist or with my husband or with the person that I've done this to, and I have never felt absolved until that night."

The group also shared prayer concerns every time they gathered. Each person would write his or her prayers on small red cards and then place them, facedown, on the altar table, which was decorated by one of the visual artists in the group every week. At the end of the service, people would take several prayer cards home with them. "We would covenant to pray for that prayer concern every day for seven days," Diana said. "I would go to different people's houses and see their little altars in their homes, and the red prayer cards would be sitting on their altars."

Diana created a religious community peopled primarily by women who never would have set foot in a church otherwise. There are thousands of communities like Diana's that gather regularly. They meet in empty classrooms, living rooms, coffee shops, art galleries, and restaurants. They form women's groups, prayer groups, book groups, house churches, Next Generation meetings, Church of Craft meetings, and meditation circles. They are drawn together by a feeling of longing, a pull toward something they might not be able to explain, and most believe they will not find what they are looking for in a church on Sunday morning. That phrase "spiritual, but not religious" often means, I do not find my beliefs and questions and politics within institutional religion. What I find there does not resonate with me. I do not feel at home.

Ministers like Diana listen to people who do not feel at home in churches and then create something new in response to what they hear. Gordon Kaufman, my theological mentor, claims theologians as artists and theology as art, a "work of art is to be *lived in:* It is the very form and meaning of human life which is here being constructed and reconstructed." Listening to the women I interviewed for this book, I began to understand ministers as artists. In *Art Objects,* Jeanette Winterson writes, "The artist is a translator; one who has learned how to pass into her own language the languages gathered from stones, from birds, from dreams, from the body, from the material world, from the invisible world, from sex, from death, from love. A different language is a different reality." Diana and Paula and Sarah and Callie and Tristy did this kind of gathering, this kind of translation, offering back to us language in which we might hear ourselves, see ourselves, find God.

In 2002, Liz Myer Boulton started Hope Church Boston. In the fall of 2002, the United Church of Christ and the Christian Church (Disciples of Christ) jointly decided to stand for unity and cooperation among Christians by starting a new, confederated church in the greater Boston area. That church was Hope Church. Liz was newly ordained, married to an ordained minister named Matt, and in her midtwenties. Although Liz told me that many church starts fail within two years, Hope Church Boston is still going strong.

Liz's father is a pastor. "So we were always the first to get there and the last to leave," she said. "When I could choose not to go to church, I never went." Reared in the church, Liz never wanted to go into ordained ministry. "It was sort of the last thing I wanted to do, but then it gets into your bones, into your system, and it is hard to run away from." Her childhood was shaped by experiences in the Christian Church (Disciples of Christ) and the Assemblies of God. During summer vacations, she attended camps run by each denomination. "I grew up with one foot in each world, which was very interesting," she said. "At Disciples summer camp we were debating things like, Christ: human or divine? And then in the Assemblies of God summer camp we were being saved and speaking in tongues." She remembers one bonfire at the Assemblies of God camp when campers were asked to burn their secular idols. "Kids were throwing in their cassette tapes and ghetto blasters and their polo shirts, taking off their polo shirts and throwing them in the bonfire." Liz's faith is shaped by both traditions, and she believes that the liberal progressive church needs to learn from the conservative evangelical church. "I feel excited to straddle the chasm between the two," she said. "We need progressive evangelical church because the conservative fundamentalist church does not have the market on what church is. There is more good news than what can be contained in that church, and so we need dynamic, vibrant progressive churches that aren't afraid of the Jesus figure and aren't afraid to grow and to share their faith."

After college, Liz decided she wanted to pursue a PhD in post-colonial literature, but before attending graduate school, she worked for the United Church of Christ and the Christian Church (Disciples of Christ) in Haiti. Liz's experience there changed her. "I was completely shattered in Haiti. I had no idea there was such a poor country in such close proximity to such a rich country, and then to walk with people—how do people's bodies hold in a life of dire poverty? How do they hold it in?" Liz asked. She witnessed the violence of the dictatorship, the sheer randomness of it that kept everyone in check. One pastor in Haiti told Liz stories about people in the militia who came into his church, took babies, and threw them in the air and shot them. "And I remember talking to him, thinking I was missing something in the translation, like this cannot be what he is saying," Liz said. "So we went over and over and over it because I just couldn't believe that I lived in a world where this could exist." In that context, Liz did not feel like talking about God at all. "But their faith is so strong," she said. "It's like you can't deny God because that pastor has faith even after..." Her voice trailed off, and then she started again. "Because his God is with him even in the valley of the shadow of death, and because he has faith, who am I to say, where is God? It would take a really pretentious person to do that. So I can have faith because he has faith."

When she returned from Haiti, Liz changed her graduate school plans. Instead of postcolonial literature, she thought she would pursue a master's degree in religious studies, concentrating on evil and suffering. She wanted to explore the questions ringing in her head: How does Haiti exist? What does church mean there? How can we call ourselves church here? She went to meet with the dean of the Disciples Divinity House at the University of Chicago, and after listening to Liz's questions, she suggested Liz attend the Divinity School and pursue a master's of divinity. Liz took her advice.

For her field education placement, she worked at Austin Boulevard Christian Church in Oak Park, Illinois. When she presided at her first funeral, she realized parish ministry was the work she wanted to be doing. "It was just such a powerful way to be present to people. I remember reading the Isaiah text at that funeral, the grass withers and the flowers fade but the word of God stands forever. Afterwards, I was driving and I saw the Chicago skyline and this big, heavy moon hanging, and it felt so right to be this present in people's lives—at birth and death and marriage, really just walking with people through these big transitions. Everything came into focus. Being torn open by the suffering in Haiti, and presiding at this funeral, and then I took a year out to do an internship at a new church start in Kansas City, and that opened my eyes to what a church start could be."

Liz had a fabulous mentor in Kansas City who shaped her experience, Reverend Holly McKissick, pastor of St. Andrew Christian Church. She was the first woman Liz ever heard preach. Hearing her, Liz felt that she was inside the gospel story for the first time, that she was part of it. "It was amazing," she said. "Through her words I felt like this is my story, too. I hadn't ever felt like that until I heard her preach. It was this beautiful awakening and sadness for realizing that I wasn't fully a part of it before." Liz's mentor is a "no-notes" preacher. Although she prepares for her sermons, she does not use any notes when she preaches. "It was very right there—there wasn't paper or a pulpit or distance. Nothing between the good news of the gospel and you," Liz said. "She talks about the sermon experience as Jesus preaching the Sermon on the Mount. It's that immediate. Through her, there is a time collapse, ideally, where the good news of the gospel is as potent and relevant as if it were coming out of Jesus's mouth."

When she was a student at the University of Chicago, John Buchanan, the editor of *The Christian Century*, visited her preaching class. He shared with the class something Liz has never forgotten. "Every week, people give you more than they give a lot of people in their lives, even their spouses," she remembers he said. "They give you their undivided attention for fifteen or twenty minutes or however long you preach, which is such a gift that they are giving you, and you need to make good on that. You need to take it seriously."

"So I try really hard to break open scripture in a way that will be relevant for the church," Liz said. She is a lectionary preacher. Three or four weeks before each sermon, she reads the appointed readings so she can, in her words, "let them marinate." She reads them again the Monday before her sermon, looking for a word or phrase that resonates, what she calls a "takeoff point."

Liz feels the responsibility of preaching. "I think a lot of sermons aren't good news," she said. "They're just sort of like random musings from a guy in a robe." She holds the experiences of her parishioners in her mind as she prepares for her sermons. "I think we need more than random musings, more than deep thoughts, more than historical criticism. It's just not going to do it." Liz returned to Paul to make her point. "I go back to Paul where he says, we are perplexed, but not driven to despair. We are pushed down, but not overcome." And then she started to preach, and I was captivated. "Walking that line between being truth tellers—miscarriage, incest, alcoholism, Darfur. We are going to name these hard, broken places. We are going to call out the valley of the shadow of death as Christians, and we can do it only because we have the hope of the resurrection. We can do it only because we are also bearers and truth tellers of the good news that love overcomes hate and life overcomes death, that behold I am doing a new thing. So that is the good news, and that is what I try to do— I try to do both, which is hard—that the kingdom is at hand, and not in a finger-shaking way but in a can't-you-perceive-it way? Even now? We need to proclaim the good news of the gospel, one to another. That God is at work and all these things will pass away, but the love and the life and the peace and the justice will reign eternal."

"Do you ever doubt it?" I asked.

"Yes!" she said. "There is a book somewhere, and I have taken the title—preaching as self-persuasion. Every Sunday you preach to yourself."

Liz understands the sermon as a bridge that Jesus walks across. "What kind of Jesus is walking across the bridge?" I asked.

"A very kind Jesus. A very mad-at-societal-injustice Jesus," Liz said. "This God who was so eager to be with us and to mend us and to heal us that this God becomes flesh and shows us everything we need to know about God's heart in this very tangible way that we can hold on to. So the healing, the hope, liberation from insecurities, from psychological evils, but also from physical evils—what I saw in Haiti was that the fact that God became flesh allowed them to stand up straighter and say, this world is bent, this is wrong." Liz paused and then added, "The fact that God became incarnate, that God became poor, liberating, kind, healing, laughing, feasting, and including and including and going to the margins and expanding the center so there is no center anymore. That's my Jesus."

After serving as a Global Mission Intern in Port-au-Prince, Haiti, graduating from the University of Chicago Divinity School, and working as a chaplain at the Dana Farber Cancer Institute in Boston, Massachusetts, and as an associate pastor at St. Andrew Christian Church in Olathe, Kansas, Liz started her own church, Hope Church in Jamaica Plain, Massachusetts, the joint venture by the United Church of Christ and the Christian Church (Disciples of Christ). She is the senior pastor, and her husband, Matt, is the associate. She realized that if she was ever going to start a church, the time to do it was then—Matt had a job as a professor at a local seminary; she had a great mentor; and (at that time) she had no children. On a drive from London, Ontario, to Chicago, she and Matt decided that if they could figure out a way to raise $110,000, they would give it a go.

Liz shared her idea for the church start with her mentor. "I called my mentor and said, Matt and I are going to try a new church start if we can raise $110,000."

Liz's mentor said, "I'll get it for you."
And Liz thought, "Oh, shit."

Although Liz admits that claiming ministerial authority is more difficult for women than for men—"The current role of 'the minister' seems to have grown out of a man's heart, so it sometimes feels like putting a square peg into a circle," she said—she has not had a problem at Hope Church with that aspect of leadership. "I think that has more to do with being a church start," she said. "We can be open and affirming because we started that way, and so we don't have to fight any battles. And I can be the person in charge because we started that way. I don't have to follow behind 'Roger' who always did it that way. I can preach on breast-feeding after coming back from my maternity leave and no one blinks an eyelash."

When I interviewed Liz, she had just had her first child. Being a mother has helped her understand God's love in a different way, what she calls the "ferocity of God's love." She said, "That story of Jesus's baptism where God tears open the heavens and says, you are my loved one. You're the pride of my life, or you're the best thing I ever did—I feel that in my stomach now. It's not just words. It's like the words have deep roots in my heart." For Liz, parenting gives her insight into God's care and protection of us. The way her child looks at her—with so much adoration and love, with such expectation of her goodness, with beautiful laughter—suggests to her how God must look at us. When her child has not seen Liz for a while and then suddenly sees her, she said, "He sees you, and it's just like this, Oh! There you are! This thrilling excitement, and I think that's what it is like when we come to God in prayer, maybe there is this, Oh! There you are!"

Throughout the interview, Liz talked openly about politics and faith. She did not seem shy or hesitant to talk about political issues in the pulpit or as a minister. For her, living a Christian life is living a political life. "I think if you walk in the footsteps of Jesus, you are walking in the footsteps of justice and peace and equality and all that good stuff," Liz said. "If you are living the Christian life, it is inherently going to be political in the sense that the good news is scandalous to the status quo."

Starting a church from scratch is unrelenting work. Liz was filled with anxiety when Hope Church first opened. In addition, church starts tend to be what Liz calls "pastor-centered." Liz did everything: set up the database, copied flyers, wrote sermons, did mass mailings. "At the beginning it felt very heavy on my shoulders, that if I had to take a week off, it would collapse," she said. "That was paralyzing." Liz has worked hard to develop other leaders in the community so that everyone does not always look to her for everything they need. "That's a struggle in ministry. It's a struggle because everyone wants a piece of you," she said. "We do this thing where we are really a priesthood of all believers. We pray for each other. We care for each other, preach for each other, prepare feasts for each other. We are all priests." And then she added, "But people want you."

Again and again, Liz emphasized the importance of community, a "community that can hold you when you think God is dead, that can preach you or proclaim you back into some semblance of belief." When I listened to her, I wanted to believe what she was saying. I wanted to be part of her community. At first, it was harder for me to listen to Liz than it was to listen to women tell me stories filled with experiences of sexism and misogyny. Although my heart broke over and over again when I listened to terrible stories, my decision to leave the ordination process was confirmed. When I listened to Liz, however, all I felt was grief. I missed being part of a church community. I missed having theological language that worked for me. I felt like I was on the outside looking in.

When I began writing this book, I imagined myself like the diver in Adrienne Rich's poem "Diving into the Wreck." Instead of wearing flippers and bringing a camera and a knife for my journey into the deep, I dove armed with a digital recorder and a keyboard, but I, too, was alone. Like the narrator of that poem, I came to explore the wreck, "to see the damage that was done," and I found that—the wreck and the damage—but I also found another world underwater that I had not expected.

Liz told me about a new lesbian couple that just started attending Hope Church. "They are a biracial couple, and they have a little baby," she said. "They came about six weeks ago, and they have been there for six weeks, and they are just loving it. Whatever happens, we have succeeded because we have created a community where they feel loved and accepted and are growing deeper into who they are called to be." And then she added, "Why am I anxious at all? It is not about me, it is about this broken vessel of a church community, that God is at work."

On Hope Church's Web site, they have posted a welcoming statement: "Welcome to all who have no church home, need strength, want to follow Christ, have doubts, or do not believe.

Welcome to new visitors and to old friends. Welcome to grandparents, to mothers, fathers, and single people. Welcome to people of all colors, cultures, abilities, and sexual orientations, to old and young, to believers and questioners—and welcome to questioning believers. Welcome to everyone!"

DEATH VALLEY BLOOMS

Connie Chandler-Ward, one of the founders of a women's retreat center in Maine called Greenfire and an Episcopal priest who was ordained with Alison Cheek (one of the Philadelphia Eleven), attended seminary before women were allowed to be ordained. Her husband was the rector of an Episcopal church. The local bishop came to her house and told her that he planned to accept, officially, Alison's irregular ordination when the general convention voted in favor of women's ordination. Connie asked the bishop to consider her own ordination. One month later, she took her ordination exams. Within a year of that conversation, Connie was ordained a deacon. When the general convention voted to ordain women as priests, she was ready.

Alison and Connie went to the bishop's "palace" for lunch and to discuss the creation of a liturgy for regularizing Alison's priesthood during Connie's ordination. "There is no liturgy for anything like this," the bishop said. "Do you have any ideas?"

Alison spoke up immediately. "How about opening with, 'Let us confess our sins, especially the sins of the church against women.'"

The bishop agreed.

When the ordination was made public, Connie received a letter in the mail that suggested she would not live through her ordination ceremony. The letter's strange handwriting was traced to a young man in a church in Virginia. He had also sent a threat to another woman, and Connie and the second woman made a citizens' arrest. The letter writer believed he was channeling the word of God. The police had him evaluated for twenty-four hours, Connie and the other woman had to face him in the hospital in the presence of a judge, and then he was released. Connie was afraid. She began to lock her car.

The FBI attended the ordination because the letter writer had been seen snooping around the alley behind the church the day before. They didn't notice that he was sitting in the fourth row. Connie's husband had to point him out to them before the service. Then the service began: Let us confess our sins, especially the sins of the church against women.

Can you imagine a service that would begin with those words today?

Because women are now allowed to be ordained in most Protestant denominations, many people do not think there is anything to apologize for anymore. Apologizing for a rule against the ordination of women is one thing. Apologizing for institutionally sanctioned sexism that continues even when the rules have changed is another. If churches were to apologize for their sins against women now that ordination is allowed, we would have to admit that sexism runs all the way through our faith, that it has perverted our prayers, our creeds, our music, our understandings of God and of human beings, that it has cut people off from and out of their relationships with each other and with God. Are we brave enough to do this work? To reclaim? Revise? Reimagine?

The week after the fateful meeting with my discernment committee, when I told them I was moving in with my boyfriend, my friend Chantal's fiancé, Charlie, was diagnosed with stomach cancer. He was twenty-seven years old. I flew to Los Angeles for their wedding. They were supposed to marry in September but rushed to marry in February instead.

"We want to be married now," Chantal told me on the telephone. "It is like a veil has been lifted, and I can see what really matters."

When I returned to Boston after their wedding—a beautiful, magical ceremony on a bluff overlooking the Pacific Ocean—a veil had been lifted for me, too. I called the rector to tell her I wanted to end the discernment process.

And then Charlie died.

While my experience was a funeral for my vocation as a priest, Charlie's memorial service was a funeral for my faith in God.

Before it happened to me, I didn't think faith was something you could lose. It's not an object, like a shoe, or a camera left on an airplane. When Charlie got sick, and when he did not get better, and when he died, I realized that my faith in God was really belief in magic, a certainty that I could say the right words, do the proper rituals, and the people I love would be kept safe. This was the kind of faith I had been cultivating, grooming my whole life. It is the faith of a perfectionist—that I could make things right when it really mattered if I just tried hard enough. That God would make it right if I just tried hard enough.

If you had asked me before Charlie died I would have told you that I knew God did not make people sick, or make people poor, or make people die. But people are sick and people are poor and people die, and, when I began to listen carefully, most of the theology and prayers and hymns I have been reading and reciting and singing my whole life promise a God who, a magician, when convinced by prayer or sacrifice or pleading, will heal some and kill others, take away from some and give to others, save some and destroy others. This version of God began to look more like a monster than a magician.

I let that God go. It seemed the most faithful thing to do.

A few years ago, after a season of torrential rain and flooding in Southern California, of mudslides and landslides that buried people alive, Death Valley, the hottest, lowest, driest desert in the United States, bloomed. Death Valley, home to the Timbisha Shoshone, is a desert of streaming sand dunes, snowcapped mountains, multi-colored rock layers, water-fluted canyons, and three million acres of stone wilderness. Temperatures sometimes soar above 120 degrees. Death Valley is a bowl. No rivers, drainages, or creeks leave it. Instead, the water that collects there evaporates, leaving behind salts. After hundreds and thousands and millions of years, the salt beds have become thick, inhospitable, toxic.

When the desert flooded, seeds that had been lying dormant in the earth, some for just a season, others for decades, had the resources they needed to flower. When I saw photographs of Death Valley in bloom, reckless, audacious bursts of color, it seemed to me the perfect image for the end of this book.

The ministers I interviewed bloomed seeds that lay dormant in me. Jessica, the woman in the ordination process in the Episcopal Church whose bishop tried to woo her fiancé to the south, told me about her prayer life. She said, "I've learned that often what is required for me is to shut up in prayer and to figure out how to spend some time in a wordless form of prayer." For Jessica, to pray is to listen. While I listened to her in the basement of her divinity school, I realized that listening to women's stories for this book was prayer for me, and I started to cry. Embarrassed, I tried to explain my tears. "I haven't been able to pray for a long time," I said. "Thank you for saying that."

My eyes welled more times than I would like to admit while I listened to the ministers whose stories are collected in this book. Ever pastoral, they ministered to me, seemed to know what was driving my questions, to intuit the pain lurking beneath the surface, to want to return some form of God to me. At the end of each interview, I always asked whether the person I was interviewing had anything she would like to add, anything she thought I needed to know, anything she wanted to tell me that I hadn't asked her about. When I asked Katharine Jefferts Schori this question, she said, "Well, maybe a prayer that you find some peace in your journey, and some clarity and direction." A prayer for peace and clarity. For me.

One of my mother's best friends, Jan, was diagnosed with ovarian cancer three years ago. Since her diagnosis, Jan and my mother attend a healing service at my mother's church every Wednesday. A group of women at the church knit prayer shawls for anyone who needs healing. Beautiful, elaborate, multicolored, soft, the shawls are created in prayer, each stitch representing healing energy and love from the creator for the person who will wear the shawl. The women knit one for Jan, and she wraps it around herself when she sits through chemotherapy treatments.

The stories in the pages of this book knit for me a kind of faith. Yes, the church is sexist. Yes, the church is racist. Yes, the church is homophobic and classist and oppressive and violent and life-threatening and exclusive. And, at the same time, the church is filled with human beings ministering to one another, nourishing one another, challenging one another.

In the Gospel of Thomas, Jesus's disciples ask, "When will the new world come?"

"What you look for has come, but you do not know it," Jesus answers.

When I began writing this book, I was extremely angry. I was grieving. I wanted to write a book that would reveal how terrible religion is, how much it hurts women, how dangerous and exclusive it is. But the women I interviewed changed my mind. Their stories, their energy, their commitment converted me. I began to feel strangely, unexpectedly hopeful. These women and men are transforming the church, renovating Christianity, altering the world. The Church of England can refuse to consecrate women as bishops, the Southern Baptist Church can ban women from teaching Sunday school, the Roman Catholic Church can excommunicate women-priests, but, in Laurie's words, "the train has left the station." At the end of one of our conversations, Laurie said, "I realize that because I am at Trinity, just being there, there is a whole generation of little girls who now know they can be priests."

Girls and boys, men and women, people all across the country, are seeing ministers like Eli and Michelle and Gari, Tristy and Callie and Sharon and Connie, Laurie and Monica and Liz and Eve, Marion and Jackie and Diana and Victoria, Claudia and Stacey and Jamie and Joan, Paula and Jessica and Catherine and Abby, Jocelyn and Shannon and Samantha and Adah, Pamela and Irene and Sarah and Nicole and Katharine, and they know that something else is possible, that they can have a church where they belong, that they can believe in a God who welcomes us all. There is no going back. We have already won.

Acknowledgments

I write with gratitude for the people who made this book possible. Thank you to Tiphany Carroll, Paula Child, Claire Este-McDonald, Terri James, Maria Maricich, Tiffany Stewart, Katherine Stiles, and Shannon Webb. Thank you to all the VAMPS and to my coaches Muffy Ritz, E. J. Harpham, and Katharine Sheldon, who challenge women to take up more space in the world. Thank you to the Runaways. Thank you to Karen King, Gordon Kaufman, and Elisabeth Schüssler Fiorenza for teaching me that theology matters. Thank you to my agent Ike Williams for helping me to become a writer, to my agent Elisabeth Weed for believing in me and in this project, and to Hope Denekamp. Thank you to my parents, Ann and Irwin Sentilles, for encouraging me to question and for lending me a beautiful place to write; to my siblings, Emily, Irwin, and Della, for making me an "m.w.p." sweatshirt when the priesthood was falling apart; to Jerry and Barbara Toshalis, for raising a son who chose a feminist; and to my newest sisters Kristine and Rebecca, strong women. Thank you to Maylen Dominguez Arlen (who originally had the idea for this book), Lynette Banks, Chantal Forfota, Tammy Massman-Johnson, Ann McClenahan, Taura Null, Mary Tess O'Sullivan, Tovis Page, Cameron Partridge, Mercer Riis, Laura Tuach, and Amy Walsh. Thank you to everyone at Harcourt, especially to my editor, Andrea Schulz, without whose vision and commitment this book would not be, Lindsey Smith, Sarah Melnyk, David Hough, Dan Janeck, Liz Demeter, Vaughn Andrews, and Susan Amster. Thank you to all the ministers I interviewed for trusting me with your stories. You give me hope. Thank you to my faithful writing companion, Cali. And, finally, thank you to Eric Toshalis, love, shelter, home.

Introduction: The Most Sexist Hour

4.   **Even though the ministry was one of the first professions to encounter pro-posals to admit women:** Paul Sullins writes about the fact that even though ministry was one of the first professions women demanded to join, it was one of the last to let them in his article "The Stained Glass Ceiling: Career Attainment for Women Clergy," published in the journal *The Sociology of Religion,* Fall 2000.

4.   **Even more, they must be feminist, which simply means, to quote my divinity school professor's bumper sticker:** This was the bumper sticker on my professor Elisabeth Schüssler Fiorenza's car while I was a student at Harvard.

8.   **In a religious context, our relationship with God and our relationship with women are inextricably linked:** This insight was developed in conversation with my good friend Chantal Forfota.

Part One

VOCATION: CALL

13. **Although there was no specific canon in Episcopal Church law prohibiting ordaining women to the priesthood:** This history is outlined on the Episcopal Church's Web site, http://www.episcopalchurch.org/women.htm, and in Carl J. Schneider and Dorothy Schneider's excellent *In Their Own Right: The History of American Clergywomen* (New York: Crossroad, 1997).

14. **Other denominations started ordaining women more than a hundred years before the Episcopal Church did:** Almost everything I learned about the early history of women in ministry in this country came from *In Their Own Right* by Carl J. Schneider and Dorothy Schneider.

14. **Historical evidence, however, reveals that the leadership of women in church communities is not new at all:** Kevin Madigan and Karen Osiek, *Ordained Women in the Early Church: A Documentary History* (Baltimore: Johns Hopkins University Press, 2005), and Elisabeth Schüssler Fiorenza, *In Memory of Her* (New York: Crossroad, 1994).

15. Even though the hierarchy of the Catholic Church partly justifies its refusal to ordain women by insisting that Jesus only ordained men, the truth of the matter is that Jesus did not ordain anyone—male or female: Fact taken from a speech titled, "Woman, why are you weeping?" by Nicole Sotelo, delivered at the 2006 event "Conversation and Celebration of Women Called," held in Santa Barbara and hosted by the Women's Ordination Conference.

15. Policies about women's ordination carry symbolic meaning well beyond their pragmatic consequences: Mark Chavez does an excellent analysis of this phenomenon throughout his book *Ordaining Women,* in particular on page 83, as well as revealing that denominational policy about women and the actual practices of women rarely correspond.

15. That was when British Quaker "Public Friends" Mary Fischer and Ann Austin landed in the Massachusetts Bay Colony, "only to be arrested, imprisoned, examined for marks of witchcraft, and shipped back to England": *In Their Own Right,* 3. I also discovered the stories that follow in the same book.

16. Although the hierarchy of the church refused to license her as a preacher, calling her instead an "official traveling exhorter," Lee described herself as the "first female preacher of the First African Methodist Episcopal Church": I learned this history in *In Their Own Right* on pages 25–26. The Schneiders refer to a study by Jean Humez that greatly helped them in their research.

16. Although many Christian denominations currently profess that ordination is open to women, such a rule does not an egalitarian system make: *Ordaining Women,* page 29.

17. Women ministers have different experiences than their male counterparts, and these different—read more *difficult*—experiences are shaped by sexism and often compounded by racism: For more information please refer to the following studies: "Reaching Toward Wholeness II: The 21st Century Survey" (Episcopal Church, 2003); United Methodist Clergywomen Retention Study (Anna Howard Shaw Center, Boston University School of Theology), 1993; Commission for Women 25th Anniversary Survey: Analysis of the Length of Time Spent Waiting for First Call (Evangelical Lutheran Church in America), 1995; "Taking the Measure of UMC Clergy—Study of United Methodist Church Clergy"— *Christian Century,* August 28, 1996; 35th Anniversary of Ordination of Women: Rostered Leader Survey 2005—Report 1 (Evangelical Lutheran Church in America, 1999); "Study: Female Ministers Face Patriarchy, Pettiness, Other Pressures," article reporting results of a University of Florida study; Clergywomen's Experiences in Ministry: Realities and Challenges, 2003: Presbyterians, published in 2005 by the Advocacy Committee for Women's Concerns; "In Search of a Pulpit: Sex Differences in the Transition from Seminary Training to the First Parish Job," Patricia M. Y. Chang, *Journal for the Scientific Study of Religion,* 1997, 36 (4): 614–27; "The Stained Glass Ceiling: Career Attainment for Women Clergy," Paul Sullins, *Sociology of Religion,* 2000, 61 (3): 243–66.

17. Consider the life of Antoinette Brown: *In Their Own Right,* pages 60–70.

CHAPTER ONE: THE CALL

25. **The central idea of Protestantism—that each human being has access to God, unmediated by an institutional hierarchy—has worked in women's favor:** For more information, see *In Their Own Right*.

CHAPTER TWO: THE ORDINATION PROCESS

38. **Most religious institutions have excluded women from ordained ministry using one of two main lines of argument: biblical inerrancy or sacramentalism:** For a thorough analysis of the roles of sacramentalism and biblical inerrancy in the exclusion of women from ordination, see Chavez, *Ordaining Women: Culture and Conflict in Religious Organizations*.

53. **For example, what we now know as atonement theology did not emerge in Christianity until the eleventh century, articulated by a man named Anselm:** For more critiques of atonement theology, see Rita Nakashima Brock and Rebecca Ann Parker, *Proverbs of Ashes: Violence, Redemptive Suffering, and the Search for What Saves Us* (Boston: Beacon Press, 2001), Anthony W. Bartlett, *Cross Purposes: The Violent Grammar of Christian Atonement* (Harrisburg, PA: Trinity Press International, 2001), and Delores S. Williams, *Sisters in the Wilderness: The Challenge of Womanist God-Talk* (Maryknoll, NY: Orbis Books, 1993).

CHAPTER FOUR: THE JOB SEARCH

69. **Across denominations, women's job searches are longer than men's, and are even longer when they are women of color:** For more information, please see the article "In Search of a Pulpit: Sex Differences in the Transition from Seminary Training to the First Parish Job," by Patricia M. Y. Chang, in *Journal for the Scientific Study of Religion*, 1997, 36 (4): 614–27. Information on the role of racism in the job search process can be found in a study conducted by Professor Delores Carpenter of Howard University and referred to in an article published in the *New York Times* titled, "Pastor Leaves Door Ajar for Other Black Women," by Samuel G. Freedman.

CHAPTER FIVE: ASSISTANT MINISTERS

82. **They have each crafted a life that makes visible the commitment in their hearts—a commitment to the belief that another world is possible, a world where we might live in ways that nourish and sustain the earth and all living beings:** This is an insight that was shaped both by my conversations with my professor and mentor, Gordon Kaufman, and by reading his books, including *In Face of Mystery*.

112. **The second issue had to do with a sermon Eve preached a year and a half earlier in which she questioned the historicity of the birth narrative of Jesus, something that has been questioned for decades by historians and biblical scholars:** For a summary of these arguments, see "The Evolution of Jesus' Divinity: An Investigation into the Birth Narrative in the Gospel of Matthew" found online at http://tiglathpileser.wordpress.com/2007/05/27/

the-evolution-of-jesus-divinity-an-investigation-into-the-birth-narrative-in-the-gospel-of-matthew/. Scholars engaged in the search for the historical Jesus include, to list just a few, Marcus Borg, N. T. Wright, John Dominic Crossan, and John Shelby Spong.

Part Two

INCARNATION: THE BODY

120. **Scientists and theorists of all kinds continue to debate what, if anything, determines biological sex, and new evidence constantly throws into question theories that used to be taken as fact:** Six factors are used to determine sex: chromosomal (XX female; XY male); gonadal (ovaries and testes); genital (penis, vulva, clitoris, testicles, scrotum, vagina, etc.); psychological (self-identification); hormonal (endocrine secretions); and secondary sexual characteristics (distribution of hair, breast development, physique, etc.). Anne Fausto-Sterling, a professor of biology and women's studies, has argued that a three-sex system (male, female, intersex) does not reflect the full spectrum of human sex development and suggests, instead, a five-sex system: males; females; "herms" (named after hermaphrodites or those born with both a testis and an ovary); "merms" (male pseudohermaphrodites, or those born with testes and some aspect of female genitalia); and "ferms" (female pseudohermaphrodites, or those who have ovaries combined with some aspect of male genitalia). Suzanne J. Kessler, a professor of psychology, has critiqued this five-sex model, arguing that it gives genitals too much weight for determining sex, when in daily life, sex is assigned without ever seeing the body hidden under clothing.

122. **As an example of this sort of argument, consider a statement issued by the Vatican in 2004 titled "Letter to the Bishops of the Catholic Church on the Collaboration of Men and Women in the Church and in the World":** This document can be located online at http://www.vatican.va/roman_curia/congregations/cfaith/documents/rc_con_cfaith_doc_20040731_collaboration_en.html.

124. **Some dioceses in the United States have gone so far as to secede, including the diocese of Virginia:** I was reminded of the similarity between Virginia's recent secession and the state's secession during the Civil War in a letter to the editor titled, "Episcopalians Against Equality," written by Harold Meyerson and published in the *Washington Post* on December 20, 2006.

CHAPTER SIX: LANGUAGE

130. **The authors report that even though ordained women personally prefer inclusive language, church worship services are no more likely to use inclusive language for God than they were in the 1970s:** The authors base this argument on a fifteen-denominational study done in 1993–1994 by Barbara Brown Zikmund.

CHAPTER EIGHT: SEX

165. In fact, Lawrence Finer, director of domestic research at the Guttmacher Institute, a nonprofit organization focused on sexual and reproductive health, discovered that not only had more than nine out of ten people had premarital sex but the rate of premarital sex has been consistent for more than fifty years: For more information, visit http://www.plannedparenthood.org/news-articles-press/politics-policy-issues/medical-sexual-health/premarital-sex-13377.htm.

176. In the United States, someone is sexually assaulted every two and a half minutes: This statistic and those that follow are from "National Crime Victimization Survey, 2005" found on the Rape, Abuse, and Incest National Network (RAINN) Web site, http://www.rainn.org/statistics/index.html?gclid=CKzLuaqsk4s CFSQOIgod4oiBSg.

CHAPTER NINE: GAY

186. As Reverend Fred Small, a Unitarian Universalist, wrote in a sermon: This sermon, delivered at First Unitarian Church in Littleton, Massachusetts, on February 8, 2004, is posted on the Web: http://www.fculittle.org/sermons/Bible_and_Homosexuality.pdf. I found the sermon beautiful and informative. Part of my argument about what the Bible does and does not say about homosexuality is based on this sermon, as well as my studies at Harvard Divinity School.

CHAPTER TEN: TRANS

214. She seems to embody in her theology and her ministry—and her body—what philosopher Richard Rorty meant when he wrote about "the priority of the need to create new ways of being human, and a new heaven and a new earth for these new humans to inhabit, over the desire for stability, security and order": Richard Rorty, *Philosophy and Social Hope* (London: Penguin, 1999), 88.

Part Three

CREATION: MINISTRY

237. "Finally she called the women to her": Toni Morrison, *Beloved*, page 88.

239. Elisabeth Schüssler Fiorenza argues that feminists must continue to interpret biblical texts critically not to keep women in biblical religions, "but because biblical texts affect all women in Western society": Elisabeth Schüssler Fiorenza, *But She Said: Feminist Practices of Biblical Interpretation* (Boston: Beacon Press, 1992), page 7.

239. Feminist philosopher Mary Daly writes that for centuries "women have had the power of *naming* stolen from us" and "have not been free to use our own power to name ourselves, the world, or God": Mary Daly, *Beyond God the Father: Toward a Philosophy of Women's Liberation* (Boston: Beacon Press, 1985), page 8.

240. "It is the creative potential itself in human beings that is the image of God": Mary Daly, *Beyond God the Father,* page 33.

240. **During her class, we read** *The Gospel of Mary:* What follows is from Karen King's book *The Gospel of Mary of Magdala: Jesus and the First Woman Apostle.*

241. **They are part of the** *Nag Hammadi Library:* For more information on the Nag Hammadi texts, please consult the following: *The Nag Hammadi Library in English,* James M. Robinson (ed.); *Q-Thomas Reader,* John S. Kloppenborg et al.; *The Gospel of Mary of Magdala* and *What Is Gnosticism?* by Karen King.

243. **The first Christians had no New Testament, no Nicene Creed or Apostles Creed, no church buildings:** In *The Gospel of Mary of Magdala,* Karen King writes on page 6, "It is important to remember, too, that these first Christians had no New Testament, no Nicene Creed or Apostles Creed, no commonly established church order or chain of authority, no church buildings, and indeed no single understanding of Jesus. All of the elements we might consider to be essential to define Christianity did not yet exist. Far from being starting points, the Nicene Creed and the New Testament were end products of these debates and disputes; they represent the distillation of experience and experimentation—and not a small amount of strife and struggle."

244. **"The central question for theology":** Gordon Kaufman, *In Face of Mystery,* 17–18.

244. **The words we use to talk about God are** *human* **words, infected with our own limitations, interests, and biases. We must engage, therefore, in relentless criticism of our faith and its symbols, always knowing we might be wrong:** Gordon Kaufman, *In Face of Mystery,* 63. He also explores this insight in *An Essay on Theological Method,* where he maintains that the only God we can know or respond to or take account of is the God *we* can know and take account of and respond to.

244. **What we call sacred tells us our most important values:** Derrick Jensen, ed., *Listening to the Land: Conversations about Nature, Culture, and Eroc* (New York: Context Books, 2002). Interview with Starhawk, page 173.

245. **In an article published in the** *Psychological Bulletin* **called "The Need to Belong," Roy F. Baumeister and Mark R. Leary argue that "belongingness"— regular and meaningful connection with a person or group of people by whom you feel included—is nearly as essential for human health and well-being as food:** Roy F. Baumeister and Mark R. Leary, "The Need to Belong: Desire for Interpersonal Attachments as a Fundamental Human Motivation," *Psychological Bulletin,* 1995, 117 (3): 497–529.

CHAPTER ELEVEN: CATHOLIC WOMENPRIESTS

264. **"to be able to call ourselves Reverend":** Elisabeth Schüssler Fiorenza, Women's Ordination Worldwide, international conference, keynote speech in Ottawa, July 22, 2006, titled "We Are the Church—a Kindom of Priests."

264. **She then quoted Rose Wu:** During Elisabeth Schüssler Fiorenza's keynote address at the Women's Ordination Worldwide, international conference, she quoted Rose Wu's article titled, "From the Ordination of Women to the Priesthood of All Believers." Wu was speaking at the twenty-fifth anniversary celebration of the ordination of Episcopal women.

CHAPTER THIRTEEN: A CHURCH OF HER OWN

296. **Gordon Kaufman, my theological mentor, claims theologians as artists and theology as art:** Gordon Kaufman, *An Essay on Theological Method,* 39.

296. **In *Art Objects,* Jeanette Winterson writes, "The artist is a translator; one who has learned how to pass into her own language the languages gathered from stones, from birds, from dreams, from the body, from the material world, from the invisible world, from sex, from death, from love. A different language is a different reality":** Jeanette Winterson, *Art Objects* (New York: Vintage, 1997), 146.

Afterword: Death Valley Blooms

307. **A few years ago, after a season of torrential rain and flooding:** For more information about Death Valley, see http://www.nps.gov/deva.

All passages quoted from the Bible can be found in the New Revised Standard Version (NRSV) of the biblical text, specifically *The New Oxford Annotated Bible*. Oxford: Oxford University Press, 1991.

History, Memoirs, and the Fight to Change the Church

Armstrong, Karen. *Through the Narrow Gate.* New York: St. Martin's Press, 1981.
———. *The Gospel According to Woman: Christianity's Creation of the Sex War in the West.* Garden City, NY: Anchor Press, 1987.
———. *Holy War: The Crusades and Their Impact on Today's World.* New York: Anchor Books, 2001.
———. *The Battle for God.* New York: Ballantine Books, 2001.
———. *A History of God: The 4000-Year Quest of Judaism, Christianity, and Islam.* New York: Gramercy Books, 2004.
———. *The Spiral Staircase: My Climb Out of Darkness.* New York: Alfred A. Knopf, 2004.
———. *The Great Transformation: The Beginning of Our Religious Traditions.* New York: Knopf, 2006.
Berneking, Nancy J., and Pamela Carter Joern. *Re-Membering and Re-Imagining.* Cleveland: Pilgrim Press, 1995.
Bonavoglia, Angela. *Good Catholic Girls: How Women Are Leading the Fight to Change the Church.* New York: ReganBooks, 2005.
Bozarth, Alla Renée. *Womanpriest: A Personal Odyssey.* New York: Paulist Press, 1978.
Bozzuti-Jones, Mark Francisco. *The Miter Fits Just Fine: A Story About the Right Reverend Barbara Clementine Harris, Suffragan Bishop, Diocese of Massachusetts.* Cambridge, MA: Cowley Publications, 2003.
Braude, Ann. *Radical Spirits: Spiritualism and Women's Rights in Nineteenth-Century America.* Bloomington: Indiana University Press, 2001.
———. *Transforming the Faiths of Our Fathers: Women Who Changed American Religion.* New York: Palgrave Macmillan, 2004.
———. *Sisters and Saints: Women and American Religion.* New York: Oxford University Press, 2007.
Clark, Elizabeth A. *Women in the Early Church.* Wilmington, DE: M. Glazier, 1983.
Donovan, Mary S. *A Different Call: Women's Ministries in the Episcopal Church, 1850–1920.* Wilton, CT: Morehouse-Barlow, 1986.

————. *Women Priests in the Episcopal Church: The Experience of the First Decade.* Cincinnati: Forward Movement Publications, 1988.

Feinberg, Leslie. *Transgender Warriors: Making History From Joan of Arc to Dennis Rodman.* Boston: Beacon Press, 1996.

Frederick, Marla F. *Between Sundays: Black Women and Everyday Struggles of Faith.* Berkeley: University of California Press, 2003.

Heyward, Carter. *A Priest Forever.* New York: Harper & Row, 1976.

Jensen, Anne. *God's Self-Confident Daughters: Early Christianity and the Liberation of Women.* Louisville, KY: Westminster John Knox Press, 1996.

Kidd, Sue Monk. *The Dance of the Dissident Daughter: A Woman's Journey from Christian Tradition to the Sacred Feminine.* San Francisco: HarperSanFrancisco, 1996.

Madigan, Kevin, and Carolyn Osiek. *Ordained Women in the Early Church: A Documentary History.* Baltimore: Johns Hopkins University Press, 2005.

Prelinger, Catherine M. *Episcopal Women: Gender, Spirituality, and Commitment in an American Mainline Denomination.* New York: Oxford University Press, 1992.

Ruether, Rosemary Radford. *Women-Church: Theology and Practice of Feminist Liturgical Communities.* San Francisco: Harper & Row, 1985.

Schiess, Betty Bone. *Why Me, Lord?: One Woman's Ordination to the Priesthood With Commentary and Complaint.* New York: Syracuse University Press, 2003.

Shattuck, Gardiner H. *Episcopalians and Race: Civil War to Civil Rights.* Lexington: University Press of Kentucky, 2000.

Winter, Miriam Therese, Adair T. Lummis, and Allison Stokes. *Defecting in Place: Women Claiming Responsibility for Their Own Spiritual Lives.* New York: Crossroad, 1994.

Responses to Sexual Violence

Coleman, Monica A. *The Dinah Project: A Handbook for Congregational Response to Sexual Violence.* Cleveland: Pilgrim Press, 2004.

Schüssler Fiorenza, Elisabeth, and Shawn Copeland, eds. *Violence Against Women.* New York: SCM Press Ltd., 1994.

Sotelo, Nicole. *Women Healing From Abuse: Meditations for Finding Peace.* Mahwah, NJ: Paulist Press, 2006.

Rethinking Biblical Texts

Kanyoro, Musimbi R. A. *Introducing Feminist Cultural Hermeneutics.* Cleveland: Pilgrim Press, 2002.

King, Karen L. *The Gospel of Mary of Magdala: Jesus and the First Woman Apostle.* Santa Rosa, CA: Polebridge Press, 2003.

————. *What is Gnosticism?* Cambridge, MA: Belknap Press of Harvard University Press, 2003.

————. *The Secret Revelation of John.* Cambridge: Harvard University Press, 2006.

Kloppenborg, John S. *Q-Thomas Reader.* Sonoma, CA: Polebridge Press, 1990.

Pagels, Elaine H. *The Gnostic Gospels.* New York: Random House, 1979.

————. *Beyond Belief: The Secret Gospel of Thomas.* New York: Random House, 2003.

Pagels, Elaine H., and Karen L. King. *Reading Judas: The Gospel of Judas and the Shaping of Christianity.* New York: Viking, 2007.

Robinson, James McConkey, and Richard Smith. *The Nag Hammadi Library in English.* San Francisco: Harper & Row, 1988.

Russell, Letty M. *Feminist Interpretation of the Bible.* Oxford: B. Blackwell, 1985.

Schüssler Fiorenza, Elisabeth. *But She Said: Feminist Practices of Biblical Interpretation.* Boston: Beacon Press, 1992.

———. *Discipleship of Equals: A Critical Feminist Ekklesia-Logy of Liberation.* New York: Crossroad, 1993.

———. *In Memory of Her: A Feminist Theological Reconstruction of Christian Origins.* 10th anniversary ed. New York: Crossroad, 1994.

———. *Jesus: Miriam's Child, Sophia's Prophet: Critical Issues in Feminist Christology.* New York: Continuum, 1994.

———. *Bread Not Stone: The Challenge of Feminist Biblical Interpretation.* Boston: Beacon Press, 1995.

———. *Rhetoric and Ethic: The Politics of Biblical Studies.* Minneapolis: Fortress Press, 1999.

Schüssler Fiorenza, Elisabeth, and Kwok Pui-lan, eds. *Women's Sacred Scriptures.* Maryknoll, NY: Orbis Books, 1998.

Segovia, Fernando F. *Decolonizing Biblical Studies: A View From the Margins.* Maryknoll, NY: Orbis Books, 2000.

Stanton, Elizabeth Cady. *The Original Feminist Attack on the Bible (the Woman's Bible).* New York: Arno Press, 1974.

Rethinking the Historical Jesus

Borg, Marcus J. *Meeting Jesus Again for the First Time: The Historical Jesus & the Heart of Contemporary Faith.* San Francisco: HarperSanFrancisco, 1994.

Borg, Marcus J., Mark Powelson, and Ray Riegert. *The Lost Gospel Q: The Original Sayings of Jesus.* Berkeley: Ulysses Press, 1996.

Crossan, John Dominic. *Jesus: A Revolutionary Biography.* San Francisco: HarperSanFrancisco, 1994.

———. *God and Empire: Jesus Against Rome, Then and Now.* San Francisco: HarperSanFrancisco, 2007.

Funk, Robert Walter, and Roy W. Hoover. *The Five Gospels: The Search for the Authentic Words of Jesus: New Translation and Commentary.* New York: Macmillan Maxwell, 1993.

Levine, Amy-Jill, Dale C. Allison, and John Dominic Crossan. *The Historical Jesus in Context.* Princeton, NJ: Princeton University Press, 2006.

Feminist, Womanist, Black, Queer, Asian, Postcolonial, Constructive, and Liberation Theologies

Althaus-Reid, Marcella. *The Queer God.* London; New York: Routledge, 2003.

———. *Liberation Theology and Sexuality.* Aldershot, England; Burlington, VT: Ashgate, 2006.

Althaus-Reid, Marcella, and Lisa Isherwood. *The Sexual Theologian: Essays on Sex, God and Politics.* London; New York: T & T Clark International, 2004.

Anderson, Sherry Ruth, and Patricia Hopkins. *The Feminine Face of God: The Unfolding of the Sacred in Women.* New York: Bantam Books, 1991.

Anderson, Victor. *Beyond Ontological Blackness: An Essay on African American Religious and Cultural Criticism.* New York: Continuum, 1995.

Aquino, María Pilar. *Our Cry for Life: Feminist Theology From Latin America.* Maryknoll, NY: Orbis Books, 1993.

Aquino, María Pilar, Daisy L. Machado, and Jeanette Rodriguez. *A Reader in Latina Feminist Theology: Religion and Justice.* Austin: University of Texas Press, 2002.

Armour, Ellen T. *Deconstruction, Feminist Theology, and the Problem of Difference: Subverting the Race/Gender Divide.* Chicago: University of Chicago Press, 1999.

Boff, Leonardo. *Jesus Christ Liberator: A Critical Christology for Our Time.* Maryknoll, NY: Orbis Books, 1978.

———. *Church, Charism and Power: Liberation Theology and the Institutional Church.* New York: Crossroad, 1985.

———. *Ecology & Liberation: A New Paradigm.* Maryknoll, NY: Orbis Books, 1995.

———. *Fundamentalism, Terrorism, and the Future of Humanity.* London: SPCK, 2006.

Boff, Leonardo, and Clodovis Boff. *Introducing Liberation Theology.* Maryknoll, NY: Orbis Books, 1987.

Boff, Leonardo, and Virgilio P. Elizondo. *Ecology and Poverty: Cry of the Earth, Cry of the Poor.* London; Maryknoll, NY: SCM Press Orbis Books, 1995.

Boff, Leonardo, Virgilio P. Elizondo, and Marcus Lefébure. *Option for the Poor: Challenge to the Rich Countries.* Edinburgh: T. & T. Clark, 1986.

———. *The People of God Amidst the Poor.* Edinburgh: T. & T. Clark, 1986.

Brock, Rita Nakashima. *Off the Menu: Asian and Asian North American Women's Religion and Theology.* Louisville, KY: Westminster John Knox Press, 2007.

Brock, Rita Nakashima, and Rebecca Ann Parker. *Proverbs of Ashes: Violence, Redemptive Suffering, and the Search for What Saves Us.* Boston: Beacon Press, 2001.

Cannon, Katie G. *Black Womanist Ethics.* Atlanta: Scholars Press, 1988.

———. *Katie's Canon: Womanism and the Soul of the Black Community.* New York: Continuum, 1995.

Chopp, Rebecca S. *The Power to Speak: Feminism, Language, God.* New York: Crossroad, 1989.

Chopp, Rebecca S., and Sheila Greeve Davaney. *Horizons in Feminist Theology: Identity, Tradition, and Norms.* Minneapolis: Fortress Press, 1997.

Chopp, Rebecca S., and Mark L. Taylor. *Reconstructing Christian Theology.* Minneapolis: Fortress Press, 1994.

Christ, Carol P., and Judith Plaskow. *Womanspirit Rising: A Feminist Reader in Religion.* San Francisco: HarperSanFrancisco, 1992.

Christ, Carol P. *Rebirth of the Goddess: Finding Meaning in Feminist Spirituality.* Reading, PA: Addison-Wesley, 1997.

————. *She Who Changes: Re-Imagining the Divine in the World.* New York: Palgrave Macmillan, 2003.

Cone, James H. *A Black Theology of Liberation.* Maryknoll, NY: Orbis, 1994.

————. *Black Theology and Black Power.* Maryknoll, NY: Orbis Books, 1997.

————. *God of the Oppressed.* Maryknoll, NY: Orbis Books, 1997.

Daly, Mary. *Gyn/Ecology: The Metaethics of Radical Feminism.* Boston: Beacon Press, 1978.

————. *Beyond God the Father: Toward a Philosophy of Women's Liberation.* Boston: Beacon Press, 1985.

————. *Outercourse: The be-Dazzling Voyage: Containing Recollections From My Logbook of a Radical Feminist Philosopher (be-Ing an Account of My Time/Space Travels and Ideas—Then, Again, Now, and How).* San Francisco: HarperSanFrancisco, 1992.

————. *Quintessence—Realizing the Archaic Future: A Radical Elemental Feminist Manifesto.* Boston: Beacon Press, 1998.

Donaldson, Laura E., and Pui-lan Kwok. *Postcolonialism, Feminism, and Religious Discourse.* New York: Routledge, 2002.

Douglas, Kelly Brown. *The Black Christ.* Maryknoll, NY: Orbis, 1994.

Dube Shomanah, Musa W. *Postcolonial Feminist Interpretation of the Bible.* St. Louis: Chalice Press, 2000.

Gutiérrez, Gustavo. *We Drink From Our Own Wells: The Spiritual Journey of a People.* Maryknoll, NY; Melbourne, Australia: Orbis Books Dove Communications, 1984.

————. *A Theology of Liberation: History, Politics, and Salvation.* Maryknoll, NY: Orbis Books, 1988.

Gutiérrez, Gustavo, and Richard Shaull. *Liberation and Change.* Atlanta: John Knox Press, 1977.

Hampson, Daphne. *Theology and Feminism.* 1980. Malden, MA: Blackwell Publishers, 1990.

Isasi-Díaz, Ada María. *Mujerista Theology: A Theology for the Twenty-First Century.* Maryknoll, NY: Orbis Books, 1996.

————. *En La Lucha = in the Struggle: Elaborating a Mujerista Theology.* 10th anniversary ed. Minneapolis: Fortress Press, 2004.

Jantzen, Grace. *Becoming Divine: Towards a Feminist Philosophy of Religion.* Bloomington: Indiana University Press, 1999.

Johnson, Elizabeth A. *She Who Is: The Mystery of God in Feminist Theological Discourse.* New York: Crossroad, 1992.

Jones, Serene. *Feminist Theory and Christian Theology: Cartographies of Grace.* Minneapolis: Fortress Press, 2000.

Kaufman, Gordon D. *The Theological Imagination: Constructing the Concept of God.* Philadelphia: The Westminster Press, 1981.

————. *In Face of Mystery: A Constructive Theology.* Cambridge, MA: Harvard University Press, 1993.

————. *An Essay on Theological Method.* Atlanta: Scholars Press, 1995.

————. *God, Mystery, Diversity: Christian Theology in a Pluralistic World.* Minneapolis: Fortress Press, 1996.

———. "My Life and My Theological Reflection: Two Central Themes." *American Journal of Theology and Philosophy* Vol. 22 No. 1, January 2001: 3–32.

———. "On Thinking of God as Serendipitous Creativity." *Journal of the American Academy of Religion* 69, No. 2 (2001): 409–25.

———. *In the Beginning—Creativity.* Minneapolis: Fortress Press, 2004.

———. *Jesus and Creativity.* Minneapolis: Fortress Press, 2006.

King, Ursula. *Feminist Theology From the Third World: A Reader.* Maryknoll, NY: Orbis Books, 1994.

Kwok, Pui-lan. *Introducing Asian Feminist Theology.* Cleveland: Pilgrim Press, 2000.

———. *Postcolonial Imagination and Feminist Theology.* Louisville, KY: Westminster John Knox Press, 2005.

McFague, Sallie. *The Body of God: An Ecological Theology.* Minneapolis: Fortress Press, 1993.

Miles, Margaret R. *Practicing Christianity: Critical Perspectives for an Embodied Spirituality.* New York: Crossroad, 1988.

———. *Carnal Knowing: Female Nakedness and Religious Meaning in the Christian West.* New York: Vintage Books, 1991.

———. *The Word Made Flesh: A History of Christian Thought.* Malden, MA: Blackwell Publishers, 2005.

Mitchem, Stephanie Y. *Introducing Womanist Theology.* Maryknoll, NY: Orbis Books, 2002.

Plaskow, Judith. *Sex, Sin, and Grace: Women's Experience and the Theologies of Reinhold Niebuhr and Paul Tillich.* Washington, D.C.: University Press of America, 1980.

———. *Standing Again at Sinai: Judaism From a Feminist Perspective.* New York: HarperSanFrancisco, 1991.

Raphael, Melissa. *Introducing Thealogy.* Cleveland: Pilgrim Press, 2000.

Ruether, Rosemary Radford. *Religion and Sexism: Images of Woman in the Jewish and Christian Traditions.* New York: Simon and Schuster, 1974.

———. *Sexism and God-Talk: Toward a Feminist Theology.* Boston: Beacon Press, 1993.

Tamez, Elsa. *Bible of the Oppressed.* Maryknoll, NY: Orbis Books, 1982.

———. *Through Her Eyes: Women's Theology From Latin America.* Maryknoll, NY: Orbis Books, 1989.

Townes, Emilie Maureen. *A Troubling in My Soul: Womanist Perspectives on Evil and Suffering.* Maryknoll, NY: Orbis Books, 1993.

———. *Womanist Justice, Womanist Hope.* Atlanta: Scholars Press, 1993.

———. *Womanist Ethics and the Cultural Production of Evil.* New York: Palgrave Macmillan, 2006.

Williams, Delores S. *Sisters in the Wilderness: The Challenge of Womanist God-Talk.* Maryknoll, NY: Orbis Books, 1993.